THE NEW DEAL
AT THE GRASS ROOTS

THE NEW DEAL

AT THE GRASS ROOTS

PROGRAMS FOR THE PEOPLE IN OTTER TAIL COUNTY, MINNESOTA

D. JEROME TWETON

MINNESOTA HISTORICAL SOCIETY PRESS • ST. PAUL • 1988

*Assistance for the publication of this book was
provided through a grant from the Minnesota
Historical Society Public Affairs Center, which is
funded by the Northwest Area Foundation.*

MINNESOTA HISTORICAL SOCIETY PRESS
St. Paul 55101

The Otter Tail County Historical Society acknowledges
the work of Roberta A. Klugman, project researcher, in
assembling the Thirties Project Papers, 1979 to 1981.

The paper used in this publication meets the minimum
requirements of the American National Standard for Information Sciences — Permanence for Printed Library
Materials, ANSI Z39.48-1984.

Manufactured in the United States of America
10   9   8   7   6   5   4   3   2   1
International Standard Book Number:
0-87351-232-4 Cloth
0-87351-233-2 Paper

Library of Congress Cataloging-in-Publication Data
Tweton, D. Jerome.
The New Deal at the grass roots : programs for the people in Ot-
ter Tail County, Minnesota / D. Jerome Tweton.
p.   cm.
Bibliography: p.
Includes index.
ISBN 0-87351-232-4. ISBN 0-87351-233-2 (pbk.)
1. Otter Tail County (Minn.) — Politics and government.
2. Otter Tail County (Minn.) — Economic policy. 3. New
Deal, 1933–1939 — Case studies. I. Title.
F612.O9T84 1988
977.6'89052 — dc19   88-21615
                                                                                              CIP

CONTENTS

Introduction *1*

1. Otter Tail County: The People, the Politics, the Place . . 5

2. Otter Tail County: The Economic Crisis and the Politics of Response 20

3. Direct Relief: "In Dire Need of Help" 37

4. CWA, FERA, PWA: "Finding Jobs for the People". . . 55

5. WPA: "To Keep Body and Soul Together" 70

6. A WPA Project and Its People: "The Boys Down at the Courthouse" 88

7. CCC and NYA: "Youth Must Rebuild What Has Been Destroyed". *101*

8. Farm Programs: "A Good Thing for the Farmers". . *114*

9. REA: "The Same as Getting God There" . . . *134*

10. Banking and Business: "You People Must Have Faith" . *147*

11. Conclusion *163*

Reference Notes *169*

Bibliographic Essay *193*

Index *197*

FOREWORD

ALMOST every local historical organization seeks to capture moments of the area's history on paper. These groups are motivated to undertake such endeavors for reasons as numerous as the organizations themselves. For the Otter Tail County Historical Society, the "Thirties Project" was the convergence of several ideas and aspirations given shape and form by volunteers, staff, and professionals sharing an interest in the happenings of the past and what they can tell us about the future.

The "Thirties Project" had a simple, innocent beginning in 1978. The society's Publications Committee, having recently completed a project, was looking for a new venture that would be different from previous publications. The goal was to produce a work that would have local significance, employ professional research techniques, generate a body of source material to complement the existing archive, and result in a scholarly publication of countywide interest.

Two volunteers, Marian Kohlmeyer and Edith Trygstad, presented the most challenging project proposal — one that emerged from their recently produced photographic exhibit on county WPA projects. During the research phase of exhibit development, they were struck by the reluctance of people to talk about the 1930s, the scant amount of research material on WPA projects, the variation in the utilization of WPA programs from community to community, and the decreasing number of people still living who could recount personal experiences during the decade and reflect on what the WPA meant to their communities. The Publications Committee recognized that researching and writing a book on the WPA and other federal programs would require special attention, and it created a subcommittee to oversee the project from beginning to end. The original subcommittee included Alvin Serkland, chair, Nanette Frick, James Daly, and Einar Saarela; later Ruben Parson, Myron Broschat, and Marian Kohlmeyer joined the subcommittee. Carol Swenson, administrator of the Otter Tail County Historical Society, served as staff liaison. The subcommittee laid the basis for the research, assisted in preparing proposals for funding, guided development, recommended persons to serve as staff, and, most importantly, kept the project close to the heart of the historical society and the people of the county.

Several other individuals merit special recognition in addition to the subcommittee members. Roberta A. Klugman—familiarly known as Birdie—served as the principal researcher on the project for more than two years; without her devotion and passion for the 1930s and her skill in working with county citizens the expansive body of research now accumulated would not exist. Marilyn Stromberg and Connie Nelson assisted her with office work and newspaper transcribing, which enabled her to devote more time to field research. Jeffrey A. Hess, who served as the society's first historical consultant, gave direction and dimension to the research when the project was in its malleable period. D. Jerome Tweton interpreted the body of research and created the manuscript that became the book you are about to read. Pamela Brunfelt, the Otter Tail County Historical Society's archivist, served as the society's liaison with the subcommittee, verified information, and coordinated work with the publisher.

Of special importance are those who believed in the project and the Otter Tail County Historical Society's ability to complete it and who provided the funds to hire outside professionals. In this category is the Minnesota Historical Society, which furnished major assistance through the State Grants-in-Aid Program to support research on the depression era. Additionally, those people who served on the board of directors for part or all of the project's duration deserve kudos of a special nature for encouraging, with society resources and personal commitment, the research, preservation, and interpretation of the county's history.

Not to be forgotten are those people of the 1930s who were the inspiration. The pain they endured and the joys they shared left a legacy that has contributed to the character and history of Otter Tail County. It is the intent of this publication to help us to listen, to learn, and to use their experiences as we contemplate the future.

CAROL J. SWENSON
Administrator
Otter Tail County
Historical Society
1977–84

ACKNOWLEDGMENTS

IN 1978 the Otter Tail County Historical Society began its "Thirties Project," an ambitious and successful effort to collect materials that would enhance an understanding of the depression decade in the county. The society's staff and volunteers combed the county, bringing together in one place materials, especially those related to federal programs, that were germane to the depression years. The project included extensive oral history interviews; preparation of a complete index and article files of several newspapers; annotated indexes of county, municipal, and township records; a search of state and national archives for pertinent documents; photographing and listing of WPA-built projects; culling the files of the Rural Electrification Administration and the local private utility for 1930s data; and photocopying these and other items for a permanent collection.

Assembling this magnificent collection was indeed a monumental task that only a team of serious and dedicated people could have accomplished. Carol Swenson's foreword to this volume names these individuals. Special recognition should be given to Roberta A. Klugman for her tireless efforts to collect records and interviews.

In 1982 the Otter Tail County Historical Society contracted with me to write a manuscript on the New Deal and the impact of its programs on the county. In the completion of this manuscript I owe a deep debt of gratitude to the society. The subcommittee of the Publications Committee served as a valuable sounding board. Members suggested people to be interviewed and helped me find obscure material. They also saved me from putting the right town in the wrong place or the wrong town in the right place. For that as well as marvelous cooperation I thank the Otter Tail County Historical Society. This is truly its book.

Several people not with the society have played important roles in this project. John McGuigan, Sally Rubinstein, and Deborah Swanson at the Minnesota Historical Society Press made important suggestions for changes that brought a much sharper focus to the study. Louise Diers and Paula Torrance Tweton typed what must have seemed like endless drafts of the manuscript. The interlibrary loan office and the staff of the Elwyn B. Robinson Department of Special Collections at the Chester Fritz Library of the University of North Dakota provided pleasant and prompt service. Finally, a special thank you to Paula for putting up with my "territorial" instinct to turn every room of the house into "my office." To Paula, my wife, I dedicate my work.

INTRODUCTION

DURING THE SPRING SEMESTER of 1970, I was lecturing to an American history survey class on the New Deal. I had just finished with the Works Progress Administration (WPA), sharing with the 150 students such information as: the WPA spent $11.3 billion on its projects, of which $4 billion had gone for highways, roads, and streets, and $1 billion to build public facilities; the WPA employed more than eight million men and women, benefiting about thirty million people; the WPA had an average monthly payroll of 2,112,000 individuals. I paused to look out the window (since bricked over in a "modernizing" project — something the WPA would not have done). As I turned back to the class, a hand popped up and a question followed: "What did the WPA do for people?" I spent a few minutes discussing, in a general way, how the WPA had assisted people to get through the difficult days of the depression and how communities benefited from the many worthwhile projects. Hoping that was sufficient, I moved on to the subjects of the Blue Eagle and the National Recovery Administration (NRA). The student, however, was not satisfied, and the hand once again waved from the back of the lecture bowl. "But what did it *really* do for people?" came the follow-up inquiry. I was not certain what exactly he was driving at and gave myself time to think with an elongated, "Well." Fortunately another hand came to the rescue. "My grandfather worked on the WPA. He helped build the post office in Tuttle, Kidder County, and. . . ." The student went on for several minutes about her grandfather's work in North Dakota during the depression and the meaning of the WPA to him and his family. In a few minutes she had turned the WPA from a lifeless jumble of statistics into a living story of people. She had gone a long way to answering the question, "But what did it *really* do for people?" That classroom experience directed my historical focus more toward people — toward teaching and writing from the perspective of how the flow of events influenced the lives of the people on Tuttle's main street or Kidder County's farmsteads.

The historian or general reader who is in search of main streets or farmsteads in the New Deal faces considerable frustration. Since Arthur

I

M. Schlesinger, Jr., began his three-volume study in the 1950s of the administration of Franklin D. Roosevelt, an explosion of scholarly studies has augmented the New Deal's bibliography and historiography. New Deal historians, however, have placed their emphasis heavily on federal-agency organization and administration in Washington. "In general, historians have focused on the Hoover administration," Bernard Sternsher wrote in 1970 about studies of the pre-New Deal depression years, "emphasizing the formulation of policy and its effects from the standpoint of men in Washington looking outward across the nation, or of men across the nation fixing their sight on the national capital."[1]

Five years later John Braeman, Robert H. Bremner, and David Brody echoed the same sentiment when they declared in their introduction to *The New Deal: The State and Local Levels* that "Students of the New Deal have traditionally tended to focus their attention upon events in Washington — Roosevelt and his advisers, the myriad of new federal agencies spawned during the 1930s, and Congress."[2] They went on to point out that since James T. Patterson's *The New Deal and the States: Federalism in Transition* was published in 1969 a "growing number of scholars" had begun to study the impact of the New Deal on states and localities.[3] For the most part, however, only the characters and setting changed. Minnesota's Floyd B. Olson, Massachusetts's James M. Curley, or Oklahoma's William H. D. ("Alfalfa Bill") Murray replaced Washington's Franklin Roosevelt, Harry L. Hopkins, or Henry A. Wallace, and the political maneuvering and administrative problems moved from the nation's capital to the state capitals. Of the thirteen excellent, chapter-length studies in *New Deal: State and Local Levels*, eleven explored the New Deal at the state level and two looked at the New Deal in cities (Pittsburgh and Kansas City, Missouri). This kind of scholarship on the New Deal in the states and cities is indeed essential and gratifying. At the same time, however, whether one is reading national studies such as Theodore Saloutos's *The American Farmer and the New Deal* and Susan Estabrook Kennedy's *The Banking Crisis of 1933* or state studies such as Francis W. Schruben's *Kansas in Turmoil, 1930–1936* and my *Depression: Minnesota in the Thirties*, a central fact emerges: main street and farmstead are lost in the political battles, agency struggles, and government statistics. Saloutos had no farmers in his book; Kennedy had no bankers; Schruben and I had few grass-roots Minnesotans and Kansans.[4]

This study is an effort to put the main street and the farmstead into the context of the depression and the government's attempts to cope with the economic crisis. In doing so I have three major objectives: to demonstrate how the New Deal's programs were translated into action at the grass roots, to evaluate what impact the policies and programs had on communities and individuals, and to explore the people's response to what the New Deal was endeavoring to achieve. To accomplish this task I have used the county as the grass roots.

When graduate students came to me over the years with suggestions of beginning-to-present county histories for thesis or seminar topics, without exception I successfully discouraged such proposals. I argued that counties are governmental not historical entities, that historical themes and movements transcend county lines, that counties are artificial historical problems. Yet for the historian who desires to probe the heart of the organization, workings, and effects of New Deal programs, the county is the ideal historical unit for several reasons. First, most New Deal programs operated in most counties. Cities may serve as appropriate places for study of the New Deal's labor policy, relief programs, or business relations, but obviously not for conservation, agricultural adjustment, or rural electrification. The urban setting presents a too limited perspective for a comprehensive investigation of the New Deal programs at the grass roots. Second, the county is close to the people. Cities, too, enjoy that status; states do not. Obviously most New Deal programs operated in some way in all the states, more so than in counties. But at the state level it is too easy to become overly involved in political struggles and state-federal problems at the expense of the people whom the programs assisted. Third, the New Deal used the county as its base of organization for most of its programs. Because the county was already equipped to handle relief, in most cases the Federal Emergency Relief Administration channeled funds through the states to county administration. The Civil Works Administration, Works Progress Administration, and National Youth Administration followed the same pattern. County committees organized and ran the agricultural adjustment programs, and most REA work sprang from county movements and organizational meetings. The Civilian Conservation Corps operated on a county-quota system in recruiting its men. With the exceptions of National Recovery Administration and Public Works Administration, the New Deal programs were operationally rooted in the county; and of the federal agencies that dispensed funds, only PWA did not maintain in-county affiliation. The New Deal essentially viewed the county as its statistical and administrative base.

Otter Tail County, Minnesota, is an ideal model county, not because of acute hardship or vast numbers of people who depended upon the New Deal, but because it experienced the broadest possible participation in New Deal programs. Almost all counties became involved with the relief administrations, the FERA, the CWA, and the WPA; participated in the farm programs; had young people who joined the CCC or took part in the NYA; and were touched by banking reform and the NRA. Fewer, but still a great many, took advantage of the PWA and its grant-and-loan program for public building. It is not difficult to find in any state counties that had these federal agencies working within their boundaries. Of the nation's 3,053 counties, about half served as CCC camp sites; 600 had a central PCA office; and 413 headquartered an REA cooperative. Otter Tail County had all three. The county also presented a unique situation in that it served as the central office for a privately owned electrical utility, providing the opportunity to explore cooperative private-power relationships. Otter Tail County is the quintessential window through which to view the New Deal in action.

In presenting the grass-roots New Deal I have used the traditional historical sources: public documents (federal, state, county, village, township), private records and correspondence, and newspapers. I have also depended upon oral history, less traditional but essential to an understanding of main street and farmstead response to and involvement in the New Deal. (See the Bibliographical Essay for an explanation of methodology.) "The historian who seeks to know the Great Depression from those who remember it faces formidable obstacles," Bernard Sternsher warned. "As in the case of every other historical development, each individual had his [or her] own unique experience, and the inquirer will unearth a bewildering variety of accounts."[5] That "own unique experience," however, is grass roots, and these recollections are helpful rather than bewildering pieces of the New Deal era's story. Extremely few farmers, merchants, and workers have left diaries or collections of correspondence. So, if one sets about to investigate the relationship between the people at the local level and the New Deal, oral history remains the historian's only alternative. And, of course, that resource dwindles with each passing day; in ten years not many people who took part in New Deal programs will have survived to relate their "own unique experience." These oral memoirs are indispensible documents in the history of the grass-roots New Deal.

OTTER TAIL COUNTY
The People, the Politics, the Place

"THE FINE SCENERY of lake and open groves of oak timber, of wind-
ing stream connecting them, and beautiful rolling country on all sides,
renders this portion of Minnesota the 'garden spot of the Northwest.' "
Captain John Pope of the United States Topographical Engineers wrote
these words to describe the area that later became Otter Tail County
that he had visited in 1849.[1] The county, which lies in west-central Minnesota, is the eighth largest county in the state and consists of sixty-two
townships, covering about 1,962 square land miles and 270 square lake
miles. The countryside is dotted with lakes, woods, fields, pastures,
farmsteads, resorts, and small towns. Some areas are broken and hilly,
and some are relatively flat. The soils differ in their agricultural productivity from poor to good, primarily due to the mixture of gravel, sand,
silt, and clay deposited as glacial till and also to the range of natural
vegetation (from prairie to mixed forest) that developed in the region.[2]
A fairly dependable annual rainfall of about twenty-four inches made
the area an appealing place for farm families to settle.[3]

Organized in 1858 Otter Tail County attracted Old-Stock Americans, largely from New England and New York, and others of British de-
scent. Names such as Sawyer, Atkinson, Baldwin, Sutherland, and Em-
ery dominated the early farmsteads and communities.[4] By the 1880s,
however, many Old-Stock Americans in Minnesota had moved to the
towns where they usually engaged in business.[5] The county did not re-
main the domain of Old-Stock Americans for long.

After the American Civil War a tidal wave of immigration turned
the region into a melting pot of almost thirty ethnic groups by 1900. Of
the thousands who found new homes in Otter Tail County, Norwegians,
Germans, Swedes, and Finns came in the greatest numbers, although
Danes and Poles clustered in certain townships. Census figures enumer-
ating persons born in a foreign country or born in the United States to
immigrant parents reveal the ethnic diversity that characterized the
county.

5

Norwegians, the largest ethnic group, began arriving during the 1870s, settling mostly in the western townships. By 1905 when Minnesota conducted a state census, 18,681 lived in the county, making up at least 50 percent of the population in Norwegian Grove, Trondhjem, Aastad, Tumuli, Oscar, Dane Prairie, Aurdal, Sverdrup, Scambler, Pelican, St. Olaf, and Tordenskjold townships.[6] Germans started to come in great numbers by 1880, although some had settled in the southern tier of townships earlier. By 1905, 11,268 Germans lived in the county. They comprised more than 50 percent of the population in Effington on the southern border and Gorman, Perham, Pine Lake, and Edna townships in the north-central section, in addition to a few enclaves in several western townships.[7] Swedes began arriving in the 1870s and totaled 1,588 in 1880. By 1905 the number had grown to 8,679. Whereas at least 10 percent of the population in twenty-three townships in 1905 was Swedish, Swedes made up more than 50 percent of the population in just one — Eastern.[8]

The first Finns migrated to Otter Tail County in the 1870s, but the influx peaked in the 1890s. The 1895 state census counted 971 immigrants in the vicinity of New York Mills, which was fast becoming a focal point of rural Finnish settlement in Minnesota; by 1905 a total of 3,671 Finns resided in the county. The last of the major ethnic groups to arrive, the Finns settled on the only available land, which was in the northeastern townships where they comprised at least 50 percent of the population in Paddock, Blowers, Newton, Leaf Lake, and Deer Creek townships in 1905.[9]

Danes reached their greatest number in 1905 with 346 immigrants and 1,026 of their children in seventeen townships. Only in Tordenskjold Township did they represent more than 25 percent of the population.[10] The Polish population totaled 498 in 1905, centered mainly in Corliss Township where about 40 percent of the people were Polish.[11]

As late as 1930, 59 percent of the population of Otter Tail County was composed of immigrants or the children of immigrants, including 7,489 Germans, 10,473 Norwegians, 4,731 Swedes, and 2,923 Finns.[12] To hear Norwegian in Trondhjem Township, German in Effington Township, Swedish in Eastern Township, or Finnish in New York Mills was still a common experience.

Religious life reflected the ethnic mosaic of the population. From whatever countries the immigrants came, they brought their religion with them. Of the 25,986 county residents who were members of denominations (about half of the people), 16,990 or 65 percent were Lutherans in 1936.[13] Norwegian Lutheranism accounted for the lion's share of the Lutheran congregations and membership (54 percent). Because of differences over doctrinal interpretation, the role of the laity, and church polity the Norwegian Lutherans had had great difficulty uniting as one church body in America. In 1917, however, most of the nation's Norwegian Lutherans came under one roof when the Hauge Synod, the United Norwegian Lutheran Church, and the Norwegian Synod merged into the Norwegian Lutheran Church of America. In Otter Tail County 28 percent (7,284) of denomination members claimed congregations involved in this merger as their places of worship.[14]

Two Norwegian Lutheran groups with congregations in the county spurned merger: the Lutheran Free Church and the Church of the Lutheran Brethren, which together accounted for about 9 percent of the county's membership. Differences over control of Augsburg Seminary in Minneapolis caused an organization called the Friends of Augsburg to leave the United Norwegian Lutheran Church in 1897 and to form the Lutheran Free Church, which was dedicated to the independence of its individual congregations and stressed personal religious experience.[15] The Church of the Lutheran Brethren broke away from the United Norwegian Lutheran Church in 1900. Adhering to a strict pietism, the Lutheran Brethren emphasized nonliturgical worship, independent congregations, and a personal conversion experience. In 1935 the Lutheran Brethren moved its Lutheran Bible Schools from Grand Forks, North Dakota, to Fergus Falls, where it maintained its headquarters.[16]

German Lutherans generally belonged to congregations of the Evangelical Lutheran Synod of Missouri, Ohio, and Other States (commonly called the Missouri Synod), which had 5,711 members (22 percent of the total county members of denominations).[17]

The Evangelical Lutheran Augustana Synod of North America, founded in 1860, was home for 2,182 people of mostly Swedish heritage — 8 percent of the county's denomination members. The Augustana Synod experienced only one serious schism; free-church groups that split off formed the Swedish Evangelical Mission Covenant Church in 1885.[18]

The Finns had three Lutheran denominations: the Apostolic Lutheran Church, the Finnish Evangelical Lutheran Church (Suomi Synod), and the Finnish-American National Evangelical Lutheran Church. The Apostolic church, whose history dates to the 1870s, was essentially a lay-led revival movement that insisted that the local congregations control their own affairs. The Suomi Synod, organized in 1890, modeled itself closely after the Church of Finland in Europe and espoused traditional Lutheran polity. In 1898 dissenting members, disgruntled over the centralization of power in the synod, established the Finnish-American National Evangelical Lutheran Church, which

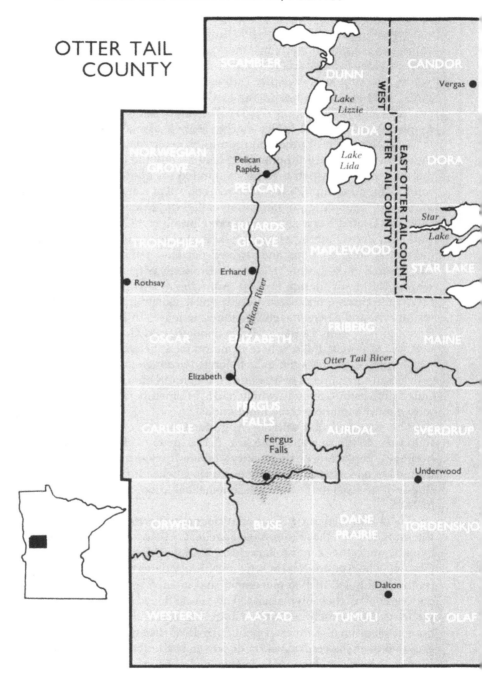

OTTER TAIL COUNTY

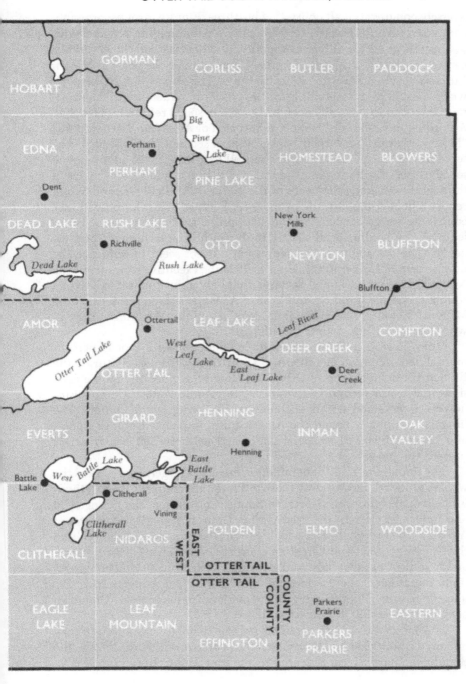

GORMAN

CORLISS

BUTLER

PADDOCK

HOBART

Big
Pine
Lake

EDNA

Perham
●

HOMESTEAD

BLOWERS

PERHAM

PINE LAKE

Dent
●

DEAD LAKE

RUSH LAKE

New York
Mills
●

● Richville

OTTO

NEWTON

BLUFFTON

Dead Lake

Rush Lake

Bluffton
●

AMOR

Ottertail
●

LEAF LAKE

Leaf River

COMPTON

West
*Leaf
Lake*

DEER CREEK

Otter Tail Lake

OTTER TAIL

*East
Leaf Lake*

Deer
Creek
●

GIRARD

HENNING

INMAN

OAK
VALLEY

EVERTS

West Battle Lake

*East
Battle
Lake*

Henning
●

Battle
Lake

● Clitherall

Vining
●

EAST

FOLDEN

ELMO

WOODSIDE

*Clitherall
Lake*

NIDAROS

WEST

CLITHERALL

OTTER TAIL

OTTER TAIL

COUNTY
COUNTY

EAGLE
LAKE

LEAF
MOUNTAIN

Parkers
Prairie
●

EASTERN

EFFINGTON

PARKERS
PRAIRIE

stressed congregational polity.[19] The three Finnish groups probably comprised about 5 percent of the county's denomination membership.

In spite of ethnic differences, polity, and practice, all the bodies accepted traditional Lutheran doctrines, emphasizing the heart of Martin Luther's teaching — justification by faith. The subordination of good works was, in part, responsible for the Lutheran reluctance to take positions on social issues or to become involved in social reform movements. According to E. Clifford Nelson, a historian of American Lutheranism, "Most Lutherans, with their background of social and theological conservatism, seemed to assume that attempts by Christians to eliminate the social causes of suffering masked the idea that one could 'cure the ills of the soul by satisfying the needs of the body.' "[20] A 1913 General Synod report reflected the attitude of most Lutherans: "The church can best contribute its great share to the solution of the various social problems . . . by holding itself strictly to the faithful preaching of the Gospel."[21] The onslaught of the depression did not seem to influence the mainstream of Lutheran thinking. In 1931 the executive secretary of the National Lutheran Council declared that only a spiritual rebirth would restore economic stability, and Walter A. Maier's radio sermons on the Missouri Synod's "Lutheran Hour" kept reminding Americans that all would be well if the country would turn to Christ.[22]

Otter Tail County's Roman Catholics numbered 4,278 or 16 percent of total denomination membership. United by doctrine and liturgy, the Roman Catholic church in Otter Tail County avoided the ethnic divisions that characterized Lutheranism. Rural midwestern Catholicism, however, remained within the conservative wing of the church. The liberals, commonly called the Americanists, supported public schools and became involved in social issues and actions. The conservatives stressed the pious, quiet, isolated life.[23]

The remaining 4,718 denomination members largely represented the well-established, mostly conservative, Protestant churches: the Methodist Episcopal church, the Northern Baptist Convention, the Evangelical and Reformed church, the Presbyterian Church in the United States of America, the Protestant Episcopal church, the Evangelical church, and the Congregational and Christian churches. The Salvation Army operated a unit in Fergus Falls, and two small Assembly of God congregations represented the Pentecostal movement. One congregation belonged to the liberal wing of American religions — a Unitarian congregation of 150 at Underwood.[24]

The conservative bent apparent in their religious affiliations in turn nurtured a political climate in which the people rarely defected from the Republican party. In presidential races Otter Tail County usually gave

The main street runs from left to right through the middle of this view of Battle Lake in about 1940.

Republicans considerable margins of victory. In 1920 Warren G. Harding received 71 percent of the county's vote.[25] Four years later Calvin Coolidge garnered 54 percent in a three-way campaign with Democrat John W. Davis and Progressive Robert M. La Follette, Sr.[26] In 1928 county voters gave Herbert C. Hoover 63 percent to aid in his victory over Alfred E. Smith.[27]

Following World War I the rise of a farmer-labor coalition altered the structure of Minnesota politics. Workers, especially in the Twin Cities, faced strong opposition to their unionization efforts. The Citizens' Alliance, an organization of business leaders formed in 1908, had effectively kept organized labor weak. The Alliance maintained that it wanted to improve working conditions and promote harmony between labor and management, but it consistently supported anti-union political candidates and employed informants who infiltrated labor's ranks. The Working People's Nonpartisan Political League, labor's political arm, did not have much influence in a state controlled by the Republican party.

Farmers, especially in the wheat counties that bordered North and South Dakota, had supported the Nonpartisan League, which during World War I moved into Minnesota from North Dakota where it had successfully captured the Republican party and established a state-owned mill-elevator and bank. Although the League was unable to gain power in Minnesota, many farmers remained in sympathy with its primary objective of improving their economic life. The Minnesota Farmers' Nonpartisan League continued as a vocal proponent of rural reform into the 1920s and was able to pressure the legislature into enacting a rural-credit plan.

During early 1922 farm and labor leaders hammered out a third-party coalition and decided to enter a full slate of candidates in the fall general election. The coalition shocked Republicans and Democrats by electing Henrik Shipstead (a Minneapolis dentist formerly of Glenwood, Pope County) to the United States Senate and two United States representatives, including Knud Wefald from the Ninth Congressional District. After 1924 the Farmer-Labor Association became the state's second-ranking party — far surpassing Democratic vote totals but unable until the depression to wrest control of the statewide offices from the Republicans.[28]

Only twice did the residents of Otter Tail County support Farmer-Labor candidates during the 1920s. In 1922 they joined other Minnesotans in retiring Senator Frank B. Kellogg in favor of Shipstead, a maverick Republican who later returned to the party. Two years later Otter Tail County gave Magnus Johnson a two thousand vote edge over the successful Republican candidate for the Senate, Thomas D. Schall. Johnson, a Swedish-born dairy farmer, was especially popular with Scandinavian voters.[29]

In the Ninth Congressional District elections, in which Farmer-Laborite Knud Wefald was usually a candidate, sometimes incumbent and sometimes challenger, county voters in five successive elections threw their support to his Republican opponents. Successful Republican gubernatorial candidates Jacob A. O. Preus and Theodore Christianson received a majority in Otter Tail County throughout the 1920s, ranging from 47 to 64 percent. The county voted for Republicans in the other statewide races.[30]

The county's farmers also followed a moderate course in organizational membership, preferring the American Farm Bureau Federation to the Farmers Union. The Farm Bureau came into Otter Tail County before World War I and emphasized the improvement of farming methods rather than political action. Organized into two divisions (East and West), the groups worked closely with the county agents. In reviewing the Farm Bureau's work between World War I and 1927, its president, Ben Kimber, cited cow-testing programs, improved fruits and grains, home-management and sewing courses, soil improvement, and boys' and girls' club work.[31] Although the national Farm Bureau Federation

The Girard Go-For 4-H Club of Perham modeled the dresses they had made in 1940. Left to right are Kitty Duddles, Phoebe Quick, Marvel Stabnow, Virginia Chesborough, ? Duddles (sister of Kitty), June Hotchkiss, Fay Stabnow, and Gail Quick.

had come, albeit slowly, to support federal legislation that would improve farm prices, Kimber gave no hint that the Otter Tail County group had political or pressure-group inclinations. By the end of the 1920s, membership stood at eight hundred, about 12 percent of the county's farmers.[32]

Compared to the Farm Bureau, the Farmers Union, which was more politically active in demanding government help, entered Otter Tail County late and did not enroll many members. The Union began a membership drive in the late 1920s in the southern townships. The county agent observed that in those places where the Farmers Union was making a bid for members, "the majority of the progressive farmers . . . are already farm bureau members."[33] The long-standing alliance between the Farm Bureau and the extension program and agents made the county a difficult place for the Farmers Union to build membership.

Otter Tail County's economy was based on agriculture. Most of its income came from farms, food-processing plants, and businesses that served and depended upon farming. Although before the turn of the century farmers emphasized wheat growing, by World War I dairying had become the primary source of income, and in 1930 Otter Tail led all other Minnesota counties in total value of dairy products[34] and ranked twelfth in the nation in volume of annual milk production — 32,094,476 gallons.[35] "Four-fifths of the 6,600 farmers in the county report dairying as one of the major projects on the farm and class their cattle as dairy cattle," the West Otter Tail County agent observed in 1932.[36] Although the total value of dairy products varied from year to year because of price fluctuations, at the end of the decade 32.5 percent of the county's agricultural income came from dairy products. Other farm income was derived from cattle and hog sales, 22.9 percent; field crops, 15.4 percent; and poultry and eggs, 10.6 percent.[37]

The use of the land in the early 1930s reflected the dependence upon dairying. Of the 1,118,189 farm acres (the most of any county in Minnesota), cropland accounted for 615,936 acres (55 percent) of which about half was in feed grains and hay. Wheat remained the largest cash crop, although it decreased in value from $610,485 in 1929 to $557,715 in 1939. Many farmers also raised flax, rye, and potatoes.[38]

Despite the primacy of dairying, the farms maintained their self-sufficiency. Farmers had other sources of income to supplement the creamery check. Of the 6,702 farms only seventy-three comprised five hundred acres or more. The average farm (about 167 acres) was diversified, had sixty-five to seventy chickens, five to six hogs, and fifteen to twenty acres of such crops as flax, rye, or wheat. Rare was the farm that did not have its garden for fresh vegetables and canning. Farm families consumed about 17 percent of the county's farm-product value right on the farm.[39]

The Ronnevik farm of 158 acres near Carlisle was typical. Jorolf Ronnevik described the operation:

> We had some thirty-five acres of corn and twenty acres of wheat, twenty acres of oats and twenty acres of hay in the pasture. . . . There were twelve milk cows; we had six work horses. As a rule we had six sows and raised one litter a year, and we had chickens. The chickens were my mother's project, and I used to carry the eggs to the little village of Carlisle and trade for groceries and a can of kerosene occasionally. . . . That's what we lived on, egg money. The milk check was steady. It wasn't large, but it was steady. And the hogs were supposed to be the one source of income to pay on debts and things of that sort.[40]

The farm also supplied the family with its food. "We always had enough to eat," Ronnevik recalled. "We had our chickens; we had our steer and a couple of hogs that we could butcher."[41]

Lincoln Avenue looking west from Mill Street in Fergus Falls in 1929

Although in 1930 most of the 51,006 people lived on Otter Tail County's 6,702 farms, almost a third called seventeen villages and the city of Fergus Falls their home.[42] The towns were tied to the well-being of farm economy, depending on farmers for most of their business. The editor of the *New York Mills Herald* emphasized the interdependence of the town and farm when he wrote:

> The farmer's obligation to the community near to where he lives are economically as great as those residing in that community. His sales outlet can only be maintained as the community prospers. If his sales outlet is removed from that community the cost of transporting his products from his farm to a sales outlet at a greater distance is increased.
>
> The farmer residing near New York Mills shares in all of the things which makes New York Mills a desirable place to live. His children attend its school after they complete the district school curriculum; in all probability, his family attends church here; and with the automobile annihilating distances his family participates in the social life of New York Mills to a large extent. Its civic activities, its library, its public gatherings, its concerts and entertainment, this newspaper — all of these agencies enrich the lives of the farmer and his family to as great a degree as they benefit the townspeople.[43]

The towns were the beehives of retail business and entertainment, especially on Saturday night when the stores stayed open to give farmers a night of shopping. The general store handled a wide variety of merchandise and dominated the retail trade. Seventy-three general stores, popular gathering places, generated about 16 percent of the county's total retail sales of $14,381,000 in 1929. Only the fast-growing filling station and automotive sector did more business — 28 percent. Of the county's 503 retail stores, specialty stores such as book, music, appliance, and ready-to-wear were few. The general store was king of the retail trade, and farm families were its main customers.[44]

1930 POPULATION OF CITY AND VILLAGES, OTTER TAIL COUNTY

Fergus Falls	9,389	Underwood	308
Perham	1,411	Dent	224
Pelican Rapids	1,365	Vining	222
Henning	731	Ottertail	221
New York Mills	667	Bluffton	204
Parkers Prairie	631	Dalton	182
Battle Lake	552	Richville	179
Deer Creek	337	Elizabeth	164
Vergas	323	Clitherall	151

Processing and manufacturing plants were small operations that did not employ many workers. Otter Tail Power Company, a privately owned utility headquartered in Fergus Falls, supplied electricity to an area that stretched into western North Dakota and ranked as the largest county employer in 1931 with 102 people. The lumbering industry in the New York Mills area had declined from its peak in the 1870s and 1880s.[45] In 1931 Northwestern Sash and Door Company of Fergus Falls, which produced finished wood products including church and school furniture, employed forty-nine people. The manufacture and sale of woolens accounted for thirty-five jobs, and Liberty Garment Manufacturing Company for twenty-nine.[46]

Several smaller factories were scattered throughout the villages. Representative of them were the Franklin Fence Company and the Schmidt Wagon Factory. Edward Franklin built a weaver for manufacturing lath-and-wire fencing during the winter of 1933–34 and by 1938 had developed a company that provided fencing and silo and corn cribbing within a 325-mile radius of his factory in Vergas. At one time the

Main Street in Pelican Rapids in about 1940

company employed twenty-eight men.[47] The Schmidt Wagon Factory, established in Perham by blacksmith L. H. D. Schmidt in 1889, specialized in constructing farm wagons. Run as a family business until 1946, the wagon factory never employed more than a handful of workers.[48]

The making of dairy products was the most significant food-processing industry. Twenty-six creameries, all but one organized as cooperatives, handled the marketing of milk and led Minnesota in manufacturing dairy products. The creameries ranged in size from the Cloverleaf Creamery Association with two employees in Heinola to the Farmers' Co-Operative Creamery Company of Pelican Rapids, which, according to the *Pelican Rapids Press* in 1932, was "one of the largest institutions in the state" and did "a business of more than a half millions [*sic*] of dollars in a year."[49] In 1929 the county, besides being a top milk producer, churned 494,728 pounds of butter.[50]

The only nondairy food-processing plant of consequence was M. A. Gedney Company's dill-pickle operation in the village of Dent. Established in the mid-1920s the company contracted for cucumbers and dill weed with local farmers and employed up to a dozen people during its processing season. Production hit about thirty barrels a day from mid-July until the first frost in the fall.[51]

Otter Tail County's bountiful lakes and beautiful landscape became a nationally recognized summer playground. Well over a hundred resorts, campgrounds, and beaches lured thousands of vacationers for

Interior of the sash and door factory in Fergus Falls in 1937

fishing, swimming, boating, and relaxation.[52] In the 1880s and 1890s real-estate developer John K. West had organized a steamboat transportation system to boost the lakes of the Pelican River valley, especially the large and remote Pelican Lake, the location of the Pelican Inn. He also persuaded Northern Pacific Railroad Company officials to make plans in 1894 for running special summer trains to bring vacationers to the area. By 1912 the railway was actively promoting tourism in "Nature's Summer Playground."[53] As developers and local governments expanded and improved the road system after the advent of the automobile, the resort business flourished.

Searle A. Zimmerman, who was born at Elizabeth in 1902 and worked as assistant cashier for the First State Bank in Fergus Falls during the 1920s, observed:

> When I went to work at the bank the economy was in pretty good shape. In 1928–29 there was a skeptical feeling about our bank's future because it had bought a lot of paper in western North Dakota farm land where things were going poorly for farming. But around the county farmers were doing all right until the thirties when the agricultural economy collapsed. Most farmers didn't carry huge

mortgages around here and just needed the two or four hundred dollar loan for operating expenses. The farmers, these Norwegians and Germans, were very conservative and believed in hard work. It took hard work to make it, but most did. They had a little bit of everything, cows, pigs, chickens, crops. That made a big difference.[54]

Zimmerman, from his vantage point in the bank, captured the essence of the county and its people as they entered the depression decade. Otter Tail County personified small-town, rural America.

2

OTTER TAIL COUNTY
The Economic Crisis
and the Politics of Response

THE STOCK MARKET CRASH of late 1929 ushered in a decade of in-security and instability, at times approaching chaos. Never before had Americans witnessed such economic depression or experienced such emotional despair. Within a few years the world's mightiest industrial nation teetered on the brink of collapse. Between 1929 and 1932 indus-trial production declined more than 50 percent. The *New York Times* weekly business activity index (which used 100 to stand for the estimated normal) fell from its highest 1929 point of 114.8 in June to 63.7 (its lowest point) in March 1933. Industrial construction tumbled from $949 mil-lion to $74 million in three years. Many factories closed; others curtailed production. Steel plants ran at 12 percent of capacity, illustrating the abyss into which business had fallen.[1]

Banking reflected the unhealthy condition of the nation's economy. Between 1920 and 1929, 5,411 banks failed — mostly small ones in rural areas that were overbanked. The impact of the failures on the national economy was slight. During 1930, 1931, and 1932, 4,921 commercial banks suspended operations, including New York City's Bank of the United States, "the largest commercial failure in American history." These failures struck at the heart of the economy and created an at-mosphere of fear that engulfed the population and eroded confidence in the system.[2]

The banking fiasco and industrial turmoil spelled the loss of millions in dollars and jobs. The income of workers fell precipitously, and the ranks of the unemployed swelled, causing widespread destitution. Thou-sands of workers lost their homes; Hoovervilles sprang up almost over-night; at least one million and maybe as many as two million people hit the road in a fruitless search for work, living off good will and sometimes thievery. Stories about city people surviving on coffee and bread, dan-

20

delions, and garbage became common. The breadline quickly became the symbol of the nation's distress.[3]

Urban squalor and hardship grabbed most of the headlines, but farmers also had their backs to the wall. The bleakest of times had struck rural America. Unlike the plight of the urban unemployed, farm woes stretched back to World War I. During wartime the government had urged farmers to produce more food and fiber to supply soaring worldwide demand. To the slogans, "Food Will Win the War" and "Plow to the Fence for Defense," they planted thirty million additional acres and took whatever measures were necessary to increase output. The demand for farm products continued after the war for a short time as American loans and credit allowed European countries to buy essential goods, and private relief agencies provided food for stricken areas. Most farmers were certain that they had entered an era of permanent prosperity.

The war, however, had created an abnormal farm economy with artificially high farm prices, and the farmers' wonderland soon faded away. Foreign markets shriveled up as American credit substantially decreased, and competitor nations such as Argentina and Australia reentered world trade. In mid-1920 farm prices began to drop sharply, signaling the end of good times and the onset of an agricultural depression. Although the nation slumped into a general recession during 1921–22, agriculture, unlike other sectors of the economy, did not recover.[4]

Having geared up for an all-out war effort, farmers could not adjust to the smaller market. Armed with new technology and scientific advances in breeding and seed development, farmers easily maintained or increased production. For example, the gas tractor and improved implements helped to cut the time needed to produce some crops by as much as 50 percent from 1900 to 1930. Corn could be grown more successfully in colder climates like that of Minnesota because of scientific seed selection. Disease prevention and better breeding and feeding methods substantially reduced pig litter losses.

The new scientific farming and the loss of foreign markets, however, were not the only culprits that undercut the farm economy. Domestic consumption dropped. A population that during the war had been encouraged to have wheatless Mondays and Wednesdays and meatless Tuesdays changed its eating habits to the detriment of food producers. Among women the slimmer flapper look replaced the bulky appearance of the prewar era, and men strove more for the Calvin Coolidge than for the William H. Taft silhouette. Annual average per capita wheat consumption fell from 224 pounds during 1897 to 1902 to 176 pounds during 1922 to 1927 and corn from 120 to 46 pounds. Consumption of beef, veal, and eggs did not keep pace with population growth, remaining about the same in 1929 as it had been in 1900. Prohibition robbed barley growers of nearly 90 percent of their market. The nation, however, drank 12 percent more milk in 1929 than it had in 1900 and consumed 9 percent more pork and lard during about the same time, but that did not offset the underconsumption of grain and the static market in beef, veal, and poultry.[5]

The loss of foreign and domestic markets, coupled with technological and scientific advances, built surpluses that plagued the farm economy, keeping prices depressed and barring many farmers and ranchers from the Republican prosperity. The initial readjustment in prices between 1919 and the years of 1922 and 1923 shocked the countryside. Wheat led the farm debacle, plummeting 57 percent from $2.16 per bushel to 93 cents in 1923; corn fell 52 percent from $1.51 to 73 cents in 1922. Hog prices tumbled from $16.39 per one hundred pounds to $6.94 (58 percent), and beef cattle from $9.97 to $5.73 (43 percent) in 1922. Wholesale prices per one hundred pounds for whole milk and value per head for chickens declined less severely, 36 percent (in 1922) and 22 percent (in 1923) respectively. Between 1923 and 1930 prices for these items rebounded somewhat but never approached the high prices of 1918 and 1919. During the six-year period, corn averaged 83 cents per bushel, and wheat, $1.19 — the most modest price recoveries. In 1928 cattle approached the 1919 price but averaged $7.62 between 1923 and 1930. Hogs hit $11.79 in 1926, averaging $9.61. Milk had a slow but steady gain of 31 cents per hundredweight, and chickens were the maverick commodity, attaining 95 percent of their 1919 price.[6] Farm income had been almost $17 billion in 1919; by 1929 it stood at less than $12 billion, a decrease from 25 to 10.4 percent of national income. Prices that farmers had to pay for goods, however, remained fairly constant, eroding the purchasing power of the farm dollar.

The decline in farm income made indebtedness and taxes a more troublesome burden. Farm debt rose from almost $8.5 billion in 1920 to a peak of $10.7 billion in 1923. By the end of the decade it had decreased somewhat to $9.8 billion. Rural taxes increased nearly a hundred percent between 1917 and 1930, intensifying the financial bind at a time when land values were skidding downward. Many farmers found themselves in an economic squeeze long before the rest of the country had heard of a breadline.[7]

Assessing the situation in fall 1929, Arthur M. Hyde, Herbert Hoover's secretary of agriculture, optimistically declared that farmers could look ahead to better times due to an improving farm economy.[8] Within three years farm prices would hit bottom, throwing farmers into an impossible dilemma. Prices, which had been fairly stable since 1925, fell more sharply than they had after the war: corn from 80 to 32 cents; wheat, $1.04 to 38 cents; hogs, $9.42 to $3.34; beef cattle, $9.47 to $4.25; milk, $2.53 to $1.28; eggs, 30 to 14 cents per dozen. Farm income dropped from $11.3 billion in 1929 to $4.7 billion in 1932. Farmers indeed faced their darkest hour.[9] The darkness of the hour, however, depended upon several factors: the nature of an area's agriculture, farm indebtedness, and growing conditions.

The inability of wheat and cotton prices to rebound as rapidly or as far as other commodities did skewed national farm income downward. During the 1920s farmers in the one-crop wheat and cotton economies of the Great Plains and the South suffered much more than did their counterparts in areas of less intense agriculture. The Otter Tail County farmer who diversified and relied on dairying was better off than the North Dakota farmer who was tethered to the wheat culture. Dairying generated 34 percent of Otter Tail County's farm income in 1929. In the postwar price-readjustment crisis, the national price for whole milk slid 24 percent, while wheat fell 48 percent; thereafter, whole milk prices remained stable. This, coupled with the increase in national milk consumption and a 55 percent increase in the county's output, meant that dairy farmers were more able to maintain incomes than were farmers tied to a one-crop economy. Poultry followed a similar pattern; the county's chicken production went up 15 percent during the 1920s, nearly off-setting the postwar price decline with new income. The county's farmers cut wheat production as much as 72 percent, devoting those acres to feed crops and flax, which commanded a relatively better price. Whereas wheat and cotton growers could not shift their crop emphasis, Otter Tail County with its diversified farms could better adjust to changing consumption patterns and market fluctuations.[10]

Farm mortgage indebtedness in 1920 was lower in Otter Tail County than the average of 52.4 percent for Minnesota, running at about 45.5 percent.[11] Many farmers had purchased land before 1900 and had paid off their mortgages. With smaller farms they did not have to buy the machinery or hire the labor that wheat or cotton farmers needed in their operations.

Ed Hintsala, who came to New York Mills in 1898 and managed the Farmers Elevator Company in the 1930s, reinforced that point when he observed:

It was mostly family farming in those days. . . . Now the combines come in. I remember [the] Allis-Chalmers [Manufacturing Company] blockman came over — combines weren't so easy to sell in this country, but I happen to know the grain so I felt I was doing the farmer a favor to sell them a combine because . . . you get better grain from it too. Saves a lot of labor. He came over one day and he said, "You can't sell combines in this country." And I asked him why. Well, he says, "Out there they were threshing and they looked like a picnic. . . . They don't want any combines."[12]

Farmers did not have to depend on the local bank for as many or as large long-term loans. Those who purchased land around the time of World War I, however, had difficulty avoiding financial trouble. Hans Ronnevik is a case in point. He moved from North Dakota to Otter Tail County in 1919, purchased a farm, worked it for one year, and sold it for a profit. He bought another farm for $135 an acre in the early 1920s when land prices peaked. Encumbered with a new mortgage, Ronnevik struggled to fight off foreclosure. Finally in the mid-1930s he lost the farm.[13]

Climatic conditions also worked on behalf of the county's farmers. Average and above-average precipitation allowed farmers to maintain high crop yields throughout most of the 1920s — an advantage that many farmers to the west and south did not have. In 1929 and 1930, however, annual precipitation slackened to about eighteen inches — six below normal. The drier conditions were, of course, uneven across the county. Both of the two county agents reported areas of severe drought, and in 1930 East Otter Tail County agent John Grathwol worried that "the past two years of drought have shown that we still do not have a large enough acreage of tame hay."[14] The drier years brought grasshoppers to some western parts of the county. In June 1932 Grathwol worked day and night, delivering a poison bait containing bran, arsenic, and molasses. The bait was mixed with water and spread on infested areas, inviting grasshoppers to a poisonous death. In spite of Grathwol's work and the bait, the hoppers destroyed some crops in 1932 and in the following dry years, especially 1934 and 1936.[15] By and large income loss due to drought and insects was minimal compared to losses that came with the jarring decline of farm prices in 1932 and 1933.

Otter Tail County farmers were better prepared to face the test of the depression than those in many other areas. Self-sufficiency played a key role in that preparation. With two-thirds of the county's people on farms, the vast majority of the county's population was self-sustaining. The Hegge, Toso, and Dillon experiences were typical.

Oscar and Martha Hegge farmed eighty acres near Dent. Oscar cut wood to raise enough money to pay the interest on the mortgage. Martha recalled that in 1936 "our cream check was down to $10, that's twice a month, so we had about $20 a month for a while — that isn't an awful

A crew of WPA workers (above) mixed poison bait each summer for the county agents to distribute to farmers. The farmer (below) then spread the bait on the grasshopper-infested field.

lot to live on if you have a family of four kids." But that year the Hegges had enough wherewithal to go dancing on Saturday nights at the White Eagle Lodge: "We didn't have any crops . . . and hardly any money and still we could have fun." The farm was diversified: the cows for the cream check and pigs, chickens, and garden produce to eat. "We got along," Martha concluded, "and it seems to me that things were not too bad."[16]

Conrad and Elizabeth Toso lived with their nine children on a mortgage-free forty-acre farm in Maplewood Township. Conrad sometimes worked for others and in 1936 took WPA employment for a brief time. He wanted electricity on the farm but could not afford the minimal cost. Times were tough for the large family, but they survived because

The Toso family of Maplewood Township posed in 1936 or 1937. Left to right, back row, are Minnie ("Grandma") Muchow, Elizabeth Muchow Toso, C. Eugene, Conrad, Mildred, Luella, Kenneth, Lorraine, and Dorothy; front row, Harvey Richard ("Dickie"), Norman, and Donald.

of self-sufficiency. Elizabeth made all the clothing, and the dairy check brought in a little cash. "What I remember about it [is that] we never went hungry," Conrad observed, although his son C. Eugene ("Gene") recalled that the children got tired of the "honey and syrup sandwiches." Gene emphasized the importance of self-sufficiency: "We generally ate beef or pork during the Winter months, and then we had no way to keep it during the summer months. So mother and dad would always get us lots of chickens." The Tosoes' daughter, Dorothy Toso Williams, summarized the depression years: "I didn't know I was deprived until about ten years ago."[17]

Susie and Robert Elton Dillon farmed with his parents, Robert F. and Josephine Dillon, on eighty acres in Lida Township near Pelican Rapids. As was true for the Tosoes and the Hegges, the dairy check provided the cash and the farm provided the food for the Dillons. One day Susie went into town to pick up the milk check and buy necessities. "My husband said if there's a nickel left get the Saturday Evening Post. But he didn't get it," she recalled. Susie made most of her children's clothing: "Everything was always made. The overalls were made from the backs of the men's overalls." Even though they carried a small mortgage and were making payments on a 1928 Chevrolet, the Dillons survived the depression, largely due to ingenuity and self-sufficiency.[18]

This is not to say that Otter Tail County wore a golden glow around its shoulders. In 1933, 6 percent of the nation's farmers gave up their land.[19] Charles M. Kelehan, the Otter Tail County agent, lamented in 1929 that "tenancy has been increasing in the county ever since the deflation of farm prices. Many farms that were operated by owners eight or ten years ago are now in the hands of Mortgage Companies or other Loaning institutions."[20] Tenancy had increased 39.4 percent during those ten years, but the figure is misleading.[21] Farm tenancy ran slightly higher than the Minnesota average, but in 1933 only 5 percent of farmland (58,738 acres) was owned by lending institutions (insurance companies, 23,298 acres; Federal Land Bank, 5,294; Otter Tail County banks, 7,424; out-of-county banks and mortgage companies, 11,745; State of Minnesota and its Rural Credit Bureau, 10,977).[22] Those who lost farms faced shattered worlds and the trauma of rebuilding broken lives. Others hung on the verge of foreclosure throughout the depression, weathering the economic storm as best they could.

Just as farmers lost farms, workers lost jobs. The unemployment problem in Otter Tail County did not approach the magnitude that it did on Minnesota's iron ranges where almost 70 percent of the mines' work force languished without employment.[23] Because most businesses were family run and the county had little nonagricultural industry, people quietly entered the ranks of the jobless without the fanfare of bold newspaper headlines. How many workers were laid off is impossible to determine. In late 1936 about 2,200 people were looking for work at a time when 1,890 were employed on government work projects. Those seeking jobs included young people, farmers who had given up their farms or who hoped to supplement their incomes, and workers who had been forced off regular jobs.[24] Although Otter Tail County's unemployment problem did not come close to rivaling that on the iron ranges, the people without work in Fergus Falls or Parkers Prairie faced the same grim prospect — no means of making a living. To individuals without work, the circumstance of geography or numbers made little difference.

The extremely hard times of 1932 caused Otter Tail County to abandon its traditional allegiance to the Republican party. In 1930 its residents ran counter to the state, rejecting Floyd Olson, the dynamic Farmer-Labor candidate for governor. Two years later, however, Olson, who ran on a platform that called for placing water and electric utilities under state control, unemployment insurance, old-age pensions, and an income tax that would put a greater burden on higher incomes, carried the county: Olson, 8,248; Earle Brown (Republican), 6,941; John E. Regan (Democrat), 1,925. Franklin Roosevelt joined the county's defection, defeating Republican Herbert Hoover, 8,805 to 7,416.[25] The rock-ribbed Republican *Fergus Falls Daily Journal* lamented, "Otter Tail county went Democratic Tuesday for the first time in a great many years if not in its history." Fergus Falls, however, did not disappoint the Republicans, providing Hoover and Brown with almost two-to-one victories.[26]

In 1934 the county did not go along with the majority of Minnesotans, giving Republican Martin A. Nelson 10,524 votes to Governor Olson's 6,240. Other Republicans enjoyed even larger majorities. Two years later, when Roosevelt swamped Alfred M. Landon, who carried only two states, Otter Tail County supported Landon, 8,899 to 8,642. County voters cast straight Republican ballots, handing Martin Nelson a 9,517 to 8,389 edge for governor over Elmer Benson, Farmer-Labor's victorious candidate.[27]

The headline, "Otter Tail Republican As Always," captured the spirit of the 1938 and 1940 elections. In 1938 thirty-one-year-old Republican Harold E. Stassen ended eight years of Farmer-Labor control of the governorship, soundly defeating Governor Elmer A. Benson, who had earned a reputation as an authentic radical. Stassen's victory in Otter Tail County was stunning: 15,064 to 5,391. Two years later Stassen won by a three-to-one margin, and Republican Wendell L. Willkie defeated Roosevelt by two to one.

The Republican party distributed this poster widely to ensure a big turnout for the rally.

Even during the grim years of the depression the county sent to the legislature mostly people who tended to be conservative. For example, Elmer E. Adams, who was elected in 1930, served in the state senate throughout the decade. Adams, in his seventies, a graduate (1884) and regent (1897–1905) of the University of Minnesota, was the editor of a newspaper and president of the First National Bank in Fergus Falls. Influential and well-to-do, he had his children educated at Yale University and at Wellesley and Smith colleges.[28]

In spite of the county's conservative political stance, it had a small but active Communist party, especially in the New York Mills area — Newton, Leaf Lake, Blowers, Deer Creek, and Paddock townships. John Hartman of Perham recalled going to dances at Heinola where the "hammer and sickle was pasted right on the walls of this dance hall."[29]

The Communists annually ran a three-week summer camp on East Leaf Lake. "Red flags flare from many tents," a reporter observed; and in 1931 about seventy children completed the training courses.[30] In 1935 the Communist party failed in an attempt to win control of the Leaf Lake Township Board. The party promised that if its three candidates were elected they would call a meeting of residents over eighteen years old to elect at least twelve residents to an advisory committee to the board. In a circular letter to township residents the Communists explained their intent:

> It is decidedly unusual for any political party to enter or endorse candidates for township elections. All the other political parties decided long ago, due to the impossibility for graft, to declare laws to be passed that candidates shall file without Party designation. The candidates whose names are written in below have pledged themselves to work for the program below. The Communist Party of this Central Section of Minnesota endorses the program whole-heartedly. We believe that if put into effect by the town boards it will really help the impoverished farmers and their townships. We ask all voters to select the men who have courage enough to come out and tell the people what they stand for.[31]

The Communist program was not very radical: support for unemployment insurance and a farm-relief bill, a relief program based on need, and a protest against appropriations for defense. Essentially, the Communists did not like the way that the township board was running the relief program.

Communist candidates usually received between 170 and 200 votes, but those totals placed Otter Tail County behind only St. Louis County in percentage of Communist voters. For example, in 1928 William Z. Foster, Workers (Communist) party candidate for president, received 185 votes from Otter Tail County, while Minneapolis and the rest of Hennepin County gave him only 451 and St. Paul and Ramsey County, 340.[32]

The New York Mills area's reputation as a center for Communist activity was augmented in 1930 when the political committee of District Nine of the American Communist party moved the headquarters of the United Farmers League from Bismarck, North Dakota, to New York Mills and appointed Rudolph Harju, a Finnish-American activist, as its national secretary. Originally formed in 1926 as the United Farmers Educational League, it became the party's rural propaganda arm. As disgruntled farmers, especially on the Great Plains, were increasingly attracted to other organizations such as the Farmers Union, party leaders hoped that a change in leadership and location might spark renewed vigor in the organization. Turning the League over to the Finnish-American Communist movement, however, did not breathe new life into the group. As 1931 came to a close organizational results had "been weak." In mid-1932, at the worst possible time for farmers, only nine hundred belonged to the party.[33]

Ethnic background rather than extreme economic hardship explains the presence of the Communist party in northeastern Otter Tail County. The Finns who lived in the area came from the farms and forests of Finland where radical socialism had gained a large following by the 1890s. Unlike the other Scandinavian groups, the Finns migrated to the United States late and brought their radicalism with them to the lumber camps and iron mines of Minnesota. They generally were more responsive to social action and reform groups than were the county's other ethnic groups.[34]

One reason the League had difficulty attracting members was the appearance of the Farmers' Holiday Association, a dynamic group that demanded immediate government assistance in militant terms. On May 3, 1932, more than two thousand farmers inaugurated the association in Iowa and chose Milo Reno, the Iowa Farmers Union leader, as its president. The Holiday Association's remedy was simple: hold back farm products until the farmer realized the cost of production. John H. Bosch, president of the Kandiyohi County Farmers Union, spearheaded the Minnesota effort and in May and June 1932 traveled through the countryside recruiting farmers for the organization. On July 29 people from western counties converged on St. Cloud to organize the Minnesota Farmers' Holiday Association. Bosch emerged as president of the Minnesota branch.

In early August the Iowa Holiday Association attempted to block all milk shipments into Sioux City in order to increase prices. On September 9 the governors of Minnesota, South Dakota, North Dakota, and Iowa met in Sioux City to discuss the price-cost dilemma. Reno presented the Holiday program: farm mortgage moratoriums, congressional action to lower the cost of farm credit, and a state guarantee of minimum prices for farm products to meet production costs.

In Minnesota the association followed a more restrained course of action. Bosch knew that only federal programs, not random strikes, could affect prices. A strike might make good newspaper copy but would have no lasting impact. Nevertheless, Minnesota farmers proceeded to withhold perishable products from market. Lack of widespread sympathy for the strike was apparent as numbers of farmers attempted to ship goods to market. On October 5 in Yellow Medicine County an irate farmer shot and killed a striker, causing the only casualty of the strike.[35] Picketing subsided after the shooting, but the state patrol had to restore order in the Twin Cities area. Although the strike had not been scheduled for termination until November 11, it had burned out by late October.[36]

The Farmers' Holiday Association began organizing in Otter Tail County after the withholding strike had begun. On September 22 a bold-faced advertisement asked, "The Farmers Strike! Shall Park Region Farmers Ignore It? Shall They Oppose It? Shall They Join It?," and invited the public to hear John Bosch at the Fergus Falls High School auditorium on the following evening. An estimated twelve hundred people from all parts of the county jammed the auditorium for the meeting. Bosch traced the history of the farm problem in his usual calm and reasoned manner, concluding that farmers needed to organize and control the market to get a fair profit. He told the crowd that he was certain that society would be willing to "pay enough for the necessities of life so that the farmers would not have to carry on their business at a loss." The *Fergus Falls Daily Journal* liked Bosch's approach because he "did not enter into a tirade on big business, as many so-called 'leaders' do in these days." Carl M. Iverson, however, launched into an attack against big business, international bankers, railroads, and the Reconstruction Finance Corporation. Iverson, who represented Grant County in the Minnesota senate, had a reputation as a staunch advocate of the Holiday Association and as a "fiery orator." John Flint, pastor of the Christian Free Church (Unitarian) of Underwood, helped to conclude the evening's speeches by issuing a call for "all honest-thinking men and women" to support the movement. The gathering had unanimously passed a motion to organize a county unit and elected a nine-person executive committee.[37]

Between September 23 and October 4 the organizational process continued with a series of meetings planned at Henning, New York Mills, Pelican Rapids, Fergus Falls, and the Inman Township town hall. Because of the county's size, the executive committee decided to have four districts, each with a chairman, and a chairman for each township.[38] After they had been selected, the township chairmen received information about circulating pledge blanks among farmers who would agree to withhold farm produce. At a Fergus Falls meeting George A. Jensen, a member of the executive committee and township coordinator for Tordenskjold Township, reported that he had secured the names of twenty-four farmers who had agreed to hold their produce off the market, but said that some were reluctant to join because they needed money to pay taxes. P. C. Peterson, a Maine Township farmer, declared that he could not pledge to withhold his livestock because he had seven pigs and only enough feed to last through the month: "I will either have to sell the hogs then or let them starve." Jensen agreed that under the circumstances it would be unfair to ask Peterson to hold the hogs. "There will be peaceful picketing when the movement gets under way," Jensen affirmed, "but absolutely no force will be used to turn back farmers on their way to market."[39]

The Farmers' Holiday Association did not attract the membership or engender the activism that it did in counties to the south. In February 1933, under the headline "Good Sense in Evidence Here," the *Fergus Falls Weekly Journal* condemned the strike action and attempts to stop foreclosure sales to the south and praised the people of the county for their moderate position: "We believe that a great majority of the people in Otter Tail county believe in our state government and will uphold it. We have had no complaints here in Otter Tail county of people being unduly forced to pay by those they owe. Everybody is showing a fine spirit in trying to grant everyone else a change [*sic*] to survive these tough times."[40]

Otter Tail County, however, did not escape Farmers' Holiday Association efforts to stop farm sales and foreclosures. Although not as frequent as in adjacent counties, Holiday Association and Communist party demonstrations broke into the news on several occasions. Three incidents illustrate how the Farmers' Holiday Association operated. In the first (in May 1933) it obtained a foreclosure postponement. The other two (in October 1933 and April 1935) demonstrated the "penny auction" in which the members would bid low and force others from the bidding. In both instances the sales had to be stopped, putting off the farmer's day of reckoning.

On May 1, 1933, Holiday Association members led a crowd onto the steps of the county courthouse in Fergus Falls to stop the foreclosure of Abraham and Anna Mattson's farm in Leaf Lake Township by the Finnish Mutual Fire Insurance Company. The crowd, described as being composed of persons mostly "from the east side of the county" along with "some . . . from Wadena county," demanded that the proceedings be stopped because Abraham had been bedridden for four or five years. George Jensen told the acting sheriff that the crowd wanted no violence but only an extension of time to give Abraham a chance to "find some way out of the difficulty." The acting sheriff said that there could be a thirty-day postponement. The crowd, however, remained to stop a second proceeding by the Iowa Evangelical Lutheran Orphans Society against a woman who had a tract of land west of Deer Creek. When the acting sheriff explained that the woman had agreed to the sale, the crowd did not protest further.

A Holiday Association leader seized the opportunity to fire up the crowd. "They took our money in good times, and now they are trying to take everything we have," exclaimed George Miller, a member of the executive committee from Fergus Falls, as he spoke about the threatened foreclosure of the Mattsons' farm and "attacked the capitalistic system." In introducing John Flint, Underwood's Unitarian minister, Miller declared, "Most preachers teach us that we shall eat pie, by and by, in the sky, but here's a preacher that thinks we should have some of the pie here." The crowd applauded heartily. Flint lashed out against international capitalism and encouraged Americans to get together to protect their homes as "They did . . . in the Colonial days against the savage Indians." Jim Flowers, a militant spokesman for radical action from Sebeka, Wadena County, quoted Karl Marx, maintaining that Marx had predicted the present economic dilemma " 'way back in 1848." He urged immediate and vigorous action: "We are waging a battle to save our homes."[41]

In October the Holiday Association broke up a sale that the farmer had requested. John C. Nelson, who rented a farm in Everts Township, had borrowed four hundred dollars from the First National Bank of Battle Lake. He was unable to repay the loan and asked the bank, although it "was not pushing him for payment," to auction off his equipment and livestock to satisfy the loan.

Holiday Association members led a crowd, mostly from Grant County and from around New York Mills and Underwood, that descended on the auction. When bids of only two cents, six cents, and one dollar were offered for a binder, a bank representative called off the sale. Then:

> The crowd demanded that he go on with it. He refused, and started for his car. The crowd gathered around the car, and threatened violence unless he would proceed with the sale. He defied them. They gathered in front of the car, and continued to make threats, refusing to allow him to proceed. Some of the leaders lifted the car partly from the ground and threatened to overturn it.
>
> As the sale was not a forced sale, or an execution sale, the sheriff had nothing to do with it, but Ed. Stai, who sometimes acts as deputy sheriff, happened to be in the audience, and drew a gun. The crowd laughed at him.
>
> State Senator Carl Iverson of Ashby [Grant County], addressed the crowd, denouncing banks and bankers, and making a typical speech for such an occasion.[42]

At the farm auction in Perham a reporter positioned in the haymow of the auction barn photographed a Communist party member selling a newspaper, probably the Farmers' National Weekly.

Jim Flowers (center, waving fist) exhorted the crowd in one of the "pep" talks given at the Perham auction.

In April 1935 the Minnesota Department of Banking, which was liquidating the assets of the State Bank of Perham, held a sale of the personal property of Gust W. Haut, a farmer in Hobart Township. Before a deputy sheriff, acting as auctioneer, began the sale, "many cars rolled into Perham. They came from Detroit Lakes, Heinola, Sebeka, Menahga and other distant places." "Farm Holiday leaders and Communists" sang " 'pep' songs" and the crowd listened to "fiery talks." After two or three cows were sold, "the angry mob dragged the buyers away." A police officer, who apparently made a bid for the banking department, was seized and thrown off the premises. Finally, to avert more violence, the Department of Banking asked that the sale be called off. A newspaper article emphasized that the protestors — members of the Holiday Association and the Communist party — "were not people of Perham and vicinity, but were strangers from a distance."[43]

The Farmers' Holiday Association did not gain much allegiance from the county's politically conservative farmers who supported the Farm Bureau with increased membership, more than eleven hundred by 1939. Those who participated in Holiday Association protests, often joined by Communists, largely came from Wadena and Grant counties and from the New York Mills and Underwood areas of Otter Tail. In Otter Tail County the withholding action does not appear to have had much success, and foreclosure and farm-sale protests were few and sporadic. By the mid-1930s Minnesota's Holiday Association membership had dwindled to less than two thousand, and in 1937 it faded back into the Farmers Union.[44]

The New Deal with its multiple farm and relief programs took the steam out of radical movements. Farmers did not come close to realizing any benefits from a cost-of-production plan, but the New Deal provided enough support to give both farmers and workers confidence that better times were coming. People whose world was crumbling, whether in Detroit or Birmingham or Fergus Falls, turned to their government for help in a time when they could not help themselves.

DIRECT RELIEF
"In Dire Need of Help"

" 'ONE MAN got off one of the trains the other night. . . . He was on crutches and was absolutely destitute. He said his home was in Ohio, but that he had been in a hospital in Canada,' " Steve Butler, the poor commissioner of Fergus Falls, told the city council in June 1927. The Canadians purchased a ticket for the man to Thief River Falls, Pennington County, Minnesota; Thief River Falls authorities bought him a ticket to Crookston, Polk County; Crookston officials sent him on to Fergus Falls. A newspaper article reported that Butler wanted to know what could be done in "a matter of this kind" because he felt that the people in Crookston had no right to "send a pauper to this city." When one of the aldermen asked Butler what he had done, he replied, " 'Oh I bought him a ticket to another city down the line.' " According to the article, "everyone felt that this was the proper and cheapest procedure."[1]

On a fall day in 1927 two women from the Fergus Falls American Legion Auxiliary drove to a small farm near Vining to investigate reports that a disabled former serviceman, now a farmer, needed help. The farmer "wasn't strong enough to do the work . . . the mother and child were without shoes and supplies of clothing were very much lacking. The only stove that the family had for heating the house was a 2-burner oil stove, and as for food, . . . if there was any in the house, it wasn't to be seen." Through talking to neighbors, it was discovered that "the husband, though really being in need of treatment in bed, was earnestly trying to do what work he could." The auxiliary provided clothes for the family, and the American Red Cross helped the farmer by "pushing" his claim for compensation with the Veterans' Bureau.[2]

The four physicians of Pelican Rapids decided that they would not treat "Poor-Pay People" whose medical bills were overdue. According to their agreement: "Debtors will receive a credit rating which determines their standing with all professional men as to whether they are entitled to service or not. An unpaid and neglected debt with one doctor disentitles the debtor entirely to the services of another doctor." In October

1927 Carl A. Snowberg responded to the physicians' new policy in his column in the *Fergus Falls Weekly Journal:*

> The doctors of Pelican Rapids will refuse to render service to poor-pay people in the future. It sounds like good business but the rule may lead to complications. Suppose, for instance, Mrs. Jones calls Dr. Healemup and says: "Mr. Jones fell on a scythe and cut an artery in his neck; come at once." Dr. Healemup consults his books and finds Jones in arrears for treatment of a carbuncle. He calls Mrs. Jones and informs her that her husband is poor-pay and he will not come. Frantically she calls Dr. Dowell, who recently read a paper at a medical meeting on "How the Physician Sacrifices His Life for Humanity." Dr. Dowell consults his list of poor-pay people and finds Jones' name on it. He tells Mrs. Jones he is sorry, but he is just leaving on a call. Hysterically, Mrs. Jones calls Dr. Payordie. This worthy gentleman tells her he does not specialize in severed arteries and recommends Dr. Mayo. By this time Jones has departed for a land that is fairer than northern Minnesota — where bad bills are never collected for lack of collectors, and where there are no ills and very few doctors. Sadly she calls the undertaker and he says he'll be right out.
>
> Moral: If you can't pay your bills don't get hurt, sick or hungry.
> A suitable epitaph on Jones' headstone might read:
>
> 1883 — Jones — 1927
> A cent for a cent
> And an eye for an eye
> If I'd paid as I went
> I'd not had to die.[3]

During the winter of 1930 the county welfare agent found living in Elmo Township a destitute mother and five sons between the ages of three and twelve. The father had abandoned the family. The sons trapped gophers for the ten-cent-per-head bounty to buy bread, the family's main food supply. "But as the fall wore on the gophers became more scarce and likewise the loaves of bread. The children are said to have eaten rose berries, leaves, and finally gophers." The family was taken to Fergus Falls where the Salvation Army and Elmo Township provided them with food, fuel, and clothing "until some other means of aiding the mother in supporting her children can be found."[4]

Newspaper reports about hardship must have shocked the residents of a county that had not tasted economic adversity since the 1890s. Although the crippled transient, the destitute farm family, the "poor-pay" of Pelican Rapids, and the abandoned family were isolated and dramatic cases, they reminded Otter Tail County that it was not immune from

An advertisement in the Fergus Falls Daily Journal for September 8, 1933, showed prices for typical foodstuffs, such as milk, bread, lard, and bacon. Note the reference to the surplus of butter.

Save Money On Your Household Needs!

A&P NRA WE DO OUR PART

CRYSTAL WHITE or **P&G** WHITE NAPTHA

SOAP 10 Reg. Bars **27¢**

5 GIANT BARS 19c

Ivory Soap Flakes . . 2 LGE PKG 39c
KIRK'S COCOA HARDWATER
Castile Soap . . . . . CAKE 5c

Camay Soap CAKE 5c
Lava Soap SMALL CAKE 5c

Bokar Coffee	LB. CAN	23c
SEAL BRAND Chase & Sanborn Coffee . .	LB. CAN	29c
Maxwell House Coffee . . .	LB. CAN	28c
GRANDMOTHER'S White Bread PLAIN OR SLICED . . .	1-LB. LOAF	6c
Peanut Butter SULTANA BRAND . . 2	LB. JAR	23c
Bisquick Anybody can make the old-fashioned Peach Shortcake now .	PKG.	32c
Calumet Baking Powder .	1-LB. CAN	25c
Whitehouse Milk 3	TALL CANS	17c

THIS YEAR'S BIGGEST FOOD VALUE—

BUTTER At this price there is no greater food value ------ **23c**

There is a tremendous surplus of fine butter—dairy farmers need help to sell this surplus, so A & P offers you butter at this low price, making not one cent of profit.

SUGAR FINE GRANULATED **10** LBS. **50¢**

ARMOUR'S STAR PURE
LARD . 4 LB CARTON **29¢**

Spring Chickens Fresh Dressed --------12c

Bacon Squares 9c

Smoked Picnics 8c

Pork Loin Roast 11c

Veal Roast 10c

A&P Food Stores MIDDLE WESTERN DIVISION

hardship and that people who were in need had few options: family help, private charity, or government relief.

During the depression government outlay of money and goods in the form of direct relief to people who were unable to, or could not, find work kept many individuals and families from starvation and illness. Direct relief went through three phases as local, state, and federal governments tried to cope with the enormous problem of unemployment. Before 1933 and the New Deal, the burden of caring for the chronically poor and the new unemployed in Minnesota rested on the county and its local governments. From 1933 through 1935 the federal government, and to a much lesser degree Minnesota state government, buttressed local relief efforts with a massive infusion of dollars. After 1935, however, the primary financial responsibility for direct relief returned to and remained with the individual local governments.

Care for the poor had been vested formally with local governments since the late sixteenth century when the Elizabethan Poor Laws came into existence in England. A local tax, called the poor rate, financed the care of paupers and required the justices of the peace to look after the poor. Local governments expected the able-bodied poor to participate in some kind of public work in return for public assistance. Although the mechanics varied from state to state and locality to locality, the philosophy of the Elizabethan Poor Laws continued to control the American relief system as the Great Depression began to cast its long shadow across the nation.[5]

In Minnesota counties could choose one of two systems. Under the county system the county commissioners administered all direct relief. The town system, under which Otter Tail County operated, made township, village, and city governments superintendents of the poor. Minnesota law, however, allowed a 75 percent reimbursement from the county to any local government for funds expended in excess of one mill of its assessed valuation on poor relief. In Otter Tail County eighty governing bodies (sixty-two township boards, seventeen village councils, one city council) handled direct relief as each saw fit.

Before 1928 the county's local governments expended little on direct relief, sometimes supporting an elderly resident at the county's poor farm or helping out a family with groceries or medicine. Between 1928 and 1933 relief outlays increased, especially in 1931 and 1932 when farm prices sharply declined. Aurdal, Clitherall, Western, and Otto townships reflected the increasing expense of caring for the poor. In 1928 Aurdal made no poor fund payments but in 1933 provided $172 in groceries, hardware, and medical care.[6] Clitherall spent between $35 and $50 annually between 1929 and 1932 when its poor relief outlay rose to

$201.49.[7] The board of supervisors in Western made only one payment of $23 in 1926; in 1930 help for the poor cost $207.22, and in 1931 the board recommended a $600 poor fund.[8] Otto's trustees granted $289.51 in 1928 and $488.09 in 1932.[9] The villages experienced similar expenditure increases. In 1927 and 1928 Ottertail had no poor fund but in 1934 spent almost $280. Dent spent $5.75 in 1929; by 1933 it needed $300. Other villages followed the same pattern between 1928 and 1933: Underwood, $100 to $400; Battle Lake, $200 to $500; Vining, $25 to $200; Elizabeth, $250 to $300.[10]

Poor Commissioner Steve Butler summed up the situation in Fergus Falls when he told the council that "the poor business is getting awful, and I've got enough business here to take up the council's time until midnight."[11] That was in March 1928 when the city was spending about fifteen hundred dollars annually on the poor. By 1933 that figure had climbed to about twenty-five hundred dollars.[12]

Private groups pitched in to help alleviate the "poor crisis," especially in 1932 and 1933. The Otter Tail County chapter of the American Red Cross distributed 138,680 pounds of flour in 1932 to those in the county who were " 'needy and distressed.' " Although Red Cross workers had anticipated only 350 needy families, 701 families representing 3,346 people received flour during the distribution. Officials of only four townships (Buse, Compton, Fergus Falls, and Leaf Mountain) and one village (Dalton) did not request flour.[13] In 1933 the Red Cross distributed 18,170 yards of material and 10,688 items of clothing received from the federal government. At least thirty sewing clubs made clothing for distribution within the county.[14]

In Fergus Falls an Associated Charities took form in late 1928 when service clubs and churches banded together to formulate "a systematic distribution . . . of charity offerings."[15] The Benevolent and Protective Order of Elks, the American Legion, and the American Legion Auxiliary held "charity frolics" to support relief work.[16] The city's 1933 Community Chest drive to raise money to help those in need set and reached a goal of $9,150, which was "less than $1 per person for every resident of Fergus Falls." To promote the drive students in city schools wrote essays on "Why All Should Help the Community Chest." Two of the winning essays, both by eighth-grade students, were poignant reminders that the depression had touched Otter Tail County. Robert Boen wrote:

> The Community Chest is an organization for the purpose of relieving want and suffering from Fergus Falls. Many people do not realize what a Chest would mean to our city. In the past few years many men have been unemployed and their families have been without

proper food and clothing. Boys and girls have been kept out of school just because of lack of funds in their families. Those of us who have had the necessities of life have remembered to help now and then with this family and that. But many cases of poverty and hardship have been overlooked. Many people are too timid to ask for help even though they deserve help.[17]

Margaret Voran stressed the plight of the unemployed in her essay:

Have you a job? If you have you should be able to contribute to the Community Chest. There are many unemployed men and women in Fergus Falls who would gladly take your job at less pay and still make a contribution to the Community Chest. When you are asked to contribute to the Community Chest, remember that the people who are asking for help would rather have a job and take care of themselves than depend upon charity. . . .

It has been proven that families in dire need of help, have often been forced to steal food or clothing in order to keep from starving or freezing to death. The Community Chest alone stands between them and their mental despair.[18]

By inauguration day in March 1933 most experts who were close to the relief problem agreed that state and local governments could no longer cope with the crisis. In some states 40 percent of the people depended upon government aid, and in some counties 80 to 90 percent were on relief.[19] Although in Otter Tail County the figure stood at less than 10 percent, probably around 7 percent, local boards and councils that had never faced the necessity of increasing poor funds thought that the situation was, to use Poor Commissioner Butler's assessment, "awful."[20]

Because of the banking crisis and disagreement within his circle of advisers over the form federal involvement should take, President Roosevelt did not immediately tackle the relief question. Finally on March 21 he asked Congress to establish the office of Federal Relief Administrator. In April Congress passed the bill that created the Federal Emergency Relief Administration (FERA) with $500 million for grants-in-aid to states. Headed by social worker Harry Hopkins, who had run Roosevelt's Temporary Emergency Relief Administration in New York, the FERA assigned half of its appropriation to states on a matching basis of one federal dollar for every three of state money expended for relief during the three preceding months. The other $250 million was earmarked for urgent need in areas where the matching requirement could not be met. Although the FERA intended to emphasize work relief, direct relief accounted for the lion's share of funding during 1933 because of the urgency of the situation. Almost at once federal money began flowing to local governments through state agencies. In Minnesota, the state Board of Control, later reorganized as the State Emergency Relief Administration (SERA), handled the funds.[21]

Before Otter Tail County could obtain federal aid, however, the county commissioners had to sign an agreement with the state Board of Control that established a countywide relief administration as an umbrella organization over the township and village superintendents of the poor. Under the terms of the relief contract the commissioners had to: (1) accept a five-member Emergency Relief Committee "with power and authority to carry out all of the orders, rules and regulations of the Federal Relief Administrator and the State Board of Control"; (2) "make every possible effort to persuade the local political subdivisions to contribute a maximum amount for the support of the poor"; (3) to recognize the county relief worker, an employee of the Emergency Relief Committee, as the one "directly responsible for the expenditure of all relief funds" within the county. The county commissioners acknowledged that they could not require the local governing bodies to authorize the relief worker to sign their relief orders but plainly warned that those townships and villages that did not comply would receive no state or federal funds.[22]

The county commissioners signed the agreement on November 14, 1933 — more than six months after the passage of the federal relief bill. Otter Tail County received its first federal funds — three thousand dollars — that same month, the thirty-third of the state's eighty-seven counties to qualify. The tardiness with which Otter Tail County organized its federal relief program mirrored the general situation in Minnesota. In October Lorena Hickok, who traveled throughout the nation and almost daily reported on the FERA's progress to Harry Hopkins, was concerned that Minnesota's FERA administrator, Frank Rarig, "didn't seem to be particularly worried about how things are going."[23] In early December Hickok visited Otter Tail County on a swing through western Minnesota. "The relief set-up in Otter Tail county is new — only three weeks old," she wrote to Hopkins. "That, obviously, isn't Olson's fault or Rarig's. The county had not asked for help previously. As a matter of fact, less than half the counties in Minnesota are getting federal aid now."[24]

Otter Tail County had not thought that federal assistance was an urgent matter. Hickok's assessment of conditions in the county supports the proposition that things were not so bad. Against the backdrop of several days in North Dakota where the situation was desperate, Hickok observed to Hopkins, "So far as destitution is concerned, I can't see that

Norman and Conrad Toso cut corn by hand on the family's forty-acre farm in 1939, a relatively dry year.

there is any comparison between what I've seen in Western Minnesota and what I saw in the Dakotas. If Floyd Olson ever gave you the idea that the need in his droht [*sic*] area could even touch that in the Dakotas, he was either crazy or a liar." In Perham, which was "supposed to be in the center of one of the worst droht [*sic*] areas," a member of the county relief committee told Hickok in response to a question about the clothing situation that, "they're a bit shabby, but they're warmly dressed." Hickok reported that there were "isolated cases of destitution. I heard of one family that had been living in a tent, and an investigator found two of the children with frozen feet." She, however, was assured that the family "had been taken care of" and did not appear to be alarmed over the situation in Otter Tail County.[25]

During the time that the FERA allotted funds through the SERA to the county (November 1933-December 1935), Otter Tail received $778,142 in federal and $53,041 in state relief funds.[26] Until June 1934 all relief money was used as direct payments, due to the winter emergency and inadequate time to plan work projects.

Because relief statistics were defined and gathered in different ways at different times, it is difficult to profile the flow and impact of federal, state, and local direct relief for the entire life of the FERA. The period from January 1 to July 1, 1934, however, serves as an example of relief orders issued from all public funds for Otter Tail County. The largest share (54.43 percent) of these relief orders was spent on food. Other expenditures included: medical care, 15.77 percent; clothing, 13.57 percent; fuel, 4.35 percent; dental care, 3 percent; shelter, 1.51 percent. Otter Tail had 2 percent of the total population of the eighty-four rural counties (excluding Hennepin, Ramsey, and St. Louis), but the funds it spent were 2.87 percent of the total funds expended.[27]

After June 1934 work projects assumed a larger share of federal relief money. Using March 1935 as a representative month, Otter Tail County's FERA allotment of $36,620 went to 1,356 families, representing 6,601 people (about 12 percent of the population). Direct relief accounted for 17 percent ($6,378) of the month's allocation. During the twenty-six months that Otter Tail County received FERA relief support, approximately $166,500 of the $778,142 was given as direct relief to unemployables.[28]

The FERA imposed a new relief structure on the county. Of the local governments with reasonably complete records on poor relief, all seem to have entered into a formal agreement with the Emergency Relief Committee to allow the county relief worker to draw orders on their poor funds "for the purpose of providing food, fuel, clothing, shelter, medical [aid], dental care, and attention in the home."[29] The townships and villages remained liable for hospital and burial expenses. For example, Gorman Township allowed the county worker three hundred dollars for poor relief within the township but retained what it hoped would be enough for hospital and funeral bills.[30] Local governments had little recourse but to authorize agreements in order to guarantee their participation in federal money.

The government's fear that local boards and councils would decrease their poor expenditures because of FERA funding was unwarranted in Otter Tail County. Of twenty-four sample townships, fourteen raised their poor levies, nine held their own, and only one decreased its poor fund, and that was by about 30 percent. The villages generally were able to maintain their poor funds in 1934 and 1935. Only Battle Lake's poor fund went up, from $500 to $600. Only Ottertail's fell, from $150 to $50. The others remained fairly constant.[31]

Because Fergus Falls held a city classification, the County Relief Administration offered it special options for the handling of relief: the city could pay 25 percent of all poor relief for employable men and take care of all other chronic cases including rents, and the government would pay the balance; the city could pay six hundred dollars per month for employables and chronic cases, and the government would pay the balance; the city could pay twelve thousand dollars per year, and the government would assume responsibility for the entire relief program.[32] The council opted for the last plan, paying one thousand dollars per month.[33]

The federal government's involvement in direct relief was a stopgap measure. President Roosevelt, as well as the majority in Congress, did not like the idea of a federal dole. By the end of December 1935 final FERA grants had been made to most states — no more federal direct relief.[34] Direct relief once again became strictly a state and local responsibility. In early 1936 the County Relief Administration informed the townships and towns that it had "of necessity made some drastic changes. . . . No new cases are being opened . . . and no applications for re-opening are being considered. All such cases are being referred to the governing bodies of the municipality in which the client has residence, this with the view of gradually tapering off the entire relief load to the local governing bodies."[35] This was ominous news for governments whose treasuries were, in some cases, already pushed to their limits. A headline on the front page of the *Battle Lake Review* reflected the concern that the county's people had: "Relief Crisis Seen in Otter Tail County." The county, which under the township system reimbursed the local governments for most of their relief expenses, had already depleted its poor fund by March 1936 and risked losing state aid due to a lack of matching funds. In an emergency meeting the county shifted funds to ensure the state funding, but the handwriting was on the wall: the exodus of federal relief support would mean higher poor-fund taxes for the county and its subdivisions.[36]

The withdrawal of the federal government from the direct relief business forced the state of Minnesota and local governments to authorize steep increases in their expenditures for unemployables. During 1936 and through June 1937 the state reimbursed each county for 37.7 percent of its total relief expenses. But after July 1, 1937, each county received a specific, and much lower, monthly allocation that covered, for example, 19 percent of Otter Tail County's total relief bill during the period July 1, 1937-June 30, 1938. From 1936 through 1939 Otter Tail

County received about $2,000 a month in state aid — $4,400 a month less than during the months of federal help.[37]

The administrative structure and system that had developed under the FERA continued with some modifications. The County Welfare Board and its office handled most of the paper work. Once towns and townships had certified a direct relief client, the welfare office executed orders for food, rent, fuel, utilities, and emergency medical care. Hospitalization, burials, and institutional care remained the responsibility of the subdivisions. The county welfare office attempted to reduce the relief rolls by applying new eligibility rules. Any person having an unpaid balance on a car or living in a nonrelief household became ineligible. Families with young men who were eligible for, but not enrolled in, the Civilian Conservation Corps could not receive direct relief.[38] In April 1937 the County Welfare Board ordered that the names of all direct-relief clients be published in the local newspapers so that citizens could report relief recipients "who make it a habit of frequenting beer parlors or liquor stores, using automobiles unnecessarily and failing to accept employment when available."[39] Local authorities added their own restrictions. For example, Fergus Falls prohibited relief recipients from using their automobiles after April 1, 1936, and threatened to confiscate license plates.[40]

In 1937 the Minnesota Supreme Court dealt the system of poor relief a severe blow. In *Village of Robbinsdale v. County of Hennepin* it upheld a district court decision that invalidated the law that allowed a township, village, or third or fourth class city to recover from the county 75 percent of its poor expenditures in excess of the one mill of the taxable valuation. The court decided that the provision violated the constitutional provision that taxes "shall be uniform on same class of subjects."[41]

The decision caused legal and legislative maneuvering — and frustration throughout Minnesota and in Otter Tail County. The legislature rewrote the law with minor changes, but the county refused to reimburse the subdivisions because it believed that the new law was also unconstitutional.[42] Fergus Falls took the initiative and successfully brought suit against the county for $2,997.70 in reimbursement for expenses incurred in 1936 and $4,629.44 for expenses in 1937.[43] The county commissioners and the County Welfare Board as of March 1, 1938, returned full administration of direct relief to the local governments.[44]

The withdrawal of federal funds in 1936 and county support in 1937 had an immediate impact on the subdivisions. In almost all cases local poor funds and expenditures skyrocketed, peaking in 1938–39. For example, the poor fund in Bluffton Township went from $50 in 1937 to $500 in 1939; Aurdal spent $39 in 1936 and $176 in 1939; Elmo from

$350 in 1936 to $500 in 1938; Gorman from $200 in 1937 to $700 in 1939; Sverdrup from $200 in 1937 to $880 plus a special one mill levy in 1938; and Parkers Prairie from $150 in 1936 to $600 in 1938. In 1938 the village of New York Mills levied only $150, but it spent $1,876. Battle Lake spent $667 in 1936 and $1,318 in 1940. In 1939 voters in Fergus Falls approved an amendment to the city charter so that the council could levy four mills for relief. Its expenditures rose from $2,661 in 1936 to $8,038 in 1938 and peaked in 1939 at $16,020.[45] Local relief costs declined in 1940, 1941, and 1942. By 1943 the relief crisis was over; the wartime economy erased deficits, and most local governments no longer needed their poor funds.

Had it not been for the passage of the Social Security Act, which President Roosevelt signed on August 14, 1935, the strain on local budgets would have been even greater between 1936 and 1941. The act provided for two separate programs: old-age insurance and old-age assistance. Old-age insurance was a totally federal program that would, beginning in 1942, provide a monthly benefit or annuity to qualified retired workers, based on their earnings and irrespective of need. Old-age assistance, which took effect almost immediately, was an attempt to give relief to the needy persons who were at least sixty-five years old and did not live in public institutions. It was a cooperative program in which federal, state, and county governments shared the cost: three-sixths federal, two-sixths state, one-sixth county. Each state administered its own old-age assistance program under guidelines that a federal social security board had to approve. In March 1936 the Minnesota program was ready to go.[46]

Much confusion heralded old-age assistance. Many people thought that it was a guaranteed thirty-dollars-a-month pension plan. The *Battle Lake Review* told readers in a bold front-page headline that twenty-four hundred residents of Otter Tail County were eligible for "old age pensions."[47] When besieged by ineligible "pensioners," the county commissioners brought in a field representative to explain the program. "The law's provisions differ widely from this idea [pension]," a Fergus Falls newspaper article stated. "The law is based on a person's needs and is thus an assistance law. In other words, it is a 'relief law.' It is intended to make up a 'budgetary deficiency.' " The article went on to explain that each applicant would be screened on an individual basis and that thirty dollars was an absolute maximum, not a guaranteed, sum of assistance.[48] Old-age assistance was a relief measure to help local governments cope with mushrooming relief costs.

Although Otter Tail County administered old-age assistance for its own people, the state Board of Control, which supervised distribution by the county agencies, established certain guidelines to ensure consistency: (1) those who received assistance were not eligible for other relief, except for medical care; (2) recipients had to be at least sixty-five years old and a resident of Minnesota for five years; (3) residents of public institutions such as poor farms or state hospitals were ineligible; (4) recipients could not own property valued at more than thirty-five hundred dollars; (5) upon the death of a recipient, the total amount of old-age assistance paid out to that person would be allowed as a claim against the estate.[49]

Otter Tail County had participated in the state's optional old-age pension program since 1933, but township boards and village councils with overburdened budgets had been reluctant to approve pensions. When old-age assistance went into operation, the county had only 16 pensioners, who were receiving an average monthly pension of $7.28.[50] By October 1936, 1,644 county residents had applied for old-age assistance, and in that month 1,253 received checks totaling $22,727.97 or an average of $18.13 per recipient.[51] For the year ending June 30, 1938, an average of 1,460 recipients — the fourth largest number in the state's counties — were receiving an average monthly sum of $18.73 (the state average was $19.70).[52]

The old-age assistance program brought about a million dollars worth of direct relief into Otter Tail County between 1936 and 1940. Clearly local governments could not have provided such benefits for the elderly. In 1938 the county closed its poor farm, largely due to the newer program's help for older citizens.

The Federal Surplus Relief Corporation, later reorganized as the Federal Surplus Commodities Corporation, also helped to remove the sting of the depression. Formed in late 1933, it distributed surplus commodities that the government had purchased in order to bolster farm prices. Those on relief were allowed to receive such items as lard, fruit, butter, vegetables, canned beef, and salt pork in addition to their relief compensation. What commodities were distributed in Otter Tail County largely depended upon what surplus the government was attempting to reduce. John Hartman, who was in the wholesale fruit and vegetable business in Perham, recalled that one year, because of overproduction in the Rio Grande valley, the county's relief clients were given grapefruit — a commodity that proved to be unpopular with most relief families: "People who had never eaten grapefruit, who never realized the nutritional value of grapefruit . . . asked [for] something we [they] could use like meat or potatoes, but grapefruit was one of the surplus commodities."[53] Throughout the 1930s commodities provided hundreds of families with additional support each month. For example,

Workers at Hopkins, Minnesota, bagged surplus commodities for distribution throughout the state.

in June 1934, 575 families received 1,754 pounds of lard; in December 1934, 576 families got 3,036 pounds of canned beef, 581 received 1,619 pounds of butter, and 576 obtained 1,678 pounds of rice.[54]

In reviewing welfare in Minnesota, the American Public Welfare Association concluded: "Most of the opportunity for constructive change in Minnesota's public welfare administration lies in the direction of organizational rearrangement. The lack of coordination of institutional and other welfare services makes necessary a duplication of service to and concern for thousands of individuals."[55] That observation was especially true of a county such as Otter Tail where eighty individual governing boards held the primary responsibility for direct relief. Each board or council set its own standards and guidelines, and depending on how voters cast their ballots, those standards and guidelines often changed.

Frustrated by increasing demands upon their budgets, governing bodies were extremely careful not to extend relief to those who could not prove that they had been residents of the town or township for six months. As boards and councils tried to force other boards and councils to accept liability for relief cases, it was a rare township or village indeed that did not find itself in court contesting a residency lawsuit. For example, the Otto Township board forwarded a bill for a five-dollar grocery order to Leaf Lake Township.[56] A man and his family applied for relief in Gorman Township. Since he had not been in the township for the required six months, the board of supervisors ordered him to return to Evergreen Township in Becker County. He then claimed that he had been a resident of Maplewood Township in Otter Tail County. When the Maplewood board refused to answer Gorman's inquiries, Gorman went to court. The judge ruled that Maplewood was responsible for the applicant.[57] When two couples from St. Olaf Township wished to move to Fergus Falls, the city agreed to allow them to stay with relatives only if the township would provide relief if it were ever needed.[58] A dispute over residency between the village of Vining and Girard Township went all the way to the Minnesota Supreme Court when Vining appealed a district court decision.[59] New York Mills wanted to get a man off its relief rolls because it was discovered that he was a resident of Wisconsin. He apparently did not cooperate with village officials who then believed that commitment to the state hospital was "the best solution." That would transfer his upkeep to the state — not an uncommon ploy. When the state hospital would not admit him, the case went to the city attorney who negotiated an agreement with Wisconsin. New York Mills paid for his return transportation.[60]

While all of the governing bodies shared the common problems of inadequate funds and residency disputes, there was little in common as to how and why they granted relief requests. The village of Bluffton allowed a man to maintain his business while receiving fifteen dollars a month for groceries for three months,[61] but the village of Elizabeth insisted that a woman "in destitute circumstances" deed over her real estate and furniture before the council would agree to allow her ten dollars a month and fuel.[62] Vergas limited expenditure for a pauper funeral to forty dollars; Battle Lake would pay seventy-five dollars.[63] While all local governments were obligated to provide adequate medical care, the methods of handling the sick and their bills varied a great deal. Several villages and townships — including Vergas and the townships of Perham, Elmo, and Folden — contracted with physicians to handle relief patients for an annual fee, ranging between seventy-five and three hundred dollars.[64] Although Fergus Falls doctors requested that arrangement, the city attorney thought the plan was illegal.[65] The villages and townships rarely paid the full bills of hospitals and physicians. Fergus Falls Township paid 90 percent;[66] Paddock Township, however, often paid only 50 percent.[67] In one case New York Mills allowed only $25 on a $322.23 hospital bill.[68] Lawsuits to recover more on a "pauper bill" were common.

In many cases the board or council decided what medical care a relief recipient should receive. The Ottertail village council sought advice from the county attorney and held a special meeting to decide whether a welfare recipient, "being ruptured," should have a truss or surgery. Although a truss would have been less expensive, the council opted for the operation. The council guaranteed his family twenty dollars a month for groceries.[69] In Perham Township three children in one family needed to have their tonsils removed. The supervisors agreed and made the arrangements, but they negotiated the payment of the bill. In this case the father worked off the bill on days he was not employed by the WPA.[70] Few local governments handled medical care in a consistent way. One exception was the Clitherall village council, which formulated a rate schedule and "rules governing medical care of indigent persons." The rules established authorization procedures as well as restrictions such as one visit per week to the chronically ill (unless there was an "acute attack") and, as was common during the 1930s, the delivery of babies in the home (unless the physician insisted on hospitalization for medical reasons).[71]

Most local governments decreed that able-bodied applicants for relief who could not find employment had to work for their groceries, fuel, or rent, thereby establishing a local work-relief program. Hourly wages for snow shoveling, wood cutting, and street and road work varied between fifteen and twenty-five cents an hour, with twenty-five cents more common. Fergus Falls purchased its own stumpage acreages, and relief clients earned between sixteen and twenty-five dollars per month cutting wood for other poor-fund dependents.[72]

Welfare recipients were essentially at the mercy of boards and councils that tried to stretch poor-fund dollars. For example, Lida Township supported a family for several months in late 1937 and early 1938 ($6 for rent, $14 for groceries, $3.60 for milk each month). In May 1938 the case came up for review. The board did not cut the relief-funding level but ordered the grocer not to allow the purchase of canned milk, Doan's Pills, or salad dressing and requested that the family use lard instead of butter in cooking.[73] In Battle Lake the council ordered relief recipients to spread their grocery shopping around town. When that did not work well, it assigned them to specific grocery stores.[74]

Often the paternalism of local governments took on a callous quality. Battle Lake told one poor resident to "pay up his bills and go straight or move out of town."[75] The Tordenskjold Township board held a special meeting in the home of one of its residents to "come to some understanding with him in regard to the support of his family." The board felt that "to feed the family would be too big an expense," so it warned that if the township had to support the children, they would be taken from him and sent to some state institution.[76] The threat of removal to the poor farm hung over the heads of the poor — especially the elderly who were reluctant to give up their local roots. In April 1934 the Leaf Lake Township board notified one of its relief recipients: "The town board of Leaf Lake has paid the rent for the place you are on till April 1st 1934 and from now on you will have to look out for yourself. If you come for more aid, the board will prepare a place for you at the co. poor farm."[77]

Although the absence of extreme-hardship stories after 1933 indicates that the poor survived under the town system of relief, some residents strenuously protested against the inadequacies and inconsistencies of relief administration. In 1935 the Communist party in Leaf Lake Township had attempted to oust the township board largely because of its dissatisfaction with the handling of relief funds. The Workers' Alliance most consistently and strongly objected to the town system of relief. Organized to promote the interests of relief recipients, the unemployed, and workers on government projects, the Alliance's committee frequently appeared before the Fergus Falls City Council and the Otter Tail County commissioners to complain about unfair relief policies. In November 1937 the Alliance alleged that the town system "is causing hardship and suffering to many of our citizens" and pledged "to do all in our power to appeal the township system."[78]

Meeting with county commissioners and the welfare board in February 1938, the Alliance demanded the abolition of the town system, county assistance in obtaining more and a greater variety of surplus commodities, supplementary relief to workers on government projects, more medical help, and house rent in sufficient amount "to allow direct relief clients to live in somewhat of a decent home."[79] A year later George Blake (state president of the Work Promoters' Association) appeared before the Fergus Falls City Council with a delegation from the local Association group and requested cooperation from the council in approving his organization's proposals. He criticized the plan to build three new "school palaces" at a time when many of the school children lived in "tar-papered shacks." Blake asked that the poor commissioner treat all relief clients the same and not favor some and said that the city relief department was exploiting poor men when it paid them only twenty-five cents an hour to do work for the city. "We do not believe the city relief department should take advantage of a worker just because he is in need of a job," Blake declared, "and put them on starvation wages." Mayor Philip

R. Monson of Fergus Falls replied for the council: "All we can do is to do our best and do as our conscience dictates."[80] Those who demanded abolition of the town system received courteous hearings, but the town system, along with its inconsistent administration of funds, remained as the 1930s came to a close.

The federal programs played crucial roles in minimizing the "hardship and suffering" that the Workers' Alliance talked about. The direct relief that the FERA, old-age assistance, and surplus commodities provided meant survival to that 5 or 6 percent of the population who were unable to work and who were in dire need of help. Without those New Deal relief programs the county's boards and councils could not have carried out their mandated charge "to be superintendents of the poor."

4

CWA, FERA, PWA
"Finding Jobs for the People"

THE UNEMPLOYMENT EMERGENCY had forced the New Deal into the "direct-relief business." Both Roosevelt and Hopkins were uncomfortable with the large numbers of people who were able-bodied workers but for lack of jobs were receiving direct relief under the FERA. Both preferred work relief, believing that it was a means of conserving the skills, work habits, and morale of people who through no fault of their own were jobless. Progress in the setting up of worthwhile work programs, however, was minimal during the summer and fall of 1933. Because the FERA was moving too slowly and unemployment statistics were spiraling upward, the president, with Hopkins's support, decided to inaugurate a large-scale federal work program to get unemployed workers through the winter of 1933–34. On November 9 Roosevelt by executive order created the Civil Works Administration (CWA), which had $400 million to begin its program.[1] Governor Olson explained to Minnesotans that "the idea is to avoid all possible red tape and throw as many thousands of persons as possible into immediate employment until the public works program (FERA) can get under way."[2]

Minnesota geared up almost overnight to administer the new work-relief program by creating an engineering division, headed by a state engineer, to handle all CWA projects. The state engineer divided the state into eight districts, each with a district engineer. Each county also had an engineer who worked with the county's Emergency Relief Committee and relief administration in overseeing projects.[3] In Otter Tail County commissioners appointed its highway engineer "to assume the duties and carry out the responsibilities of the Civil Works Administration program."[4]

To expedite the gigantic undertaking, the township boards and the city and village councils made applications for approval of work projects directly to the Otter Tail County Emergency Relief Committee. The federal government allotted quotas to the state, and the state allocated resources to the counties based on population and relief-load costs. The first half of the workers had to come directly from relief rolls and the second half from the National Re-Employment Service registration with preference given to some workers, including veterans with dependents.[5]

In late November the state allowed 899 CWA positions for Otter Tail County. Each town and township received a specific allocation. The average worker earned about fifteen dollars for a thirty-hour week, but a worker was replaced when he or she earned a maximum of one hundred dollars. Because of the urgent need to employ people, most CWA projects involved projects that "can be undertaken quickly" and "can be done by hand labor," such as road work or the repairing of public buildings. For example, New York Mills received sixteen hundred dollars for sixteen workers to make street and other public improvements. The council decided to gravel the streets and improve its park and cemetery, although later it put six women to work "cleaning and painting the jail, fire hall, library, city hall, and school."[6] At Henning seventeen CWA workers finished a skating rink, calcimined walls in the schoolhouse, and were to clean and decorate the city hall.[7] Twelve workers in Underwood refinished schoolhouse floors, cleaned up the lakeshore, and completed a skating rink.[8] In Fergus Falls workers replaced seventy-two thousand feet of water mains[9] and remodeled school buildings. The *Fergus Falls Weekly Journal* was especially pleased with the school improvements. Under the headline "Money Is Well Spent on High School Here," it commented, "One of the CWA projects which is returning a hundred per cent of value for the money [three thousand dollars] expended is the work that is being done in the public schools of the city."[10]

The CWA provided only a handful of jobs for white-collar professionals in its experimental night-school program. Beginning in late January 1934 four teachers conducted the first programs in the county at Elizabeth and Carlisle. A teacher met with interested people in various communities to discuss topics such as farm management, parliamentary practice, social and economic problems, windbreaks, public speaking, and dramatics during one of five sessions offered each week.[11]

These representative experiences were duplicated in all the county's political subdivisions. Paul Schroeder, who worked closely with the CWA as district statistician of the National Re-Employment Service in Fergus Falls, recalled that CWA projects ranged from "road construction work and repair of public buildings, and, of course, all the way from [the] township up through the county."[12] Although not more than nine hundred people were employed on CWA work at one time, from September 1933 to February 17, 1934, 2,778 Otter Tail County residents received CWA placements and took part in the New Deal's effort to put people to work with a minimum of red tape.[13] The CWA pumped

$285,310 into the county's economy at a critical time and helped local relief burdens during the difficult winter months.[14] Searle Zimmerman of Fergus Falls recalled that "1934 was the toughest winter. The federal program put people to work doing this, and that sure helped. You could see it."[15]

The CWA projects at times seemed makeshift and loosely organized. Roads and public buildings were, of course, improved, but the CWA's main objective was relief for the unemployed like Jacob O. Hatling, who at age eighty-two was one of the nation's oldest persons on the CWA payroll. Working as a carpenter on the Dalton school got him through the winter.[16]

Roosevelt terminated the CWA at the end of March 1934 because the winter emergency had passed and the program had become too expensive. Since Minnesota had not yet fully organized its work division to implement FERA work projects, the state Board of Control hurriedly put together the Relief Work Administration (RWA) to complete the projects that were caught in the demise of the CWA.[17] Improvements at the Otter Tail County courthouse, for example, were to be continued.[18] The state Board of Control had to approve each project that the RWA was to take over from the CWA and earmark FERA funds for its completion. For example, the board authorized the RWA to finish four Fergus Falls projects: Vine Street sewer ($750), courthouse painting ($1,500), city hall painting ($500), and wiring and painting of city schools ($750).[19]

During the RWA interlude the State Emergency Relief Administration (SERA) scrambled to put its Work Division into operation so that FERA work projects could begin as soon as possible. Using the CWA format as a general pattern, the state was divided into ten districts, each headed by a supervising engineer. By May 1 the SERA's Work Division began full-scale operations. Its field engineers did a great deal of promotional work with local governments to "sell" ideas and to "whip" proposals "into shape for approval." Each political subdivision was eligible to apply for SERA projects (because the SERA administered FERA projects, the projects were commonly referred to as SERA projects or even ERA projects, not FERA projects), but the application blanks were "quite complicated," and boards and councils were inexperienced in the new bureaucratic ways that were engulfing them. The engineers were crucial in launching work-relief projects.[20]

Once the SERA approved a local project, two people played key roles in assuring that it would be completed successfully: the field engineer in each county and the project foreman. Herlin L. Sandin served as Otter Tail County's field engineer. In addition to assisting local governments

The Vine Street sewer project in Fergus Falls was one of those caught in the changeover from CWA to FERA.

with applications, Sandin assigned workers to projects, attempting to adapt projects to the skills of the workers. Once a project started, he worked with the foremen and ironed out problems if they arose.[21]

The overall responsibility for a project fell on the foreman who worked full time at sixty cents an hour and did not have to meet relief-need standards. The foreman saw to it that workers used their allotted hours, that time sheets were "accurate in every respect," that the rules of job safety were followed, that the workers were physically and mentally fit for the job, and that all tools were accounted for at the end of each day. The foreman's most difficult job, however, was supervision of the project's progress. While most workers gave a full day's work for their wages, that was not always the case. The administrators of SERA's Work Division realized that slackers would give the program a bad name and often reminded foremen of their duty:

> Some of the men in some of the crews have the impression that while working on relief they are not required to do a day's work and are inclined to stall. This must be stopped. You are the foreman and have the rights and duties of foremen on any job. If you were working as

a foreman for some contractor, he would require you to make a showing, and see that the men were doing an honest day's work. . . . We are in exactly the same position. . . . We want to make good or we get the axe.[22]

A worker on a SERA project had to come from relief rolls and was allotted work hours based on need. Four projects in and around Pelican Rapids provide a grass-roots view of work relief: Project 56-B2-24, street repair, January-March, May 1935; Project 56-B7-25, sewer work, December 1934, July 1935; Project 56-B1-32, sidewalk work, October-December 1934; Project 56-D3-38, woodcutting, February-April 1935. Each worker earned fifty-five cents an hour, but take-home pay varied from project to project and person to person because the number of hours worked varied. The average monthly wage on the sidewalk project was twenty-seven dollars, but on the sewer it was thirty-one dollars. One worker was employed on all four and, because of his large family, had the highest monthly salaries; for example, sewer, $46.20; street, $48.95; sidewalks, $50.05; woodcutting, $51.60. The Pelican Rapids projects indicate that each town or township had a relatively stable relief work force. The street-repair crew of May 1935 employed twenty-seven men of whom sixteen were assigned to the July sewer work. Eight of the twenty-seven worked both the sidewalk project in November 1934 and the woodcutting project of February 1935.[23] Without these public-works projects, the Pelican Rapids men would have been dependent upon the village's already overdrawn poor fund.

Most FERA-financed projects in Otter Tail County were similar to those in other counties in Minnesota and across the United States: the improvement of roads, streets, sidewalks, public buildings, athletic fields, parks, sewer systems, and waterworks. The SERA, however, especially singled out three Otter Tail County projects that were unique or exemplary. The construction of the Leaf Mountain-Inspiration Peak road, a three-and-a-half-mile gravel road in Leaf Mountain Township, was an extremely difficult task. It required the moving of eighty thousand cubic yards of dirt and gravel, a twelve-thousand-yard fill across a swamp, and four "major cuts" of about twenty-five feet each. The old road was shortened by two miles and six hazardous curves were eliminated.[24]

The Fergus Falls Cooperative Packing Company's plant was one of the few Minnesota cooperatives that received a FERA loan. The depression had closed the plant, but the federal government urgently needed slaughtering facilities to handle cattle that it was purchasing as part of its drought-relief cattle program. The SERA loaned the cooperative $4,671 for new equipment and materials to be used in renovation. Fif-

The Otter Tail County employees who managed the FERA program posed on the courthouse steps in 1934. Left to right, back row, are Herlin Sandin, F. F. Vaughn, Thor Moe, Afton Glorvigen, Neils C. Neilsen, Gus Fargeland, C. Arthur Anderson, William I. Prince, Jr., and Bill Potter; center row, ? Dreught, ? Pelant, Elsie Oelslager, Mary Gray, Solveig Henrikson, Corrine Helleckson, Charlotte Wangness, Bette Vanderslius, Florence Baumgartner, and ? Scanlon; front row, Alice Malmstrom, Stella Hanson, Gertrude Rosholt, Louise Noren, Inez Breen, Violet Eckstrom, Mildred Estlick, Ethel Fetvedt, Dorothy Christianson, and Maybelle Charlson.

teen SERA "relief clients" provided labor for the project. The SERA gave the cooperative a contract to slaughter the government cattle, which was canned at another plant for later distribution as a surplus commodity to the needy. Between August 10 and November 29, 1934, the cooperative killed and dressed 9,072 head. With the profit on the contract, it paid off almost all of the SERA loan.[25] "The rehabilitation of the Fergus Falls farmers cooperative packing plant," the SERA concluded, "rehabilitated not only the plant, but also 210 farmers who were stockholders."[26]

Although twenty counties carried on SERA woodcutting projects, the district engineer singled out the one in Otter Tail County as efficient and even enjoyable. During winter 1934–35, a hundred men per day cut wood for distribution to relief clients at a cost of $8.75 per cord, "which compared favorably with a commercial price of $7.50 to $8.50 per cord." Each day the men were trucked out to the woodcutting camp. Each worker "contributed 5 cents a day to a pool and the money was used to buy meat, vegetables, coffee, sugar, milk, bread and butter. . . . A satisfying hot meal consisting of old fashioned 'mulligan', coffee and bread and butter was served at noon each day." The engineer was impressed with the Otter Tail camp: "The men enjoyed wood cutting and many of them reported for work even beyond the requirements of their budget. It may have been the wholesome mulligan or the wholesome nature of the work, but it was a fact that these projects were popular with the workers and filled the requirements for fuel production in a satisfactory manner."[27]

Many relief clients had SERA gardens, and some towns had SERA community gardens, but Otter Tail County operated a county SERA-sponsored garden. On twenty-two acres four miles north of Fergus Falls, workers planted and tended potatoes, carrots, beans, cabbage, sweet corn, squash, beets, peas, and rutabagas. Although the garden provided fresh vegetables for the needy, much of the produce was canned at SERA projects in Fergus Falls, Henning, and Perham for distribution during the winter.[28]

The adult-education program that began under the CWA continued as a SERA project during 1934 and early 1935. Between ten and thirteen unemployed teachers offered evening courses in music, civics, dramatics, home economics, handicrafts, and social and economic problems.[29] For instance, the night-school class in School District Number 179 near New York Mills studied American government and had fun in the process: "The lesson on courts was very interesting. After the recess of games, we had a mock trial which caused much merriment as well as making the previous lesson more easily understood."[30] In studying state government the class held a mock legislative session that passed laws "which we were sure would help the farmer."[31] Five rural schools in the eastern area of Homestead Township held classes in dramatics and presented a group of short plays for the public in the Homestead hall.[32] In the spring of 1935 the SERA sponsored a countywide contest in which twenty-two classes presented one-act plays. After judges selected the best four productions, a final competition in Fergus Falls determined the county winner.[33] The child hygiene division of the state Department of Health, in conjunction with the county relief administration, offered nursing classes in six communities during late October to mid-December 1934.[34]

The adult-education project not only gave jobs to teachers at an average salary of $64.50 per month from January to October and of $77.85 per month after October 1, 1934, but also provided Otter Tail County residents with a sound educational experience. During the first half of 1934, about two thousand persons per month took advantage of the opportunity to enhance their education.[35] Although it continued into the summer of 1935, beginning in the fall of 1934 the program was gradually reduced in scope.

For winter 1934–35, the SERA organized a statewide recreational and leisure-time program that took over the dramatics and music activities of adult education and also offered art classes and athletics. Under a headline, "SERA Sports Program Will Be Active Here," the *Battle Lake Review* explained that "Anything similar has never before been attempted in an American state" and enthusiastically announced that a "wide variety of opportunities for exercise and diversion" would be offered to "people of all ages and conditions." The program had two objectives: to give employment to trained workers in the fields of recreation and to "provide worthwhile programs of leisure time activity which may contribute to the upbuilding of morale and community spirit."[36]

During the fall of 1934 fourteen recreational workers directed activities throughout the county. In Fergus Falls, women ran story hours, assisted the Camp Fire Girls, worked with handicraft groups, and assisted churches with social and recreational programs. Two young men helped with Boy Scouts of America troops in Fergus Falls, Pelican Rapids, Underwood, Battle Lake, Dalton, Western Township, Perham, New York Mills, Richville, Vining, Henning, and Parkers Prairie. SERA sports leagues took shape quickly. The slap of hockey sticks, the swish of basketballs, the smash of volleyballs echoed throughout the county in Underwood, Parkers Prairie, Battle Lake, Homestead Township, New York Mills, Fergus Falls, Perham, and Pelican Rapids. Battle Lake and Pelican Rapids had music programs: a band and drum and bugle corps. An average of 2,810 county residents participated in these activities per week.[37]

The adult-education and the recreation programs gave jobs to a few people; its real significance, however, was the raising of people's spirits. "[Those things] kept people's minds off the tough times," recalled Searle Zimmerman. "Lots of folks did those things. Games. Schooling and the like. They sure helped."[38] Through these programs the federal government recognized that uplifting the mind and spirit was a vital factor in conquering the depression.

The president and Congress had begun the FERA as an emergency agency and had intended to phase it out as soon as a federally operated work program could be devised. On December 31, 1935, the FERA ended, and Congress replaced it with the Works Progress Administration (WPA), a federally funded and controlled public-works program that would sponsor projects similar to those of the FERA.

Both the CWA and the FERA had been measures to relieve the unemployment crisis. The third public-works agency, authorized in 1933, had a more far-reaching objective: recovery. Roosevelt included $3.3 billion for public works in the National Industrial Recovery Act that Congress passed in June 1933 and named Secretary of Interior Harold L. Ickes to head the Public Works Administration (PWA).

The PWA hoped to bolster the economy by stimulating the terribly stagnant construction industry and providing jobs for the third-largest group of workers in the nation, the building trades. "Industry could not be stimulated solely by slogans of 'confidence,' " the PWA maintained. "Here was a country with a great and growing need for more schools, more highways, more bridges, more waterworks. . . . Here was industry hungry for orders for the needed materials. The idea was to bring all of them together."[39] The agency had several ways to bring workers and materials together: its own projects as a construction agency, allotments to other federal agencies to carry on construction work, and a combination of loans and grants to states and their subdivisions for nonfederal building. For the most part the PWA worked through private contractors who were not tied to the hiring of relief-role workers. PWA projects demanded advance planning, exact specifications, engineering surveys, blueprints, and detailed cost estimates. Obtaining authorization for a project was a slow process since every contract and plan was painstakingly reviewed en route to a final scrutiny by Ickes himself.[40]

The PWA focused its program on major construction, such as schools, courthouses, hospitals, sewage and water plants, and highways. Between July 1933 and March 1939 it aided in construction projects on approximately 70 percent of the nation's educational buildings, 65 percent of the courthouses and city halls, and 35 percent of the hospitals.[41]

In Otter Tail County the PWA assisted in the construction of seven building and two highway projects. Fergus Falls received help for three new schools and a hospital, waterworks, and sewage-treatment plant expansion. New York Mills built a new water plant and system. Of the county's PWA projects the water system for New York Mills, school construction in Fergus Falls, and highway work are representative and illustrate how the PWA functioned at the grass roots.

The PWA program almost immediately sparked renewed interest among the people of New York Mills in a water plant. Two years earlier a bond issue had lost with 140 votes against and 86 in favor.[42] "The idea of establishing a water works system in the village is not a new one," the *New York Mills Herald* commented in 1933. "Those favorable to aforesaid public improvement have received new inspiration from the new public works program of the federal government."[43] Water proponents circulated a petition, demanding that the village council "submit the necessary question to the voters of the Village."[44] The council, as it had two years earlier, studied the water issue. With the possibility of PWA assistance the council called for a larger and more complete system with greater storage capacity and sixteen thousand feet of water mains. By fall 1933 the engineer had completed the plan, and Minnesota's sanitary commission approved it in December.[45] The New York Mills water proposal was on its way to Washington.

In mid-February 1934 the PWA announced a $34,000 grant and loan to New York Mills; $10,200 was an outright government grant. The village would pay off the $23,800 loan over twenty years at 4 1/4 percent interest.[46] Three hurdles remained to be cleared: a favorable vote by the people, the letting of bids, and PWA authorization of those bids. The people said yes on March 20 with a vote of 216 in favor and 118 against. The bids were let, and in July 1934 PWA officials in Washington approved the bids. New York Mills would finally have its water system. On August 13 Mayor John Mark turned the first shovel of sod on the lot next to the jail, signaling the beginning of construction.[47]

The well went down in August, and the tower went up in November. The water tower became a badge of honor for New York Mills. The village's editor captured that when he wrote:

> The village of New York Mills is joining with other large "small towns" in this section and the water tower for the new water works system is now up, and the tank is being put together. Where it was possible to see the village from but a short distance out of town before, it can now be seen for several miles as the water tower extends high above the buildings. It will not be necessary for outsiders to question about the size of New York Mills in the future. They will be able to see that it is one of the bigger "small towns" in the state and that it is getting into the city class.[48]

The PWA project in New York Mills did more than provide an essential improvement for the village. It gave work to *all* the town's unemployed men and a shot in the arm to the Jacobs Brothers of Bird Island, Renville County, who laid the mains; to P. G. Thein of Clara City,

Adams School (above) and Jefferson School (below) of Fergus Falls show the variations that one building design could have. The roof of the old Jefferson School appears on the right.

Chippewa County, who drilled the well; to J. A. Shaw of Fargo, North Dakota, who built the pump house; and to the Challenge Company of Batavia, Illinois, which raised the tower.[49] To the people of New York Mills and to the contractors the project meant water, employment, and business.

The New York Mills water system, the county's first PWA project, was a typical early PWA effort: small in scope and relatively untroubled by red tape. The school building program in Fergus Falls, the county's last building project, illustrated the federal agency's shift toward larger and more closely supervised projects. In 1938 the Fergus Falls Board of

Education decided to construct McKinley School, a new third-ward elementary school to relieve the enrollment pressure at Lincoln School, and in July voters approved a forty thousand dollar bond issue to qualify the school district for a thirty thousand dollar PWA grant. In October voters again approved a bond issue: forty thousand dollars to replace Adams School (which had probably been built in 1884) in the fourth ward and thirty thousand dollars for an addition to Jefferson School (an 1885 structure) in the second ward. Both were PWA projects. The board, with PWA approval, met and then rejected as too high the bids for McKinley School. Consequently the board decided to replace Jefferson School and to bid the three new buildings as one project, hoping for a lower bid.[50] The board received some criticism from people who claimed that the construction of the three schools at once would necessitate the employment of workers who did not live in Fergus Falls.[51] In April, however, the board awarded the contracts. Hungry for business, eleven general construction companies submitted bids with the lowest bid of $144,725 coming from Carl Swedberg of Wheaton, Traverse County. William Galena and Sons of Fergus Falls was awarded the plumbing, heating, and ventilating contract at $32,399. The total bids came in lower than expected at a cost of $181,424 of which the PWA would provide 45 percent.[52]

During construction the school board or its committees met almost daily to "iron out all the little difficulties that arise in a building program of this magnitude," and Fergus Falls school and city officials made a number of trips to the PWA regional office in Omaha, Nebraska. For instance, in July the PWA clashed with the school board over bricks. The PWA maintained that it would not "stand 45% of the cost of the brick on the grounds there was not open competitive bidding." A trip to Omaha straightened out the matter.[53]

On December 15, 1939, about two hundred residents of Fergus Falls and PWA officials gathered in the Washington High School auditorium to dedicate the three new schools: McKinley, Adams, and Jefferson. Although each had a similar one-level floor plan, including six classrooms, a library, a playroom, a teachers' office, and a kitchen, the exterior design gave each an individual style that featured glass blocks and curved and straight lines. "With the completion of the three new grade school buildings," a Fergus Falls newspaper observed, "few cities the size of Fergus Falls can boast of better elementary educational facilities."[54]

Between July 1933 when New York Mills dreamed about a water system and December 1939 when Fergus Falls celebrated the construction of its new schools, the PWA was involved in two highway projects in Otter Tail County. People who lived in Elizabeth, Deer Creek, Henning,

Perham built curbs and gutters as part of a PWA project. A gutter-cutting machine (above) carved out a level track, and the men (below) set the forms for the cement truck to fill.

Parkers Prairie, Vergas, and Vining, and farmers from Eastern to Norwegian Grove and from Eagle Lake to Corliss townships benefited from PWA road construction.[55] A large PWA road-building project, sponsored by the state Department of Highways, upgraded Minnesota 78, the highway that went from Ashby, Grant County, through Battle Lake, followed the southeast shore of Otter Tail Lake, and ended in Perham. Beginning in April 1934, a total of three hundred men and one hundred teams of horses worked their way slowly through the sometimes thickly wooded countryside.[56] The largest county-sponsored PWA road project began in spring 1939 to improve or build nineteen pieces of county highway covering sixty-one miles in twenty townships. Six contractors were awarded jobs totaling $152,032. The PWA paid 45 percent ($83,604) of the cost of the road building. County highway engineer Herlin Sandin estimated that the project would excavate about one million cubic feet of dirt.[57]

The PWA did not provide the economic relief that the FERA and the CWA had. Since most contractors who were awarded jobs were not residents of Otter Tail County, that profit, although it stimulated the overall economy, left the county. Some contractors, such as Carl Swedburg, the Fergus Falls school contractor, purchased most of his material locally, helping local vendors. The PWA's greatest contributions to Otter Tail County, however, were the employment of local people and the value of the projects.

Contractors had to hire the county's unemployed — preferably but not necessarily those on the relief rolls — for the common labor on a project. The number of workers on the county's PWA projects rose and fell depending on the building activity generated by the agency's grants and loans. Between September 1933 and February 17, 1934, the National Re-Employment Service had placed 513 persons with PWA projects.[58] PWA employment figures after that date are sketchy, but it is likely, with the exception of the road construction in 1939, that the numbers rarely surpassed five hundred men at any one time. Those who found PWA employment earned more than those on other government programs, between $68 and $115 per month. PWA grants to Otter Tail County totaled about a million dollars, of which a large share went to the workers.

The three agencies that gave people employment during the early years of the New Deal functioned in different ways and with different objectives. The CWA was a five-month crash program that sought to put money in the pockets of workers so that they could survive the hardship of the 1933–34 winter; the projects were secondary. The FERA was an emergency program administered through the SERA to give work relief to those who needed and wanted to work but could find nothing in the private sector; the projects, however, were as important as the monetary relief. The PWA was a long-range, public-construction program in which the value of the project and stimulation of the nation's construction industry were primary, and employment relief was secondary. All three helped lessen the strain on local relief funds, provided useful community improvements, and gave bona fide work to the unemployed.

5

WPA
"To Keep Body and Soul Together"

THE WORKS PROGRESS ADMINISTRATION (WPA) became the
New Deal's response to the need for a more controlled and systematic approach to the relief problem. The PWA was not providing enough jobs
for enough people, and the FERA placed too much emphasis on direct
relief — the dole.[1] Roosevelt adamantly opposed continuation of federal
direct relief, which he increasingly saw as "a narcotic, a subtle destroyer
of the human spirit." He told Congress in early 1935 that "The Federal
Government must and shall quit this business of relief." Congress passed
the Emergency Relief Appropriation Act of 1935, which allocated almost $5 billion dollars to implement a new work-relief program. The
president then created the WPA to distribute $1.4 billion of the initial
funding and named the FERA's Harry Hopkins as its chief administrator.

Like the FERA, the WPA was a relief agency. Unlike the FERA, it
provided only work relief. Direct relief again became the responsibility
of state and local governments. The WPA also differed from the FERA
in two other significant ways. First, federal, not state, officials ran the
program. In 1933 the use of existing state agencies had been an expedient
way to begin a relief plan as quickly as possible. But inconsistent
management and intergovernmental bickering convinced Hopkins and
Roosevelt that the work-relief program should be federalized. Second,
the WPA required no matching state money — often a sticky problem under the FERA. Instead, it required a project's sponsor to furnish building
materials.[2]

Although some special WPA programs were administered directly
from Washington on a nationwide basis, the overwhelming share of
government funds went to main-street America. Any political subdivision, such as a school district, county, township, village, or city, could
apply for a WPA project, provided that the applicant furnished most of
the materials. In one instance the Parkers Prairie village council applied
for WPA funds in 1935 to extend water mains. The village pledged

70

$8,489 in materials, and the WPA provided $12,659 for labor and an additional $1,200 for materials. In 1937 School District Number 5 of Underwood asked for $2,689 to meet labor costs and match its $1,041 in materials for a bus garage.[3] The application procedure was not complicated. The sponsoring agency merely had to complete a form that called for a detailed budget and a full description of the proposed project.

Four WPA offices were involved in facilitating and reviewing proposed projects. Each county had a WPA office and a countywide committee to help applicants. Perham lawyer Michael James ("Jim") Daly, who served on the Otter Tail County committee, recalled that, "We were supposed to have projects lined up for the WPA men in the county."[4] The WPA district office in Detroit Lakes, Becker County, coordinated the work in the eighteen counties that made up the seventh WPA district. Although district officials played no role in the review process, its district engineer assisted government bodies with the preparation of proposals and the organization of the projects. The Minnesota WPA director reviewed all proposals and kept the state's requests within its allocation. Final decisions officially rested with the president, but he routinely approved proposals that the national WPA office forwarded to him.

Once a project was authorized, the WPA district and county officials helped the sponsoring agency put it together, allocating personnel and selecting foremen and timekeepers. When the project was underway, the district office and engineer kept a watchful eye on its operation and progress.

The crew for each project consisted of the workers, a foreman, and a timekeeper. Townships or municipalities had to certify workers as relief cases, for without that certification a person could not work for the WPA. Workers were paid according to an elaborate pay scale that was based on their ability and their county's "area." A county was assigned to one of three state areas, depending upon the size of the population of its largest municipality in 1930. Therefore, workers in Otter Tail County earned slightly more than those in Cook County and somewhat less than those in Hennepin County because the population of Fergus Falls fell into the five thousand to twenty-five thousand category.

The wage rates in 1938 for Otter Tail County included those for five wage classes: unskilled, intermediate, skilled, professional and technical, and project supervisory. Although within each class the hourly wage varied, take-home pay was about the same because the hours to be worked were adjusted to achieve a nearly common salary.

Most Otter Tail workers fell into the unskilled class. Hourly rates for the eighteen types of manual workers in this class ran from 35 1/2 cents for watchmen, who had 136 assigned hours of work per month for $48.28, to 44 cents for cement handlers, laborers, teamsters, and eight other types, who each worked 110 hours for $48.40. The eleven types of nonmanual workers, such as bookmenders, elevator operators, and office boys, worked 120 hours at 40 cents for $48.00 per month.

The intermediate class included 69 manual workers who earned from $54.27 for 83 1/2 hours to $55.00 for 100 or 110 hours per month. Cobblers, second cooks, power-machine seamstresses, and four other types received the lowest hourly rate of 45 1/2 cents for $54.60 monthly, while terrazzo-base machine operators got the highest of 90 cents, but were allowed to work only 60 1/2 hours for $54.45. Almost all of the 36 nonmanual types, ranging from junior bookkeepers to practical nurses to typists, worked 120 hours for $54.60 a month; the remaining 3 types earned $55.00 for 100 hours (intermediate artists) or 110 hours (gang bosses and subforemen).

The 75 manual workers in the skilled class took home between $68.75 and $69.30 per month. Bakers, first cooks, and power-machine clothing cutters earned the lowest rate of 57 1/2 cents, working 120 hours for $69.00. Dredge operators and structural ironworkers received the same monthly amount for 46 hours at the highest rate of $1.50 per hour. Nonmanual skilled workers accounted for 49 types who each earned either $62.40 or $69.00 per month for 120 or 100 hours of labor. The lowest hourly rate of 52 cents went to 18 types, including barbers, photographers, and senior stenographers, while 30 types such as senior editors on research projects, interviewers dealing with "difficult subject matter," and elementary or junior high school teachers got 57 1/2 cents. Only skilled artists worked 100 hours, at a 69-cent rate.

Most of the highest monthly WPA wages of $75.00 to $75.90 were in the professional and technical class. Twenty-six types, such as senior architects and librarians, office managers with six or more full-time assistants, senior high school or college teachers, and laboratory technicians, got the lowest rate of 63 cents but were allowed to work 120 hours for $75.60 a month. The other 17 types included professional artists and 16 varieties of foremen; ironworker foremen received the highest rate ($1.65) and lowest number of hours (46).

The project supervisory class had 6 grades each of foremen and timekeepers, under the heading of security, who worked 110 or 120 hours at rates from 45 1/2 to 69 cents for $54.60 to $75.90 per month. Under nonsecurity, there were 6 grades of foremen, 5 of timekeepers, 4 of engineering aides, 2 of engineers, and 4 classes each of superintendents, assistant superintendents, and job-safety inspectors. They had no assigned hours or monthly earnings, only rates of 63 cents to $1.46 per hour.[5]

The Otter Tail County project of the state Historical Records Survey (HRS) illustrates the system. Four men who began work with the project in early 1937 were senior interviewers at 57 1/2 cents per hour, 120 hours per month for $69. They remained at that rate until July 1939 when the WPA reduced all wages, theirs to 53 cents per hour — but increased their working hours to 130 for $68.90 into August.[6]

Foremen were responsible for the successful completion of a project, but their task was more complicated than that. They had to make sure that workers were certified, that the project stayed within budget, and that safety standards were maintained. Foremen also submitted monthly progress reports to the district office in Detroit Lakes and validated the timekeeper's records.[7]

Timekeepers recorded and reported the time spent by each WPA employee (including "Drought Relief" workers) on a project keeping track of time lost ("due to weather conditions or temporary interruption") and to be made up by employees, and handling the paper work for transfers, reassignments, changes in work status, and reclassifications.[8] Few positions reflected more vividly the bureaucracy that accompanied the growth of an agency such as the WPA. From August 1936 through June 1937, timekeepers received twenty-seven bulletins containing detailed instructions concerning procedures and new policies and explanations of old guidelines.[9] They were given information about filling out and submitting ten WPA forms: 502 (for "recording time for personal services only"), 508 (for "relief employees driving personally owned teams or trucks"), 719 (for "recording time of equipment and machinery hired on a contract basis"), 325 (for "new non-relief assignments"), 402 (for "all other transfers or assignments"), 403 (for use "whenever a worker leaves your project for any reason except a transfer"), 404 (for indicating "a change in occupational classification or wage rate"), 713 (for "tools or equipment . . . needed on a project"), 714 (for "tools and equipment . . . no longer needed"), and 715 (for "Stolen or lost tools").[10]

Since few timekeepers had had experience with government employment, the district office sent out directions not only for record keeping but also for behavior. "It is expected that they will at all times conduct themselves so as to avoid public criticism," the office stated. Timekeepers were warned to be honest, to avoid "conversation with the workers," and not to rely on memory alone.[11]

Within four months after the president established the WPA, proposals inundated the Minnesota administrator's St. Paul office. In one September week 2,019 proposals crossed his desk.[12] By November announcements of approved Otter Tail County projects became common news items. During 1935 the WPA authorized 218 projects totaling $1,523,129 in federal money for the county and ranging from $245 to paint classrooms in Battle Lake to $162,110 for remodeling at the Fergus Falls State Hospital. Most projects were small, in the area of between $1,200 and $1,700, but almost overnight the WPA transformed Otter Tail County into a beehive of activity. Crews of men armed with shovels and teams of horses pulling scrapers raised swirls of dust in most townships and villages as roads and streets took new shape. In the villages workers laid water and sewage pipes; painted schoolrooms and fairground buildings; enlarged dance pavilions; fashioned baseball and football fields, tennis courts, and race tracks; improved parks; remodeled municipal and school buildings; poured concrete for sidewalks and streets; built gymnasiums, auditoriums, and garages; sewed clothing;

A WPA crew put the finishing touches on a sidewalk along Union Street in Fergus Falls. Elsewhere in town the men built retaining walls alongside the sidewalks.

collected historical data; and arranged courthouse records. In the countryside, laborers erected bridges, constructed dams, improved schools, built new rural schools, and dug drainage ditches.[13]

After the initial burst of activity in late 1935 and early 1936, WPA allocations to Otter Tail County and to most counties decreased substantially. The WPA began to emphasize fewer but larger projects for two reasons. First of all, in 1935 President Roosevelt wanted to give the economy an immediate and hefty shot in the arm, especially since he was up for reelection in 1936 and wanted as many places as possible to benefit from the WPA. Second, the WPA found that so many small projects were difficult to administer. Larger projects would be more efficient.[14]

Otter Tail County received only $131,955 for 1936 and $417,634 for 1937. In 1937 the twenty-four projects averaged $17,401 each and stressed larger buildings such as the New York Mills municipal building at $41,091.[15] For 1938, a critical congressional election year for the Democrats, the WPA allocation shot up dramatically; Otter Tail County was awarded $1,375,985 for thirty-five projects, averaging $39,313 each. Henning built a sewage system and plant; Fergus Falls laid out a golf course, expanded its sewage system, and began a park development program; Underwood started work on a sewage system.[16]

In 1939, $276,323 supported twelve projects, and in 1940, $202,976 provided for ten. During those two years the largest grants went to Fergus Falls for sewer, street, recreational, and school improvements.[17] By this time small grants to townships and villages were a thing of the past. The year 1941 was the last big one for the WPA and Otter Tail County: $776,173 for fifteen projects — an average of $51,744 per project. Again Fergus Falls captured the largest share for schools and sewers, but Henning was close behind with $79,711 for streets and water-system work. Perham, Parkers Prairie, and New York Mills were able to pave streets and continue work on sewage systems.[18] In 1942 the WPA made its last grants. Otter Tail County received only $125,247, of which Pelican Rapids and Perham spent $116,750 for water and sewage projects.[19] When workers finished up the Perham job, the WPA had thrown its last shovelful of dirt in Otter Tail County.

The county commissioners used the WPA to improve roads, especially farm-to-market, and bridges. When Harry Hopkins explained the objectives of the WPA in 1935, he promised that the unemployed in small towns would find plenty of work on the upgrading and construction of secondary roads. The *Battle Lake Review* applauded that as "good news for farmers, rural mail carriers, and every business man in agricultural areas."[20] When the WPA called for proposals, the county commissioners asked for $23,456 to match its $3,500 in materials.[21]

The county commissioners were disappointed when the WPA did not approve the request in 1935. The WPA director for Minnesota, Victor A. Christgau, explained that money for the state would be gone by March 15 unless more allotments were made. The *Fergus Falls Weekly Journal* observed that "No headway can be made on road work in the winter."[22] In the spring of 1936, however, the WPA funded the county's road program; a force of 475 teams of horses and 27 trucks were engaged in roadwork throughout the county by October. Because roads were constructed with shovels and horse-powered scrapers, progress was slow on the eighty-five miles of new construction and improvements. The project went well until the WPA cut the work force by almost 60 percent due to lack of funds. The county commissioners called a special meeting with WPA officials in Fergus Falls on October 21. Herlin Sandin, the county engineer, argued that building farm-to-market roads was a way to use WPA money "in gainful work." "Roads are far more important to the public than leaf-raking and boondoggling," he declared.[23]

The severe drought of 1936 that left many of the county's farmers with no crop worked for the benefit of the road program. A WPA rule prohibited farmers from working on its projects. In 1936, however, the WPA relaxed that rule, allowing farmers in drought-stricken counties to apply for WPA work. During July few areas of the county had rain. "Pastures are burned brown from the torrid sun," the *New York Mills Herald* lamented, "and drouth and heat have made grain crops . . . almost a complete loss."[24] By mid-July the county had not been designated as drought stricken, even though Senator Elmer Benson "saw no crops worth harvesting." The commissioners claimed that they could not assist farmers without WPA help since budgets were overdrawn because of $650,000 in tax delinquencies.[25] In a resolution they asked that the WPA get farmers working on road projects "prior to severe winter weather conditions."[26] Hopkins declared Otter Tail County drought stricken in July as dust storms obscured the sun in some parts of the county. Farmers went to work for the WPA. Each was allotted employment lasting a few weeks to a few months, according to need. The number of the county's farmers on WPA averaged fifteen hundred through the summer. By mid-November when it was announced that the drought-relief work was to end, about that number were still employed. Between November 15 and December 15, the ending date, the farmers were phased out of WPA.[27]

The influx of so many workers into the WPA, even for two or three months, gave an unexpected boost to Otter Tail County's road projects. Although 150 farmers helped clean up the Otter Tail River, most were assigned to a road crew near their own farms. The massive paper work

Road construction in Maplewood Township kept a WPA crew busy in 1936. Bulldozers filled a cut (above), while horse, man, and truck (below) leveled the roadbed.

caused by approximately fifteen hundred new workers nearly exhausted the district office, but the farmers were grateful for the income.

The county road program was the largest benefactor from the WPA funds — close to a million federal dollars, about 20 percent of Otter Tail County's eight years of WPA funding. The road projects usually gave work to between 275 and 350 men during the construction season.[28]

County road building and municipal improvements accounted for much of the county's WPA employment and funding. Two statewide projects, however, provided additional jobs for scores of men and improved the natural surroundings. The state Division of Forestry initiated an eight-county project that included Otter Tail. Beginning in 1938 a crew of fifty men undertook such forestry projects as planting trees and constructing firebreaks, truck trails, and small dams.[29] The state Department of Conservation carried on a large WPA project to restore the state's lakes, rivers, and water supplies. As early as July 1934 the county's lakes were "going down rapidly"; and the state conservation experts reported that only Pine, Rush, and Otter Tail lakes were "up to normal." The 1936 drought dictated that something be done. The building of dams raised the level of lakes to normal and increased water-storage capacities. For example, at a cost of $6,922 (WPA, $5,176; Department of Conservation, $1,746), fifteen men constructed a dam that increased Pelican Lake's storage capacity, guaranteeing a steady water supply for towns on the Pelican River.[30] Besides a WPA grant of $41,484 that cleaned up the Pelican River, the Department of Conservation restored sixty-three lakes in Otter Tail County at a cost of $487,613.58, of which the WPA paid $429,803.64. The cost of lake projects ranged from more than $20,000 on Silver and Blanche to under $1,500 on Long and Stalker. The lake restoration project, which ran from 1936 into 1941, gave county residents 534 "man years of work" and enhanced the county's lake country.[31]

The WPA projects were essentially manual labor jobs. Of the $4,829,422 of federal money that was allocated to Otter Tail County, only $119,207 or 2.4 percent was earmarked for work considered suitable for women and white-collar unemployed men.[32]

Women who were heads of households found WPA employment on sewing and bookmending projects. The countywide sewing project continued for most of the WPA's years, employing between twenty-five and forty women at any given time. They made a "wide variety of clothing for men, women and children. They were distributed to the needy by welfare agencies," and at Christmastime crafted stuffed toys for hospitalized children. Between 1935 and 1939 Otter Tail County women put together 28,287 garments. "Besides producing articles that otherwise

Adeline F. Karst

would have to be purchased with local relief funds," state WPA director
Linus C. Glotzbach observed in 1939, "they provided work this past year
for 4,652 Minnesota women who are the breadwinners of their
families."[33]

Adeline F. Karst, a former home-economics teacher whose husband
Edward N. ("Ed") Karst was a Fergus Falls businessman, oversaw the
county sewing project for a year and a half before taking a position in
which she supervised all the sewing projects in the WPA eighteen-county
district. She especially recalled four aspects of the project: the dedication
of the workers, the difficulty some women encountered as WPA workers,
the essential qualities to run a successful project, and the WPA
bureaucracy.

"My women were conscientious workers — they needed it [the
work]," Karst observed. She focused on a young woman who supported
her four children:

> She was a worker, diligent as she could be; she worked so hard, and
> she was so glad to have a job. She did all our cutting . . . we'd lay
> out probably 4 or 5 bolts of material at one time and she'd put the
> pattern on and she'd cut through all that material; she'd get such cal-
> louses on her thumb from the scissors and never complained.[34]

The hard work was sometimes accompanied by heartache. Karst
pointed out the difficulty that some women faced because of traditional
attitudes that discriminated against women in the workplace. In 1939

Women from the WPA sewing project in Fergus Falls (above) took a break from machines and yard goods. The WPA Sewing and Pattern Service in Minneapolis demonstrated how one basic pattern could be varied by using assorted trimmings (below). This procedure would save in cutting time and increase the creative ability of women on the project as well as offering different-looking dresses to the relief department.

the WPA required workers to take a thirty-day leave, hoping that they might find employment in the private sector. According to Karst:

This lady, she was a lovely lady, she had her problems, she had one very poor eye and I remember she was just sick when she was terminated [for the thirty-day leave]. . . . I got a notice that she'd be coming back on the project and she didn't show up for a couple of days, and I thought that was kind of strange. Her husband didn't want her to work because when she got the check he felt subordinate to her and he didn't like to have her have the money — [even though] they needed it badly. . . . He had destroyed the slip notifying her that she was supposed to come back on the job.[35]

Running a project often called for extraordinary diplomacy. Karst had to keep bill collectors from interrupting the work and had to keep peace among the workers. "I had two ladies . . . who liked the same widower and I had to have them sitting in opposite ends of the room because they couldn't stand each other," she recalled.[36]

Adeline Karst received great satisfaction from her years of work as a WPA project director and as a district supervisor. But the burgeoning bureaucracy irked her. The WPA seemed loosely organized, inconsistent, and, at times, wasteful. "I'd get a letter from St. Paul telling me I was supposed to do something, go out on the projects and tell them this or tell them that and you made 5 or 6 copies of everything," Karst declared. "And you could hardly get back to the Detroit Lakes Office and you would have a letter rescinding what you had been out and said two weeks before."[37] Poor planning especially got her goat:

We got gorgeous woolen material to make dresses, now the people we gave those dresses to should never have had woolen material in the first place because they didn't know how to handle it. . . . We had a group of dresses that we're supposed to make and . . . [the] girls even did some embroidering on them. Why, you'd wear them anyplace, they were just beautiful.

A project worker spotted one of the dresses hanging on a clothesline. It had been laundered incorrectly and had shrunk. "That was poor purchasing," Karst maintained.[38]

The book-mending and bookbinding project, housed in the basement of the courthouse, gave work to women and older men from its inception in 1936 into 1941. The crew rebound and repaired public school text and library books that "would otherwise be thrown away." The *Fergus Falls Daily Journal* in 1936 explained that the cost of repairing a book was about eight cents and that John M. Henderson, the superintendent of schools for Otter Tail County, had stated that "this project has saved the school districts of the county a great amount of money."[39]

White-collar projects that might have employed men were more limited than projects for women. Less than one percent of the county's funding went to projects that, probably but not necessarily, had jobs for men who were not by training or inclination cut out for manual labor. Small projects, mainly during the first years of the WPA, included codification of Fergus Falls ordinances, a survey of Fergus Falls real property, a countywide recreational program, adult education, collection of county historical data, and mapping. It is doubtful that these projects provided jobs for more than twenty or thirty people.[40]

Of the five nationwide artistic and professional work-relief programs of the WPA (the Federal Music Project, the Federal Art Project, the Historical Records Survey, the Federal Theatre Project, and the Federal Writers' Project), the music, art, and history projects touched Otter Tail County in tangible ways. These federally sponsored projects were the New Deal's way of providing work for artists and stimulating the nation's creativity during depressed times.[41] Although they were centered in urban areas, these projects attempted to reach out to rural America. For example, the New York Mills high school band went to Brainerd, Crow Wing County, to participate in a one-day clinic sponsored by the Federal Music Project. Members of a WPA band helped the children with musical problems and in the evening joined the high school bands in a concert for the public.[42]

The Minnesota state director of the Federal Art Project (FAP) cooperated with the Otter Tail County Historical Society by creating a poster for the society's summer 1936 meeting. The society provided the cost of most of the materials, and the project produced one hundred copies of the poster.[43] From July 1938 to November 28, 1940, the state FAP sent the society twelve oils and five watercolors of Otter Tail County scenes painted by artist Charles J. Grant of Minneapolis and based on photographs that the society had provided. The paintings captured early Fergus Falls scenes as well as *Market Day in Pelican Rapids* and *The Saw Mill at New York Mills*.[44] Although at least one was returned so that Grant could correct a historical detail, Edward T. Barnard, secretary of the society and a prominent Fergus Falls funeral director, summed up the appreciation of county residents: "The paintings have been praised by everybody who has seen them."[45]

Barnard also furnished photographs of thirteen items in the society's collection for possible inclusion in the Index of American Design, a research project of the FAP, whose purpose was to "uncover articles of good design made in the United States between the years 1620 and 1890, and to record them by photographs and color drawings." The Minnesota FAP office forwarded the photographs to Washington for selection, and several were chosen to be drawn for the index: "Horse collar and hane, handmade chair made by Daniel Chapin, carrier, ribbon making machine, and flour barrel made from a basswood stump."[46]

Otter Tail County took what advantage it could of the music and art programs, but the Historical Records Survey had considerably more impact and stayed for almost the entire life of the WPA. The HRS employed workers to catalog county records, interview old settlers, index newspapers, write sketches of institutions, and undertake other projects that preserved and interpreted the history of the county.

Whether blue collar or white collar, village or country, countywide or nationwide, WPA projects stood for employment and physical improvements. The number of jobs varied from year to year and month to month. The high point of WPA employment came in the fall of 1936 when farmers were allowed on WPA projects for a short time. By December 23 the state WPA office planned to issue checks to 2,200 WPA workers, of which about 1,600 went to farmers.[47] The county's work quota usually ranged between 500 and 750 for those years of prime WPA activity.[48] Although the WPA could not give jobs to everyone who was looking for work, it took care of about 40 percent of the county's unemployed — at least in 1936.[49] But the WPA meant more than a paycheck for hundreds of Otter Tail County people; those jobs stimulated the county's economy. During the first two years of operation, WPA checks increased the county's buying power by $957,938.[50] A 1939 survey showed clearly the impact that WPA checks had on main street. In mid-1939 WPA workers spent an average of $44,156 per month. Of that, $17,221 went to food stores; $7,507 to landlords; $4,416 to clothing stores; $4,416 for fuel and other home necessities; $1,766 for transportation; and $1,766 for medical care. Grocery and meat markets received 39 percent of every paycheck. And if the largest share of that $17,221 went to food merchants who reported their 1939 income, then WPA paychecks accounted for about 9 percent of food sales.[51]

The physical improvements that WPA projects brought to Otter Tail County affected most people's lives. Some communities, such as Deer Creek, Battle Lake, Vining, and Bluffton chose not to take full advantage of the WPA. Other towns, especially Parkers Prairie, New York Mills, Perham, Pelican Rapids, Fergus Falls, Underwood, and Henning, did. The water-sewage systems, school additions, recreational facilities, upgraded streets, and other municipal improvements raised the quality of life. For example, the towns of Parkers Prairie and Perham could not have made the physical progress that they did without a federal program

The Perham sewage disposal plant in 1939

such as the WPA. Between 1936 and 1942 Perham expanded its sewage and water systems; improved the old and laid out new streets and sidewalks; remodeled and added to school and village buildings; and constructed new facilities at the fairgrounds. Accomplished through thirteen WPA projects, the improvements cost the village $91,683 of the total cost of $303,343. Parkers Prairie, through four large projects, built a new sewage system and treatment plant, expanded its water works, upgraded its streets, and constructed an addition to and refurbished its school. The village provided $84,014 of the $271,691 that was needed to complete the projects.[52]

Henry Holmgren, who was elected mayor of Henning in 1935, was a staunch advocate of WPA projects. He recalled a conversation that took place on a town street:

Mr. X:	"What the hell are you doing now? Putting in [a] sewer?"
Holmgren:	"Yes, we are."
Mr. X:	"You just got through putting in water last fall and now you start on the sewer again and our tax is going to be so damn expensive here in Henning that people [will] have to move out . . . the town is going . . . plum to hell."
Mrs. X:	"Don't pay any attention. . . . He used to bluff me too like that first when we got married but I told him to save that. . ."

Parkers Prairie school showing the new addition in about 1936

Mr. X:	"How come that [my wife] will stick up for you, instead of me?"
Holmgren:	"She is a real lady and she knows what's going on and . . . that we are getting a good deal."[53]

Some workers who viewed the WPA as relief rather than employment, however, tarnished its public image. Edward Barnard sent two WPA historical workers in 1936 to record information from the back issues of the *Perham Enterprise-Bulletin*. Harvey D. Smalley, Sr., the publisher and editor of the newspaper, wrote to Barnard, "If they are like some of the workers on our sewer project shooting would be the only profitable way of handling them."[54] On another occasion Barnard protested the assignment of a certain WPA employee to his historical project because the man "does not know what the word 'work' means nor has he any idea of giving the government any value for the money they pay him."[55]

In June 1937 the Oak Valley Township Board attempted to convince surrounding townships to join it in a drive against WPA "loafers." Alex Freedland of the Oak Valley board laid out the plan:

This letter is about WPA and direct relief. Our town Board is planning on firing every man on WPA and direct relief. . . . I was wondering if our neighboring Town Boards would be willing to cooperate in firing this bunch of tax-eating loafers, as it would not help very much just to fight them in Oak Valley Township.

There is no reason why these men could not get private employment, as there is going to be a big crop of hay and grain. . . .

Dickie and Donald Toso loaded their wheelbarrows and played at being WPA road builders like their father.

If we permit these men to stay on WPA and direct relief, there never will be any reduction in the relief expenditures and I believe that now is a good time to start house cleaning.[56]

The Inman Township Board agreed "to take up the question of firing that bunch of loafers we have on hand with the exception of one, who is a hopeless case and we are better off by having him on than otherwise."[57] What happened to the "purge" is unknown, but the exchange of letters indicates that some people were dissatisfied with the performance of WPA workers. The rural concern over a supply of harvest workers and an overburdened tax system may have colored their view, but clearly the Inman and Oak Valley boards reflected the opinion of some persons that the WPA was a boondoggle.

Detractors of the WPA, however, represented the minority view. The WPA was a powerful and positive force in the lives of the people. "It was a job, a job for money," observed Conrad Toso. Without WPA work he, his wife, and their nine children might not have made it through the drought of 1936. The family's farm in Maplewood Township supported them during good times, but when the WPA allowed farmers to work during the drought, Conrad tried to sign up. He was refused WPA employment because the Tosoes owned their farm, so Conrad and three of the children went to help pick potatoes on his brother's farm near Moorhead, Clay County. "I got a letter from the sheriff to bring the children back because they should be in school so I wrote back to the sheriff . . . if you put me in jail, why, I understand I'd get three meals a day but what about the children?" Conrad recalled. "I got a letter from my wife that they put me on [WPA] and they kept me on [WPA] until my first cream check."[58] The WPA meant jobs.

John Mark, the mayor of New York Mills, was extremely proud of the track and the football field that the WPA built for his village; New York Mills hosted the district and regional track meets. Once a friend took Mark to the stadium at the University of Minnesota where they ran into football coach Bernard W. ("Bernie") Bierman, who gave them a tour of the facility. Mark looked around and then commented to Bierman, "You might have the bigger the grandstand than we have in New York Mills but we've got the better the track."[59] The WPA meant facilities.

Laura Dunlap, a homemaker who lived on the edge of Fergus Falls, voted for Republicans Herbert Hoover in 1932 and Alfred Landon in 1936, and her husband had steady private employment throughout the depression. Yet, in looking back at the WPA and its projects, she maintained: "There really were good things. . . . I feel in those days they spent every dollar for something they got a dollar's worth out of."[60] John Hartman of Perham reflected on the WPA: "Shovels were the main thing, so they had something to lean on. We can laugh about it now, but . . . those were rough times, very rough times . . . fellows would do anything to keep body and soul together."[61] Laura Dunlap and John Hartman captured the spirit of the WPA: it created useful things and helped people keep "body and soul together" in a time of crisis.

6

A WPA PROJECT AND ITS PEOPLE
"The Boys Down at the Courthouse"

56-713 under W-316 began P-862 of 165-1-71-147(2) in 71-522-56. In WPA language this means: Roy A. Baker, under this order, began historical-type work on a local project of the Historical Records Survey in Otter Tail County.[1] The WPA's massive bureaucracy reduced people and what they did to numbers. The number of people who worked on a project, its cost, and its objective is relatively simple to catalog. Fifteen workers were assigned to build a dam to restore the water level on Pelican Lake for $6,922.[2] That, in and of itself, is worth knowing, but almost impossible-to-answer questions remain. What were those workers like? What did they do day after day? How did they feel about their work? How did the WPA affect their lives? Could they have survived without government employment? The story of "the boys down at the courthouse" — as the people were often called whose headquarters were in two basement rooms of the county courthouse allotted to the Otter Tail County Historical Society — provides a rare glimpse into the day-to-day world of WPA workers.

In the summer of 1935 a WPA official invited Edward Barnard, as the secretary of the society, to "suggest something that a few 'white collar' men might do for the Historical Society." Barnard, an avid promoter of local history, jumped at the opportunity. "I explained how it was getting harder and harder all the time for me to answer correctly the hundreds of questions asked me," he wrote to Theodore C. Blegen, the superintendent of the Minnesota Historical Society. He hoped that Blegen would lend his support to a proposed project that would select and record on cards the "date of all important happenings, elections, prominent deaths, buildings burned, etc." mentioned in the county's newspapers, thus increasing the county society's reference capabilities.[3]

Barnard later told Blegen that the officials of one of the newspapers were "very enthusiastic about this project," but he was still being realistic: "I am a little skeptical about the project going through because of the great number of projects that have been suggested. I sort of feel that the only pulling card is the fact that this is a 'white collar' job whereas most of the others require muscle."[4] It appeared that his "pulling card" might not work. By mid-December he had heard nothing from the WPA. So Anton Thompson, the president of the Otter Tail County Historical Society and a judge of the Seventh District Court, sent off inquiries to the state WPA office and the state historical society.[5] The WPA office had "overlooked" the application; by December 28 it found that the project had been approved by the president "but that to date no funds have been allotted." The WPA district office in Detroit Lakes, Thompson was assured, was being advised of the project and the district engineer urged to "contact the sponsors of that project to the end that they may be kept informed of developments."[6]

In February 1936 Thompson heard from Alma B. Kerr, the director of the Division of Women's and Professional Projects of the state WPA, that the project was "authorized to commence work." The district engineer, Kerr promised, "will be able to take care of this project for you."[7]

By March Barnard had three people busy reading back issues of county newspapers, "for the purpose of recording the dates of the various happenings in Otter Tail county from the beginning." In April the WPA assigned the two men who were to go through the *Perham Enterprise-Bulletin* files.[8] Publisher-editor Smalley was not entirely pleased with his new role: "I am very much surprised to find myself appointed timekeeper and nurse for the two WPA boys who are doing historical stuff here." He did, however, have kind words for their attitude and ability: "They took hold in a workmanlike and intelligent manner."[9] Barnard felt that he should tell Smalley that his salary "for watching these young men will be the same as mine — $000.00 per month."[10]

The recording project was affected when the WPA began to handle historical projects through its Historical Records Survey program. The Minnesota Historical Society acted "as sponsor to certain district-wide local historical projects, and as adviser to others" in cooperation with the survey. The state society developed standards and procedures for project units, providing unified guidelines.[11] By April 1937 Barnard learned that the county society "has been granted another 'project' in the new set up and that *one feature* of it will be the visiting and writing-up of the pioneers that are still living." He planned to have county people meet with a district representative "who will tell us all about *what* we can do, *how* to do it and *who* will do it."[12]

Although the Minnesota Historical Society sponsored projects and established objectives, local units had an autonomy that gave each its own identity. The Otter Tail County project, supervised by the Otter Tail County Historical Society, is a prime example.

Edward C. Budack (left) and Edward T. Barnard (right) posed with items donated to the Otter Tail County Historical Society Museum. Budack is holding a flour barrel that was hollowed out of a basswood tree.

The Minnesota Historical Society suggested that local projects inventory records of county officers, townships, municipalities, school districts, and state institutions; locate and list records of organizations such as churches, fraternal organizations, and political groups; interview "old settlers" and take down their reminiscences; and copy original manuscripts in private hands, as well as index newspapers and undertake other historical work.[13]

A crew of six worked in the courthouse basement. Five each earned 57 1/2 cents an hour for a 120 hour work month. Edward C. Budack oversaw the project as office manager, earning 63 cents per hour or $75.60 per month. In July Albert G. Muske joined the team. These seven workers formed a permanent crew until February 1939 when Roy Baker replaced Budack. Other workers came and went, maintaining a fairly constant group of eight or nine people.[14] And the progress of the project pleased Baker: "The Project Workers have entered into the spirit of the work in good shape and I feel that we are accomplishing something."[15]

After Baker had been with the project for some five months, he wrote about how impressed he was with the workers: "I have six good men . . . who have been on this project for nearly two years, and they know their business."[16]

Barnard watched the project closely and acted as its coordinator and troubleshooter. Problems, however, were few. He tried in vain to have a Finnish-American woman added to the project staff, believing that she would be invaluable in interviewing Finnish pioneers. "To me the Finnish language is about as hard to learn, or understand when spoken, as Chinese," he explained to a district WPA official. "I visited New York Mills for one week . . . and the only word I really learned was 'raha' — money."[17] When the WPA attempted to reclassify one of the "boys down at the courthouse" downward in status and pay, Barnard successfully convinced the director to drop the matter.[18] A serious dilemma came in late 1938 when the district office assigned the unwelcome employee to the project. Barnard objected strenuously:

> I want you to know that we *do not want him on the project* or even loafing around the room. You will remember that he was the overseer of the book binding project and became such a nuisance with the young ladies that *you fired him.* I had to make complaint to the W. P. A. office up stairs before we got him out of our rooms. . . . I don't care where you send him so that he is not allowed around our project.[19]

The new worker was not around for long.

The Otter Tail County crew accomplished a great deal, employing as many as nine or as few as five workers each month. Beginning in April 1937 and continuing to the project's apparent end in November 1939, they logged 27,482.50 hours of work: 2,638.50 indexing newspapers and pictures, 5,903 calendaring newspapers, 17,973 conducting and writing up interviews, 392 rearranging and labeling exhibits, and 576 making reports for the Minnesota Historical Society. Day after day they worked with the county newspapers, compiling a card index listing "almost every important historical event from 1871 to date showing date, paper in which it appeared and a few words telling what it relates to." They traveled at least 3,085 miles to conduct more than one thousand interviews with "old settlers" and other people living throughout the county. And while they were on the road, they collected material for the county historical society, including "pioneer," Indian, and military artifacts; clothing; firearms and accessories; household, agricultural, and medical tools; articles brought by immigrants; and photographs, pictures, newspapers, books, and pamphlets — in all about 860 items. They

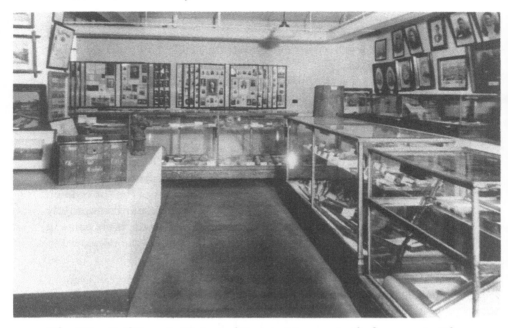

The Otter Tail County Historical Society Museum in the basement of the county courthouse

ranged from a handmade flail, homestead certificates, and a "Stone scraper used by mother of Chief Pokenahga" to G.A.R. memorabilia, spinning wheels, and an "Old style lunch box brot from Norway in 1878." The crew played a part in putting together the 184-page book that contained the record survey and history of the county. What these Otter Tail County WPA workers did was useful and significant: the first systematic inventory of records, the first countywide collection of artifacts, the first effort to recreate the past through oral history, the first thorough cataloging of the county's history. Although much of the work would not be appreciated until a generation had passed, the effort was vital to the preservation of the county's heritage. The project provided food, shelter, and clothing for the workers and their families and gave the county materials through which residents could better understand their past.[20]

Of the men who worked on the historical project Albert Muske and Roy Baker were with the WPA almost as long as it existed. Their cases reflect the WPA as it influenced and interacted with their lives. On July 20, 1937, Albert Muske of Fergus Falls joined the "boys" who were working in the courthouse basement on the WPA historical project. As a senior clerk and later senior interviewer, Muske was classified as a skilled worker who earned sixty-nine dollars for a 120-hour work month. Although they indexed newspapers, especially during the heart of winter, Muske and the other interviewers also spent many hours visiting their subjects, sometimes driving considerable distances. "The Interviewers have been on the road during a large part of the month and have traveled a total of 805 miles," reported Baker one spring. "They have completed for filing 45 interviews with old settlers and have compiled their biographies." When the interviewers returned to Fergus Falls, each wrote a thorough report based on his notes. Although an interview may have lasted for two or three hours, writing the report could take several days.

When the project's work force was reduced in late summer of 1939, Muske remained, but at a reduced monthly income of $57.20.[21] In early December 1939 he and the four others who were still on the project became nervous about rumors that the project would be terminated. Usually workers would be transferred to another project, but there was no guarantee of a job. The bad news came: the project would end on December 31. Muske's reputation as a knowledgeable and dedicated worker, however, had caught the ear of Jacob J. Hodnefield, the supervisor of the Historical Records Survey for Minnesota. He asked Muske to continue on as a worker who would list the churches and cemeteries in Otter Tail County.[22] By the first week of January 1940 Muske was paging through courthouse records, plat books, and other sources, making a list of churches and their locations.[23] For each church he had to supply its official, corporate, and popular names, location, conference, and pastor's name, address, and telephone number. Hodnefield inspected a sample of Muske's work in early April. "We appreciate that on the whole you have the right idea in mind about the proper way to do the church directory forms," the director commented. "We feel you are progressing the way we should like to have you."[24]

On May 1 Muske left the survey work for temporary private employment as an assistant to the Fergus Falls city assessor, who was making an annual assessment of personal property. Since the WPA regulations required that no worker could stay with a project for more than eighteen months without a layoff, the city job worked to Muske's advantage because he had income during his lay-off time. He was reassigned to the WPA project on June 17 and conducted research on the church survey during the summer.[25]

In early August Hodnefield wrote to Muske that "while we are entirely pleased with the work you have shown evidence of performing so far, we do think you have spent a little too much time with the church directory for Otter Tail County." Two months was more time than most workers spent on such a task.[26] Muske replied that Otter Tail County's size and large number of churches called for more time: "I am certainly sorry to learn that I have not been doing as much as has been expected of me, because I have always endeavored to give my best."[27] Hodnefield agreed that "Otter Tail is a large county, and travel is a difficult thing to overcome," but reminded Muske that he had been on the church directory work for more than six months and the "publication date is coming nearer and nearer."[28]

After Muske finished this church directory, Hodnefield asked him to undertake the same task in Wilkin County, emphasizing that it "should be a minor task in comparison to Otter Tail County."[29] Now experienced in such research, Muske was asked in early October to do more work in Otter Tail County after he finished the Wilkin project: detailed, informational lists of townships, school districts, municipalities, and cemeteries.[30] Muske pointed out that preliminary work on school districts had already been done. Hodnefield acknowledged that that was true but asserted that "This office realizes just what work needs to be done" and told Muske, "Please comply with this assignment."[31]

Muske worked until mid-December when he questioned the assigned methodology. The cemeteries list needed more information than the original cemetery plats and county plat books provided. Muske was not content with what he considered to be an incomplete approach. "Just to satisfy my self how near accurate that procedure would be I made personal contact in a number of townships and I found that it would hardly average more than 50% accurate. . . . I feel that in order to have it fairly accurate I will have to make personal contacts in nearly every township."[32] Hodnefield was not happy with Muske's search for accuracy. "We had no intention of having you drive throughout the county in order to obtain a listing of cemeteries. . . . it is sufficient now to send in the best list you can without driving."[33]

During December 1940 and January and February 1941 Muske divided his time between the church directory and the cemetery survey. For example, from December 30 through January 24 he mostly took notes on churches from township files, transferred the notes to church history forms, and wrote historical sketches of churches. On January 27 and 28 he compiled data and typed a preliminary cemetery report. From January 29 through February 17 he worked again on the church information, and during the rest of February also put together and typed his final cemetery report.[34]

As he labored, he became increasingly dissatisfied with the church and cemetery history forms that the survey used, and asked if he might make some suggestions for changes.[35] Hodnefield wrote Muske that "We would be very glad to receive any suggestions you have," but warned him that "Whether we can use them or not, however, may depend not only on us but also on the Washington office."[36] The implication that "Washington" might not like his suggestions did not deter Muske. He fired off five single-spaced typed pages of suggestions that he felt would improve the forms.[37] Hodnefield replied that "we will not be able to decide much until next week. We will inform you of any changes in instructions."[38]

Muske's list of cemeteries was acknowledged with high praise: "This is one of the best so far received."[39] With this list out of the way, Muske concentrated on church histories, often working on his own time. Hodnefield told him that in April "As soon as the roads improve, it would be well that you spend more time in the field completing some of the church histories on which you are working. The . . . main reasons for this are that we would like to be able to catch any misunderstandings before you have spent too much time, so that the monthly work report will show some work turned in by you, and so you will not be forced to do too much driving all at once, later on."[40] Muske then detailed what he had accomplished and remarked, "let me assure you that with the method that I have adopted I can turn out more and better work in the end. . . . But if you should feel that you have a better way of going about it, I shall be glad to adopt it . . . or a[t] least give it due consideration."[41]

By July 1941 Muske had submitted most of his church history work, but before he could put the finishing touches on it, new orders arrived: "Commencing very shortly after the 4th [of July], this project will drop all past work until a directory of community service and defense organizations has been completed. . . . Calls will be made and forms filled for each group such as Commercial Clubs, Parent-Teacher Associations, and Boy Scouts, etc."[42] Almost before Muske could begin the new assignment, it was withdrawn, and he was back working on the church directory.[43]

Muske continued his work for the Historical Records Survey into 1942 when the war removed the need for public-work programs. The WPA was in its last months. On March 19 he was allotted fifty-six hours for "his last pay period."[44] He asked Hodnefield if he could continue "for another month or so," but Hodnefield, while observing that Muske's work was "entirely satisfactory," left the decision on termination with the district WPA office in Detroit Lakes. So Muske worked his last day for the WPA, ending a career of nearly five years as a historical worker for the government.[45]

Like Muske, Roy Baker was dependent on the WPA for a livelihood. In 1879 he, as a boy of about six, had arrived in Otter Tail County with his parents. The gold rush of 1898–99 lured him to Alaska, but by 1902 he was back in Minnesota, where he worked at the Rochester State Hospital until 1911. That year he entered the real estate business with his father in Fergus Falls. "I made good in this and loaded up with high priced lands and city property," he recalled, "and when the bottom dropped out in 1920, I dropped with it." Before the depression he was an insurance salesman and served as a deputy sheriff for six years.[46]

In his sixties, Baker found work in October 1935 as foreman of a WPA construction crew that was building a grandstand on the county fairgrounds. From that time on, Baker was a WPA employee. The few private jobs that were available were simply not suited to a man of his age; government work was his only option. In December 1935 the WPA transferred him to a repair and construction crew at the Fergus Falls State Hospital, where he was foreman until February 1939. Because of his age, his interest in history (he had written a history of early Fergus Falls), and his acquaintance with many of the county's pioneer families, the WPA then transferred him to oversee the historical project. The new job was up Baker's alley: "I like this historical work very much, and feel that I am in it heart and soul," he wrote a few months after he joined "the boys down at the courthouse."[47]

As office manager Baker earned $75.60 a month (63 cents per hour). In addition to handling the project's paper work, he did what the others did. Things went smoothly for Baker until July when the new WPA rule that required those who had worked for eighteen consecutive months to take a thirty-day layoff went into effect. With a family to feed and shelter, the prospect of thirty days with no income was indeed grim. While Baker explored private employment, Barnard tried to convince the secretary of the Minnesota Historical Society to make an exception in Baker's case. "It would be a very severe loss to our society to have him laid off," he told Theodore Blegen.[48] "He met reverses like hundreds of others but it did not dull his ambition to work and to try to take care of his family," he explained to Hodnefield. "The government has got full value for every cent he has been paid."[49]

Baker found harvest work for two weeks, but the rule specified thirty days — not two weeks. "Is there any possibility of making an exception 'for the good of the order' in this case," Baker asked the WPA office in Detroit Lakes. "I have no work in sight and with a family of four youngsters on my hands, I do not know how I am going to keep them eating, to say nothing of rent, also water and light bills."[50] The WPA office responded by letter the next day: "We regret that this action is necessary but it is only within our line of duty that your termination is being made."[51]

Roy Baker

For whatever reason, bureaucratic error or bureaucratic benevo-
lence, the WPA let Baker stay on until the end of the project on December 30, 1939, with just a two-week layoff. As early as June he had in-
quired about the future of the historical project because "I . . . am
getting along in years, and I do not want to be out of a job."[52] Four days
before Christmas the workers did not know what work the new year
would bring. It was a gloomy holiday season. "This crew is wondering
what is to be done after that date. . . . We would all rest easier, if we
knew what the future held in store for us," Baker wrote to the district
office. Two days after Christmas the good news came. The workers
would be transferred to other projects, but Baker would continue the
work for the historical society.[53]

Baker began 1940 as a worker at the Otter Tail County Historical Society under the sponsorship of the Historical Records Survey. He operated the museum, interviewed old-timers who dropped in, and made
notes from old newspapers. His description of the first two weeks on the
job is typical of his activities for the six months that the project operated:

> During the past period, we have had, probably, 125 visitors . . . and
> I have talked with, probably, 50, [from] some of whom, I obtained
> data in regard to their parents, who were old timers; others have
> promised to bring in relics for our museum, etc. I have gone through
> the yearly bound volum[e]s of the Fergus Falls Journal for the years

of 1873–74–75–76, and have picked up quite a little historical data. I have received some museum relics.[54]

Now and then Baker answered specific questions for the Records Survey. In spite of frequent difficulties with WPA forms and officials, Baker's work went smoothly — until June 1940. He began to worry on June 17 when he received no time schedule for working days after June 25.[55] "I am so interested in the work that I often work evenings and week ends, at home, on it," he tried to explain in a later letter to the Detroit Lakes office. "My understanding is that I have been working, since the first of the year, in a line of historical work, that has not even been authorized by the W. P. A., hence, the closing of the project."[56] Baker wrote the Detroit Lakes office, "I am very sorry that the project has been discontinued and I sincerely hope that there may be something in the historical line come up again, in the near future, so that I may be able to continue this work."[57] Baker had been transferred to the bookbinding project at a much lower salary. He was grateful but apprehensive: "I wish to, also, thank you for giving me a transfer to another project . . . as I need the where-with-all to keep the kids eating and clothed. I have a hard time making both ends meet on the $68.40, and it remains to be seen what $44.40 will do. I do not believe that I will open up a bank."[58]

Barnard was outraged at what he considered to be shabby treatment: "I feel it would be a shame to put a man of his ability on to a bookbinding project when he is so badly needed on our historical survey project," he lamented to Arthur J. Larsen, superintendent of the Minnesota Historical Society.[59] Larsen replied sympathetically that he had "been trying to get to the bottom of things."[60]

Baker worked on the binding project for less than a month. On July 15 the WPA notified Barnard that Baker would soon be assigned to "do library work in the museum."[61] Baker was soon back doing what he did best: indexing, preparing exhibits, and conducting tours.[62]

In October 1940 a proposal for a project, with the board of county commissioners as sponsor, was submitted to the WPA. Washington approved provision for "a competent man in the museum rooms" for the next two years. Baker had not enjoyed that kind of promised job security for some time.[63] But he faced another crisis: the mandatory thirty-day layoff. This time the WPA insisted on the full thirty days — until April 25, 1941. It was a difficult month for Baker and his family. On April 25 he asked the Detroit Lakes WPA office for immediate reinstatement. "Our finances are getting pretty low," he explained, "and it is tough to see our kids come home from school, hungry, with but little in the house to feed them."[64] The WPA put Baker back on his old job. But because of shifting national priorities, the government began closing most of the nation's historical projects, and on June 13, 1941, Baker's project ended.[65]

Beginning August 29 he was assigned to an intermediate-class job at $52.80 per month with the Minnesota Statewide Archaeological and Historical Research Survey Project, a WPA program administered by the University of Minnesota. Baker was back in the Otter Tail County courthouse — this time researching historic markers, monuments, sites, buildings, trails, abandoned villages, and abandoned and private cemeteries.[66]

Although the return to history-related work overjoyed Baker, he was afraid that the intermediate classification salary would not be enough to make it through the winter. "Previous to this project," he wrote Richard R. Sackett, the project's director, "I have been classified in the Skilled and Professional Classes, on the historical work. Naturally, I would like to get as much salary as possible, especially with a family on my hands and winter coming on. . . . We are not an expensive family as we live very plain, yet we would like to keep warm and have enough to eat."[67] He asked the WPA to consider a reclassification: "I am not blowing my own horn, but I honestly feel as though I was entitled to more pay. I need it bad."[68]

When near the end of October he had received no word from Sackett or the district WPA office concerning reclassification, his patience began to wear thin. "Now, if each office is waiting to hear from the other," he complained, "I am afraid that I will have to take up a few more holes in my belt, (or the family will)." With no hope of making enough money on the archaeological project to survive the high costs of winter, Baker asked to be transferred to a new project with the clerk of court's office. He had heard that the project had a skilled job with a monthly salary of $74.10. "By economizing, we can live on this," he told Edward F. Landin, the WPA area supervisor.[69] In December he was on the job, checking old birth records in the clerk of court's office — a new task with more money, and he was still one of "the boys down at the courthouse."[70]

Muske and Baker demonstrate several points: the WPA was essential to the two men's survival; they were dedicated and knowledgeable workers; their work was useful; the WPA complicated, but protected, their lives. Both depended on the WPA to provide the necessities of life for their families and themselves. They needed the employment to survive. In his sixties Baker's chances of private employment were nil. He went from project to project with a sense of gratitude, even when his salary was cut a third on the bookbinding project. It was work! He had four children to feed, clothe, and shelter. When Muske's project finally ended in April 1942, he hoped for "just one more month," just another paycheck that would provide the essentials of life. For both Baker and Muske the WPA meant survival.

They were hard workers who knew what they were doing. They loved their work, and their highest priority was a job well done. Muske was frequently disturbed with his orders from St. Paul because he wanted to do a more complete job than was required. Often Muske and Baker knew better how to go about their tasks than did those in far-away offices in St. Paul or Washington. They frequently worked on their own time, not content with monthly time allocations. Their attitude and work goes far to dispel the popular notion that "WPA" stood for "We Putter Around."

What they did was useful. Both made valuable contributions to the history of the county and the state. In many ways they built the foundation for a successful county historical society and made possible a better understanding of the heritage of Otter Tail County's people. They collected and pulled together the basis of today's historical interpretation.

The endless paper work, the bureaucratic maze, and the uncertainty of employment frustrated both men. The flow of new forms and directives irritated Muske; the monthly reporting system vexed Baker. The WPA often appeared to be an impersonal governmental monster. Yet it somehow cared for them. Baker was transferred to numerous projects during his career with the WPA. With the help of Barnard, who desperately wanted the Otter Tail County Historical Society work to go on, historical projects kept Baker employed after 1938. When historical projects disappeared, bookbinding — although at lower pay — was always an option for him. During the years with the WPA, Baker and Muske were without government checks for only the shortest times. They needed the checks, and the WPA seemed to need and care for them.

CCC AND NYA
"Youth Must Rebuild
What Has Been Destroyed"

THE ENTRY of young people who were of working age into the market place augmented the nation's unemployment problem. About 2.5 million young people were looking for jobs with little chance of finding work.[1] At the same time dry winds were ravaging the nation's heartland, a sixth of the continent's soil was gone, and soil erosion was rampant. The New Deal attacked the villains of both unemployment and waste with one agency — the Civilian Conservation Corps (CCC).[2] Roosevelt had been keenly interested in conservation since he entered the public sphere in 1910, and as governor of New York he had implemented an unemployment relief program in 1932 that gave jobs to ten thousand men in conservation work.[3] Roosevelt placed a high premium on a federal program that would rescue the nation's quickly depleting natural resources and extend hope to young men who were groping for survival. On March 21, 1933, he presented the CCC measure to Congress. "More important, however, than the material gains will be the moral and spiritual value of such work," Roosevelt told Congress. "The overwhelming majority of unemployed Americans . . . would infinitely prefer to work. We can take a vast army of these unemployed out into healthful surroundings. . . . It is not a panacea for all the unemployment but it is an essential step in this emergency."[4] Before the month had elapsed, the national conservation crusade had been launched.

"Roosevelt's Tree Army" took shape during the spring of 1933. The Department of Labor was to select the men; the Department of War to enroll, feed, clothe, house, condition, and transport them and to run the camps; the Department of Agriculture and the Department of the Interior to select and to oversee the projects. Rarely had government agencies cooperated so closely.[5] Initial enrollment was limited to single men aged eighteen to twenty-five, most of whose families were on the relief rolls. Of the thirty dollars each man was paid per month, twenty-two to twenty-five went directly home to help his family. On April 17 Camp Roosevelt, the first CCC camp, was established in Luray, Virginia.[6] Problems with organization, however, got the CCC off to a slow start. By May 10, 1933, only 52,000 men had been enrolled. A year later the CCC was in full gear with 353,000 men involved in conservation projects. In September 1935 the CCC reached its highest enrollment: 502,000 men in 2,514 camps. (On June 30, 74 of the then-extant 2,110 camps were in Minnesota.)[7] Between 1935 and 1941 only a few new camps opened, and old ones began to close as the government gradually reduced the CCC funding. By 1940 Roosevelt's goal was to cut to only 1,227 camps housing 230,000 men.[8] After the attack on Pearl Harbor on December 7, 1941, the question became: can the CCC help win the war? The answer was "no"; and the CCC, like most New Deal relief programs, ended in 1942.

Initial response to the CCC was overwhelming. "Quite a number of young men from all parts of Otter Tail county have called . . . in regard to securing jobs on federal reforestation projects," the *Fergus Falls Weekly Journal* reported in April 1933.[9] The young men had to wait for nearly six months, however, while the wheels of bureaucracy turned slowly, organizing the Corps. By fall the CCC was ready to enroll Otter Tail County men and send them off to camps. Each county received a quota, and Otter Tail County's was disappointing. Only twenty-three could join the CCC during the first enrollment. The local man in charge of enrollment for the county explained that "As a great many more than this number will apply" he wished to point out that "those who are accepted will be young men who are unemployed and who have relatives who will be dependent upon the money they will make at the government camp."[10]

The 1934 drought and the completion of additional camps allowed more Otter Tail County young men to join the Corps. In April and July 1934 about 159 men entered the CCC, and in 1935, 120 enrolled. In 1935 when the national CCC enrollment reached its peak, Otter Tail County had 224 of its "boys" scattered throughout twenty-two of Minnesota's camps.[11] The dismal harvest of 1936 sent 61 of the county's young men into the CCC in April, May, and July. In October Otter Tail County recorded its largest class: 115. "The district court room at the court house looked like headquarters for a nudist colony Saturday, when 150 young men were examined for CCC duty," a Fergus Falls reporter observed. "All applicants were obliged to shed their clothing and take a physical examination. . . . The men must . . . be able to hear the tick-tick of a watch a foot from either ear."[12]

The hundreds of Otter Tail County men who joined the CCC represented a broad cross section of the county's urban and rural areas. For example, in July and October 1939, of the ninety-six men who enrolled, thirty-four came from the towns (Fergus Falls, ten; New York Mills, nine; Parkers Prairie, four; Henning, three; Vining and Richville, two each; and Pelican Rapids, Vergas, Perham, Ottertail, one each). The other sixty-two left rural areas for the CCC adventure.[13]

The CCC experiences of four Otter Tail County men provide a view of life at camp and the meaning of the Corps to its participants and their families. Harold R. Davis had just graduated from Fergus Falls High School. Leonard Hovland was twenty-two years old and living on his parents' farm near Pelican Rapids. Clinton Thun and Alex Klimek lived five miles apart — Thun in Parkers Prairie, where he worked in a garage, and Klimek on his family's farm near Urbank. The four had two things in common: the future looked dim, and they joined the CCC in 1934. "If work of any kind was available, it was filled by married men with families to support. My first application to join the C.C.C. was turned down as our family was not on relief," Davis recalled. "Within a month this rule was abolished and I was accepted."[14] Hovland entered the Corps because of the farm crisis in 1934: "We had a drought that year and no rain hardly and we didn't see that there was going to be any crops. So a bunch of us young boys got together and decided that we were going to join the CC's."[15] Thun and Klimek enrolled because quotas were raised due to the drought. "There was such a real dry summer," Thun remembered, "they took in an extra group and that's the way we got in."[16]

The four passed their physical examinations in Fergus Falls, and, like other Minnesotans, journeyed to Fort Snelling, in the Twin Cities area, for a final physical, a general briefing, issue of World War I olive-drab uniforms, and assignment to a camp. "We were sent to Fort Snelling and there we took our physicals and at the time I was there there was [sic] about five thousand boys . . . sleeping in tents all over and we stayed there about four days," Hovland recalled, "and then we were sent out to camp in Northern Minnesota around Duluth. We were all split up. . . . We rode by train from Duluth and then we were hauled in Dodge trucks with cattle racks . . . to our camps."[17] Klimek and Thun spent about two weeks at Fort Snelling, working around the grounds. "They put us in a train and off we went and the next morning we woke up and we were in the north woods," Thun recalled. Davis, Thun, and Klimek ended up, along with many others from Otter Tail County, at Camp Kabetogama Lake (Camp S-81, Company No. 724) in Kabetogama State Forest, St. Louis County. The post office for the camp

Harold R. Davis at the CCC camp

was about ten miles west on U.S. 53 at Ray, Koochiching County.[18] Hovland found himself in an isolated camp twenty miles inland from the shore of Lake Superior.

Most CCC camps were similar in appearance. Usually each consisted of four or five barracks (each one hundred by twenty feet), a mess hall, a recreation hall, administration buildings, officers' quarters, a hospital, a garage, and sometimes a schoolhouse. Ordinarily the buildings were laid out around three sides of a rectangle with an open grassy space or recreational ground in the middle.[19] Camp Kabetogama Lake was unique. According to Davis, "The camp was built around a recreation room with passageways to and from the barracks, offices, supply room, mess hall, showers, hospital, etc. So in bad weather there was no need to go outside."[20] Not many camps enjoyed that luxury.

The enrollees were at camp to work. The men at Camp Kabetogama Lake during its first year of operation (June 17, 1933, to June 30, 1934), among other projects, reduced the fire-hazard potential on 998 acres, cleared 20 acres along roads, strung 37 miles of telephone lines, cleared 13 acres for tourist camps, brought 33 fires under control, cut 1,200 tele-

The mess hall (above) and barracks (right) at Camp Kabetogama Lake

phone poles, sawed 132,000 board feet of lumber, thinned 253 acres of dead timber, and cruised 3,811 acres, looking for good lumber. Davis observed that "the first crew I was assigned to was sent to a side camp on an island at the upper end of Lake Kabetogama where we cleaned up the area which had been logged off during the winter of 1933."[21] Working except in downpouring rain and in temperatures twenty below zero or colder, Davis cleared roadsides, planted trees, thinned out forest, and cleaned up a cedar swamp, fighting off mosquitoes all the while. When winter snow stranded deer and cattle, he and his fellow CCC workers hauled hay to feed to the animals.[22]

Hovland also did a variety of jobs during his three months with the CCC. In the summer he worked in a nearby stream, "Building up shelters for fish," and in the fall planted "acres and acres" of firebreaks with pine trees. During the winter the "boys" who stayed on cut wood and worked on firebreaks.[23] Thun and Klimek built roads, thinned out woods, cleared and burned brush, cut logs, and made telephone poles.[24] The work was not always pleasant. Thun recalled about their footgear that "We wore rubber bottoms, leather tops and that always got all soaked up. We came in with wet feet every day — we'd work in the deep snow." In the evening they dried out their boots and rubbed them with saddle soap or oil, but "The next morning then the oil kinda soaked through again. We worked all day with wet feet."[25]

"All day" meant from 8:00 A.M. until 4:00 or 5:00 P.M., although time was allowed within that day for travel to and from the work site and for lunch and coffee breaks. During the work week of Monday through Friday the state Division of Forestry directed the work at Camp Kabetogama Lake. The United States Army oversaw the men after work and on weekends. Davis observed that "we were under the army and army regulations. The officers and the first sergeant saw to it that we did what we were supposed to do. They would give us extra duty, confine us to camp, and things like that. Just like it was during the war."[26]

The army provided a doctor for each camp. According to Davis, "The camp was equipped with a dispensary and a hospital. Sick call was held each morning immediately after breakfast. An orderly took care of those reporting and dished out aspirin, etc. If in his opinion the doctor's attention was necessary, you got to see the doctor, who made [h]is examination and put you in the hospital if necessary. Surgery was not performed at the camp. You were taken to a hospital in International Falls if surgery was necessary."[27] Hovland thought that "We were taken real good care of there" and observed that a doctor and medicine were readily available and that he had been taken to Two Harbors to have a tooth extracted.[28]

Davis (far left) and fellow CCC workers tackled an unaccustomed week-end chore — laundry.

The army also provided "plenty to eat." Hovland complained a little about the two cheese sandwiches and one summer sausage sandwich for lunch every day but thought that "We were real well fed" and remembered that he had gained "quite a bit" of weight.[29] Davis agreed, "The food was good and plentiful."[30] Thun characterized meals as "pretty good."[31]

The CCC workers could relax during the evenings and weekends. Poker, pool, horseshoes, hiking, kittenball, and reading were favorite pastimes. The weekly movie was a happy occasion, and the men looked forward to dances. At Camp Kabetogama Lake "trucks were dispatched to International Falls for dances." Sometimes the army would bus in girls from International Falls for a dance in the camp's recreation hall. A guard was placed at each door so, according to Thun, "you couldn't run out in the woods with the girls."[32] Hovland went to a dance occasionally when the fellows were taken to the Cascade Lodge, about forty miles away.[33]

The CCC men worked hard for their monthly paycheck. "I made more money with my five dollars than I ever did in my life," Klimek claimed.[34] Hovland spent his five dollars on tobacco and confessed "They weren't supposed to do it but every two weeks the folks would send me two dollars . . . you couldn't get along on the five hardly when you smoked."[35] The Otter Tail County men were proud that they could help their families at home with twenty-five dollars a month. How did Klimek feel about the money that went home? "Good." For Thun's family, "It kept them alive. It kept them going."[36] Hovland agreed, "It really helped them, cuz there really wasn't much income."[37]

Hundreds of Otter Tail County's young men shared the CCC experience with Davis, Hovland, Klimek, and Thun. The impact was threefold: they received the training of a lifetime; they provided the nation with some of the most long-lasting and useful work of the New Deal programs; and they made life more tolerable for the families back home in Otter Tail County.

Although the vast majority of CCC camps were in northern Minnesota, Otter Tail County benefited directly from two CCC initiatives. In June 1934 Walter S. Olson, the director of the Division of Drainage and Water for Minnesota, contacted Fergus Falls officials about a project that would clean up and restore the water level of the Otter Tail River. To Fergus Falls, suffering from a water shortage, this was welcome news. Olson suggested that the city support the idea that the CCC undertake the work with camps at Fergus Falls, as well as at Breckenridge in Wilkin County and at Frazee in Becker County. The proposal called for each camp to have 250 men. The city council approved the plan and promised to provide a ten-acre tract of land for the camp.[38] Within ten days Olson and a United States Army officer inspected sites in the city and decided on Park Region Luther College, which had recently closed, at a suggested rental fee of two hundred dollars per month.[39] The advantage of the college site was clear: camp buildings would not have to be constructed.

The CCC worked to put the new quarters in shape after the arrival of the first contingent. During the first week of August 238 men moved onto the college grounds and began repairing the college building before cleaning up the Otter Tail River between Otter Tail Lake and Breckenridge.[40] Later in August the CCC planned to assign additional men to Fergus Falls, raising the work force to 313.[41] Fearing that the camp would disband when the river project was finished, the city council approved a plan to maintain the CCC camp in the city. Upon the recommendation of the Parks and Playgrounds Committee, the council authorized one thousand dollars to help to carry out nine proposed CCC projects for the city.[42] The city's concern was well founded. Before the onset of winter, the CCC had completed its task in the Fergus Falls area. "As a result of CCC work," reported E. Victor Willard, the state commissioner of conservation, "water is now flowing into the Otter Tail river in places where it was completely dry this summer."[43] Fergus Falls gained a more plentiful water supply, but the termination of the project closed its college-campus CCC.

In January 1935 the *Fergus Falls Weekly Journal*, under the headline "CCC Camp to Be Established Here if People Want It," urged the city to make a bid to secure another camp for the city.[44] The city council acted swiftly and at its February 4 meeting passed a resolution asking for the establishment of a new CCC camp in the city.[45] Perham did the same.[46] Both efforts were in vain.

In 1940 the Otter Tail County agent, working with the Soil Conservation Service, urged farmers to support the establishment of a CCC camp in that part of the county where drought had hit the hardest. The effort paid dividends, and in the spring of 1941 when many camps were closing, the CCC announced that a new camp would be constructed on the north end of Wall Lake in Section 33 of Aurdal Township. The camp's work area encompassed an eighteen-mile radius, including the townships of Elizabeth, Friberg, Buse, Dane Prairie, Tordenskjold, Tumuli, Aastad, Aurdal, Western, Oscar, Erhards Grove, Maplewood, Star Lake, Maine, Amor, Everts, Clitherall, and St. Olaf.[47]

The Otter Tail County camp (SCS-MN-21) began to take shape in June; by early July the *Fergus Falls Daily Journal* observed that the "new CCC training camp at Wall Lake is fast becoming a neat little city of tents and frame buildings."[48] Seventy carloads of materials and one hundred men arrived from the Lake City, Wabasha County, camp, which the CCC had closed. Captain Frank W. Brunson, commanding officer, encouraged local young men to sign up, hoping to increase the work force to 160. The men could enroll at the camp or at the county welfare office or at five other locations in the county. With economic conditions improving, however, fewer men qualified for the CCC, and in late July the camp was still short about forty workers.[49]

The Soil Conservation Service's main objective for the camp was to improve land-use planning through soil conservation. The Service entered into contracts with farmers and worked out a comprehensive plan for each farm. The CCC workers provided the labor. If the plan called for the rearrangement of fields or pastures or both, the CCC constructed new fences.[50] Where drainage was a problem, the men built "broad-based terraces to control the run-off water." In many cases the CCC planted trees as a part of a soil-erosion control plan.[51] By mid-August the CCC workers, under the supervision of the Service, were busy at work on several farms, including those of Edwin J. Wold near Underwood, Onan Torgerson and John Svendsgaard in Aurdal Township, and P. E. Winters, Elmer Stock, and Tilford Christopherson in Buse Township.[52]

During the 1941–42 winter, camp workers cleared out diseased and dead trees from woodlots in preparation for the planting of seedlings in the spring. CCC and Service personnel, especially during the winter months, carried out a conservation education program, giving talks to Farm Bureau units, Parent-Teacher associations, 4-H clubs, and other civic organizations.[53] The CCC was pleased with the reception of these programs: "From the short period of observation since the inception of the camp it is anticipated that cooperation with groups . . . will be exceptionally good."[54]

CCC camp SCS-MN-21 was short-lived. A year after the first tents went up in June 1941, Congress terminated the CCC — a casualty of better times and the war. Harry Burau, who farmed near the camp, recalled its final days:

> They went around and they . . . trimmed out bad trees in little wood lots that there were. And they planted grass and . . . had a pretty big tree planting program. . . . So they advertised in the paper that anyone that wanted any of the trees there could have them . . . as long as the boys were there, they would send the boys out to plant them.[55]

The demise of the CCC and Otter Tail County's camp in 1942 ended one of the New Deal's most successful and popular programs. An article in the *Literary Digest* claimed that "attacks on the New Deal, no matter how sweeping, rarely or never extend to the Civilian Conservation Corps."[56] "Roosevelt's Tree Army" had made a lasting contribution to the nation. It turned the tide against the spoilage of the land, regenerated the lives of almost three million young men, and helped to provide the necessities of life for their families.

The CCC was in its third year when the president authorized the National Youth Administration (NYA) in June 1935 under the auspices of the WPA. Roosevelt articulated a dream for the youth of the nation: part-time, wage-paying work, providing funds for needy secondary-school, college, and graduate students; job training, counseling, and placement assistance; encouragement of constructive leisure-time activities; and beneficial community projects.[57]

The NYA work program gave aid to those who came from needy families and who wished to continue their education, as well as to those who were unemployed and out of school. High-school students who became NYA workers earned their lowest monthly average wage of $4.12 in 1941–42 and their highest of $5.41 in 1935–36, repairing equipment, landscaping school grounds, and serving in library or clerical positions. College students (excepting graduate students) earned their lowest monthly average of $11.54 in 1938–39 and their highest of $12.90 in 1940–41 — to help to finance their educations while they performed useful work on campus.[58] Wages generally averaging between $15 and $22 a month gave some youths a chance to work in their hometowns. Involved in projects such as construction (small buildings, roads, sewers), conservation, sewing, and recreational programs, these young people provided valuable community services.[59] Between June 1935 and July 1943, the NYA assisted 4,800,000 young people between the ages of sixteen and twenty-five and spent $662,300,000 — including $467,600,000 in wages for those out of school and $169,500,000 for those in school — on its programs. To Minnesota it allocated $14,317,097 for wages, with out-of-school work programs receiving $10,312,393 and student work programs, $4,004,704.[60] Aubrey Willis Williams, NYA's executive director, adamantly defended his agency's expenditures. "The urgent need in this crisis is that we shall not throw away or spoil our human resources, and particularly that we shall conserve the health and the enthusiasm of the young," he declared. "Youth must rebuild what has been destroyed. It is the nation's most precious asset."[61]

Unlike the CCC, the NYA received no bold headlines and only a rare news story. Otter Tail County's newspapers proudly listed the names of young people who entered the CCC but paid little attention to those who took part in the NYA program.[62] The NYA's work was quiet, and it did not employ many of the county's youth. The proceedings of the Fergus Falls City Council indicate the NYA's low profile. While the PWA, the WPA, the FERA, and the CCC consumed meeting after meeting, the NYA received scant attention. After the council read a communique that announced the NYA work program on January 6, 1936,[63] it found work for sixteen young people and three years later briefly discussed three city construction projects: concrete street markers, warehouse repairs, and toilets at a city park.[64]

Each month Otter Tail County's NYA programs provided about seventy-five young people with in-school and out-of-school work. Two examples illustrate the kind of projects that the NYA, through local government agencies, sponsored. In 1936 and 1937, sixteen NYA young people worked for the Fergus Falls Park Board supervising activities and improving facilities. They organized and coached kittenball and tennis programs and supervised playground activities and at swimming pools. About 215 children took part in the program on a daily basis. A crew of ten NYA youths, under the direction of NYA area-supervisor Gerry M. Houg, worked for the Park Board, improving recreational facilities and taking care of equipment. They reclaimed a slough near the tennis courts and transformed it into a playground, laid out courts for horseshoes, basketball, and badminton, repaired playground equipment, and built a new diving board and children's slide.[65]

The Otter Tail County Historical Society sponsored and oversaw other NYA projects. In 1940 NYA workers constructed a historical marker in Tordenskjold Township that commemorated the site of the first county seat.[66] The society provided the plaque and cement, and the NYA supplied the labor.[67] The following year, the NYA fashioned a marker for the village of Henning as a memorial to "the Virtues of the

Judge Anton Thompson (left) and Mayor Henry Holmgren (right) at the dedication of the NYA monument in Henning

Men, Women and Children who pioneered in this section of the County" and the arrival of the Northern Pacific, Fergus and Black Hills Railroad in 1881.[68]

The NYA had little impact on the county's economy, but that was secondary to Aubrey Williams's dictum, "Youth must rebuild what has been destroyed." Lorna Anderson Olson, who worked on a NYA park program in Fergus Falls and later went to college with NYA assistance, agreed wholeheartedly with Williams. "It gave me a chance I wouldn't have had," she explained. "We moved to Fergus Falls from the farm in 1936, a drouth year. Dad worked the harvest and at this and that. NYA work helped the family, but in the long run it really helped me." With three children and unsteady employment, the Andersons could ill afford expenditures for a college education. "It was fun working with those kids and I earned . . . about fifteen to eighteen dollars a month that summer," she recalled. "I learned a lot about people. It was a good experience, but going to college opened a new door to me. That was something."[69]

The CCC and the NYA gave young people jobs in a time of massive unemployment. Youths such as Harold Davis, Alex Klimek, Clinton Thun, and Leonard Hovland found the CCC to be a rich experience. It gave them work when there was none, a sense of self-worth, and support for their families when they needed it the most. Young men and women such as Lorna Olson found the NYA to be a valuable experience. It provided help for her family at a bleak time, important training for life, satisfaction in having provided fun for the children of Fergus Falls, and a college education. The CCC and the NYA told the young people of Otter Tail County that their government had not forgotten them.

8

FARM PROGRAMS
"A Good Thing for the Farmers"

THE PROLONGED SLUMP of the 1920s, the sharply increased hardship of the early 1930s, and rural protest activities, especially the Farmers' Holiday Association, had focused the nation's attention on the agricultural dilemma and the need to cope with that situation. In 1927 and 1928 President Calvin Coolidge had vetoed the McNary-Haugen plan under which farmers would sell on the American market the amount of production that could be sold at a price that would provide them with the purchasing power that they had enjoyed before World War I. A government corporation would buy the surplus at the going price and "dump" it abroad at the world price.[1] In 1929 the Herbert Hoover administration advanced the Agricultural Marketing Act, which had two main objectives: to strengthen producer-owned cooperatives and to establish stabilization corporations that would help steady commodity prices. Armed with $500 million, a Federal Farm Board made loans on crops to single commodity cooperatives to bolster sagging prices. Created to raise prices over a long period of time, the board could not cope with the disastrous consequences of a national depression. By 1931 it had 257 million bushels of wheat and 3.4 million bales of cotton. The board ran out of money, and the program failed.[2] Support for McNary-Haugen and the Agricultural Marketing Act on Capitol Hill, however, clearly indicated that Congress was prepared to do something about the farm problem.

When Roosevelt called Congress into special session to deal with the banking crisis in early March 1933, he had intended to limit the session to banking, but because of pressure from farm groups and his agricultural advisers, he changed his mind and decided to ask for remedial farm legislation. In less than a week the administration, with the advice of farm organizations and journalists, hammered out the Agricultural Adjustment Act of 1933. "There were no long speeches," wrote Secretary of Agriculture Henry A. Wallace. "There was no rehashing of familiar facts. There was solid agreement on the necessity for action."[3] Because the farm problem had been under scrutiny and study for more than ten years, the basic ideas were already on the table. The bill's objective was to establish and maintain a balance between the production and consumption of farm goods so that the prices of commodities would be raised to a level that would allow them to be exchanged for the same amount of nonfarm goods as had been the case from August 1909 to July 1914. This concept of "fair exchange value" became known as parity. Marketing of farm produce would be regulated and controlled. Farm purchasing power would thus be raised to a position of equality with other sectors of the economy.

Although Roosevelt submitted the bill on March 16, Congress did not approve the legislation until May 12. The administration's decision to present Congress with a list of other relief measures delayed action somewhat, but disagreements on the Hill over the bill itself held up consideration for longer than Roosevelt had anticipated. The final compromise measure, one of the New Deal's most complex, embodied six major concepts: the control of farm production, benefit payments for voluntary participation, self-financing through a tax on the processing of farm products, a role for farmers in the administration of the program, the sale of surpluses on foreign markets, and agreements among processors and distributors as to the prices they would pay for farm goods.[4]

Organizing the Agricultural Adjustment Administration (AAA) within the Department of Agriculture and working out the details of the various programs was a monumental task. The establishment of an agency of three thousand employees in Washington was difficult enough, but the creation of a network of trained and effective field workers who would implement the various and complicated programs at the local level was impossible. Like the FERA, the AAA decided to use an existing agency. The Extension Service already had farm experts in each county where the AAA needed to inaugurate its programs. Although not ideal, extension agents became the AAA's field force. They would act as the AAA's local coordinators, but farmers would run their own programs at the grass roots.

In a way the AAA was organized from the bottom up. Farmers who signed up for a government program became members of a community producers' association. Each community association selected three representatives—one to a countywide committee and two who organized program sign-ups, checked contracts on which benefits and allotments (the crop that a farmer was allowed to produce) were based, and provided the state AAA director with a list of county farmers from which contract-compliance officials were selected. The county agent called the first meetings and acted as secretary to the county committees, but farmers ran the AAA wheat and corn-hog programs at the county level.[5]

Under the AAA wheat program, farmers had to cut production not more than 20 percent beginning in 1934. In return for signing a voluntary three-year wheat-reduction contract, the farmer would receive a thirty-cent-per-bushel benefit check on 54 percent of the farm's average wheat output for the years 1930, 1931, and 1932. For example, if a farmer's average yield were one thousand bushels during those three years, that farmer would receive an annual $162 benefit payment on 540 bushels. The program placed no restrictions on the sale of wheat, and even if drought destroyed the crop, the farmer would get the benefit check.[6]

During the summer of 1933 the county's two agents, who had been briefed at meetings in St. Paul, conducted organizational meetings in all the townships. With a sign-up deadline of October 2, no time could be wasted. By mid-August the Perham postmaster observed, "This wheat business surely must be something important. The number of forms, which you [county agents] have received this past week, clearly indicate that the Government plans on doing something for the farmers of this community."[7]

In Otter Tail County 865 farmers (152 East; 713 West) signed up to take more than twenty-two thousand wheat acres out of production.[8] The program's popularity was affirmed in May 1935 when preliminary returns of a wheat referendum showed that 527 signers and 113 non-signers advised the government to continue it; 52 signers and 16 non-signers voted against.[9] During the three years that the first AAA operated, Otter Tail County's farmers received $127,040 in wheat benefit checks, about $146 per farmer. That does not seem like much support, but in Otter Tail County few farmers had more than twenty or thirty acres in wheat. Moreover, the wheat payment was but one of several income sources.[10] The county agent for West Otter Tail County, pleased with the success of the program, reported that, "In all cases the farmers lived up to their contracts. . . . A good many farmers that had not signed a contract last fall now regret it. . . . Some explained they didn't understand it, some that they were afraid they would get entangled in difficulties, others too independent for any cooperation whatever."[11]

The other AAA reduction plan that assisted Otter Tail County farmers was the corn-hog program. Although the government carried out an emergency pig-sow slaughter in August-September 1933 to reduce hog production and to bolster farm income, the corn measure was not ready for operation until 1934. This program set up a system of forty-five-cent-per-bushel loans for corn on the cob, secured by a new government agency, the Commodity Credit Corporation. The corn had to be stored under seal; the farmer could pay off the loan and feed or sell the corn or let the corporation take it over to satisfy the debt.[12]

For corn the objective was to cut acreage by at least 20 percent in return for cash payments of thirty cents per bushel for the corn the farmer did not grow. To reduce the number of hogs produced for market and the number of litters, a minimum 25 percent reduction was mandated in return for a five dollar bonus per head for the hogs that the farmer was permitted to raise. The 1935 contract called for a 10 percent reduction on both corn and hogs; the corn payment was increased to thirty-five cents and the hog bonus to fifteen dollars.[13] East Otter Tail County agent John Grathwol tried to explain the corn-hog program to a meeting of farmers:

> If a farmer's "retired" corn acres have produced an average of 30 bushels to the acre during the past five years he will be entitled to benefit payments of $9 an acre. If the 20 percent reduction equals ten acres, for example, the farmer's total corn acreage payments for 1934 will be $90, less the administrative expense.
>
> Hog adjustment payments will amount to $5 a head on 75 percent of the average number farrowed and marketed during the last two years. If a farmer has raised and sold an average of 100 hogs during the years 1932 and 1933, he is entitled to raise and sell 75 hogs for 1934. And his benefit payments at $5 a head on these 75, will total $375, less the necessary expenses.[14]

The two agents held educational meetings throughout the county during the first three months of 1934.[15] As in the case of wheat, committees of farmers administered the local programs, authorizing applications and checking on compliance. For example, 137 farmers (65 West; 72 East) served on township corn-hog committees and as compliance inspectors.[16]

Unlike the wheat-program contracts, the corn-hog agreements operated on a yearly basis. For 1934, 3,597 (2,421 West; 1,176 East) signed contracts; for 1935, 1,863 (955 West; 908 East) took advantage of the program. During the two years of the AAA, corn-hog operations took about thirty-three thousand acres out of corn production and cut hog output by about thirty-eight thousand animals. In all, the AAA paid West Otter Tail County farmers $465,000 in corn-hog benefit payments, or about $138 per farmer over the two years. East Otter Tail County farmers received $105,000 in 1934 or an average of $89 per farmer.[17]

Hans Ronnevik's participation in the corn-hog program demonstrates the mechanics of the AAA plan for one Otter Tail County farmer.

Of his 158 acres he had planted an average of thirty-seven acres in corn during 1932–33. This allotted him a reduction of eight acres. Because his per-acre yield was estimated at 35 bushels, Ronnevik received benefit payments on 280 bushels. His corn reduction payment at thirty cents per bushel came to $84. Because he had raised an average of 38.5 hogs for market in 1932 and 1933, his contract called for a 1934 reduction to 29 with a limit of four litters. At his guaranteed AAA price of $5 per hog, Ronnevik got $145 for his reduction payment. For 1934's participation he earned a total of $229.[18] In 1935 he kept 11.1 acres out of corn production, which represented 406 bushels. At thirty-five cents per bushel the program gave him $142.10 for his participation. His reduction of market hogs from 38.5 to 34 paid him $60 at $15 a head. His corn-hog income, however, dropped from $229 in 1934 to $202.10 in 1935 because his hog reductions were not as great. Ronnevik's AAA checks for the two years — $431.10 — placed him significantly above the county average of $213.[19]

Aid for dairy farmers came slowly and indirectly. Although Secretary of Agriculture Wallace believed that milk production should be restricted to improve prices, dairy interests could not agree on the formulation of definite control plans. Dairy interests essentially had dairy products included as a defensive measure since they were uncertain as to a course of action. Although the AAA approved several producer milk agreements for large consuming centers such as Chicago, New York City, and the Twin Cities, areas remote from centers of population, such as Otter Tail County, had no such arrangements. The secretary of agriculture agreed to the government's purchase of $12 million worth of butter and cheese, mostly for relief distribution, as an interim measure while dairy organizations and the AAA worked out a feasible control-of-production plan. In January 1934 the AAA announced its dairy plan: farmers cutting production 10 to 20 percent would be eligible for payments of 40 cents per pound of butterfat and $1.50 per hundred pounds of milk. Strong resistance to the program arose among dairy farmers. Wisconsin farmers rejected the plan, but in Minnesota it never came up for a vote.[20]

Essentially the Otter Tail County dairy farmer was dependent upon the government's purchase of surpluses to maintain or raise prices of dairy products. The occasional purchases of butter, cheese, evaporated milk, and whole or dry milk for distribution to relief clients raised dairy product prices at various times. In one case in July 1935, it was announced that the government would make large purchases of cheese and dry skim milk. The *Battle Lake Review* reported that John Grathwol, the East Otter Tail County agent, said, "Dairy farmers of Otter Tail county will be aided substantially by the plans of the government to purchase approximately one million pounds of cheese, [and] five million pounds of dry skim milk."[21]

The county's dairy farmers were also helped by the government's emergency purchase of cattle, many of which were milk cows. Because of the drought, especially in 1934, certain counties — including Otter Tail — became eligible for the program. "It was a drought relief program where farmers were liquidating their herds because they couldn't get feed to feed them," Harry Burau explained. "I was asked to take the veterinarian around because I knew the area pretty well . . . and . . . he'd go into the herd and . . . the farmer'd point out the ones that he wanted to ship and the veterinarian would grab ahold of the cow's tail and give a hard pull, and if the cow stood up and didn't fall down . . . the cow was strong enough to be shipped and the government bought them."[22] Conrad Toso, who farmed in Maplewood Township, recalled that he sold cows because all he had to feed them was Russian thistle and that was tough on the cows. "It wasn't too much milk. But I pulled them through and then . . . the government . . . bought up the cattle to help us out and we got $20 a head for good cattle. . . . I sold them all except four."[23]

The county agents organized the buying plan, and each township had a committee of three or four men that oversaw the purchases in their respective townships. The emergency cattle purchase saved farmers who could not find feed or looked toward an outlay of twenty to fifty dollars to carry a single animal through the winter of 1934–35. Farmers received ten to twenty dollars per head, depending upon the animal's age and condition. The farmers of Otter Tail County sold 22,913 head (12,786 East; 10,127 West), reducing herds by roughly 20 percent and providing farmers with about $320,000.[24] The agent for West Otter Tail County put it well when he commented that "the Dairy Reduction Program turned into a cattle buying program."[25]

In early January 1936 the United States Supreme Court dealt the AAA its death blow, declaring the Agricultural Adjustment Act of 1933 to be unconstitutional. Under the "first Triple-A" Otter Tail County farmers benefited indirectly from surplus-commodity purchases and directly from AAA payments and government cattle purchases. Those direct payments amounted to about $922,000. During the period of the first New Deal agricultural program, farm income in the nation increased strikingly. In 1935 farm income was more than 50 percent higher than during 1932. About 25 percent of that increase was due to the New Deal's AAA.[26]

The abrupt curtailment of the New Deal's first farm program left both farmers and government planners in the lurch. Overplanting, sur-

pluses, and lower prices loomed on the horizon if farmers were left without a new, constitutionally sound program. Upon the recommendation
of the Department of Agriculture and farm-organization officials, Congress acted quickly, passing the Soil Conservation and Domestic Allotment Act (SCDAA) on February 29, 1936. Under this plan, which was
inaugurated in March, soil-conservation payments were made to

*Harry T. Burau and his farm in Dane
Prairie Township in about 1940*

farmers who shifted acreage from soil-depleting crops such as wheat and corn to soil-building crops such as legumes and grasses. The AAA entered its second phase. During 1936 and 1937 the soil-conservation program was the heart of the government's farm program.[27]

The responsibility for educating farmers about the new scheme fell on the county agents, who, as they had done three years earlier, blanketed the county with meetings. "Getting farmers to take part in an agricultural conservation program seems to be more of a matter of education than anything else," wrote Charles M. Kelehan, Otter Tail County agent. "Undoubtedly many more farmers would have been in full performance this year [1936] if they knew exactly last spring what the requirements were. It is a rather difficult job to have operators of farms understand the principles of the program by just attending one or two meetings and talking the program over between their neighbors."[28]

In spite of that difficulty 95 percent of Otter Tail County's farmers signed up for the new program to plant a certain number of acres in soil-building crops. As with the earlier AAA program, farmer-run committees for the county and the townships oversaw the programs. And each fall local committees of "reporters" checked each farmer's compliance with the conservation agreement.[29] For 1936, Otter Tail County farmers received $739,801 for participating in the conservation program. The average farmer got $125.[30]

Because the severe drought of 1936 boosted farm prices, fewer farmers signed up for the 1937 conservation programs, hoping to make more money with cash crops. "High prices of grain crops last spring undoubtedly influenced some farmers in their decision to plant more depleting crops, particularly wheat, than they would otherwise have done," Kelehan speculated.[31] The sum of $468,284 in conservation payments went to farmers in Otter Tail County; in West Otter Tail County an average payment of about $124 was made to 3,247 farmers.[32] Hans Ronnevik was one of those farmers who signed up for the 1937 soil-conservation program. He put 21 1/2 acres into alfalfa and 15 acres into sweet clover, retiring wheat acreage. In return he received a $193.45 payment.[33] With wheat at fifty-nine cents per bushel a good crop could have made more money for Ronnevik, but, of course, the drought experience of 1936 had taught Otter Tail County's farmers that a good crop could not be guaranteed.

The SCDAA did not work well as a crop-reduction plan. When surpluses increased and prices declined during the dip in the economy in 1937–38, Congress supplemented the soil-conservation approach with the Agricultural Adjustment Act of 1938. The new legislation embodied three main features: (1) it empowered the secretary of agriculture to fix a marketing quota whenever it was determined that a surplus of a crop (such as cotton, wheat, rice, tobacco, or corn) threatened the price level; (2) it authorized acreage allotments to individual farmers after two-thirds of the farmers affected had by referendum expressed their approval; and (3) it incorporated the "parity payment" principle and established the "ever-normal granary" arrangement by authorizing the Commodity Credit Corporation to make loans to farmers on their surplus crops at a level slightly below parity. Such excess crops were to be stored under government auspices, and the farmer was to market the surplus during crop failure years when the price was at parity or above and repay the loan. Since disposal of surpluses would prevent the market price from rising too high above parity, this arrangement, according to the AAA, would stabilize agricultural prices and stored surplus crops without loss to individual farmer income.[34]

In Otter Tail County about the same number of farmers who had taken part in the 1937 soil-conservation program continued to do so in 1938, 1939, and 1940. The county's payments ran at an annual average of three hundred thousand dollars with most checks to farmers ranging between one hundred and two hundred dollars each year.[35] The wheat-loan program, administered by the Commodity Credit Corporation, was the county's most widely used in 1938 and 1939. According to agent Kelehan, "Commodity loans proved quite popular during the 1939 crop year for the wheat growers particularly those that had 10 or 15 acre allotments." The allotment for West Otter Tail County was forty-three thousand acres with an average yield of 11.7 bushels per acre. Farmers numbering 359 borrowed $57,654 on 75,500 bushels.[36] Wheat-loan rates as well as marketing quotas and parity payments changed slightly from year to year, but generally wheat rates were between fifty and eighty-two cents per bushel depending on grade and the year's surplus.[37] The government parity payment on the 1938 reduction program was twelve cents per bushel, but because of that year's large harvest, the 1939 subsidy was raised to twenty-six to thirty cents in an effort to cut production. The AAA explained the government subsidy program in a news release in August 1938:

> To obtain maximum subsidies under the federal program, a grower must not plant more than the acreage allotted him by the AAA. The amount he may receive will be determined by multiplying the amount of what he normally produces on his acreage allotment by the subsidy rate.
>
> For example, should the rate be fixed finally at 30 cents, a grower with a 60-acre wheat allotment would receive $216 if his normal

yield were 12 bushels to the acre. Rates of benefit payments for other crops . . . will be calculated in a manner similar to that for wheat.[38]

By 1939 both loans and parity payments were in effect for rye and corn. Rye-program loans were offered at thirty-eight cents a bushel. The loans on rye, however, the *New York Mills Herald* pointed out, "will differ from the loan on wheat in that it will be a 'demand' loan. . . . The Commodity Credit Corporation retains the right to call this loan at any time." Loan rates were forty-three cents per bushel for noncommercial corn and fifty-seven cents for commercial corn.[39]

Government purchases of surplus commodities continued to support dairy prices. For instance, during 1938–39 it bought more than $33 million worth of surplus butter. The Agricultural Marketing Act of 1937 allowed the dairy industry to form regional and local marketing agreements that would fix minimum prices handlers had to pay producers. Marketing agreements, however, affected only populous consuming centers.[40]

The farm programs that the New Deal designed to stimulate the agricultural economy were complicated because the nation's farm sector was complicated. Louis O. Sieling, county chairman of the Agricultural Conservation Committee, explained, as clearly as anyone could, how the programs could have affected a mythical farmer in 1939:

Mr. D. is a farmer in East Otter Tail County. He runs a 160 acre farm, of which 110 acres are cropland and 45 acres non-tillable pasture and wasteland. Mr. D. has 80 acres in his total soil-depleting allotment. His wheat allotment is 12 acres, his potato allotment 8 acres, and his general soil-depleting allotment 60 acres. In 1939 Mr. D. will grow 20 acres of alfalfa, 15 acres of sweet clover. Cropland in excess of the total soil-depleting allotment totals 35 acres, which, multiplied by 50 cents (the rate for figuring allowance on soil-conserving crops) gives him his soil building allowances of $17.50. To earn this, he must put into effect 12 soil-building practice units (35 times 50 cents times two-thirds). The percent of productivity for the farm is 97.0, the normal yield of potatoes 88 bushels, and the normal yield of wheat 11.7 bushels per acre.

With this set-up, Mr. D. can estimate his 1939 payment as follows:

AGRICULTURAL CONSERVATION PAYMENT:
12 (wheat allotment) times 11.7 (normal yield)
times 17 cents (rate of wheat payment)......................$23.87
8 (potato allotment) times 88 (normal yield)
times 3 cents (rate of potato payment).........................$21.12

60 (general soil-depleting allotment) times .97
(percent of productivity) times $1.10 (rate of payment)...$64.02
Soil building allowance of $17.50 (which is earned by
seeding 6 acres of alfalfa or 12 acres of sweet clover).......$17.50
TOTAL: $126.69[41]

The AAA did more than provide conservation benefits and parity payments and facilitate crop loans. Beginning in 1939 under the Federal Crop Insurance Corporation (FCIC), it offered voluntary wheat-crop insurance, which was expanded to other grains later in the 1940s. Accepting premium payments in bushels of wheat or cash, the FCIC insured the farmer's crop against losses of 50 or 75 percent from unavoidable causes such as drought, flood, hail, and disease. In 1940, 350 Otter Tail County farmers took out the insurance, covering forty-eight hundred acres.[42] During 1941, 225 farmers insured their wheat crops. The cash equivalent of 1,509 bushels went to seventy farmers who reported losses. Their collective premium had been 635 bushels of wheat.[43]

Because of the indirect support for dairy farmers and the complexity of loans and parity payments during the "Second AAA," it is difficult to arrive at a precise dollar figure for New Deal farm programs in Otter Tail County. The first AAA and emergency cattle purchases netted the county's farmers $922,000. Soil conservation payments, 1936–40, totaled about $2 million. The second AAA generated in the neighborhood of $2 million through loans and parity payments, bringing the adjustment programs for Otter Tail County to nearly $5 million — an average of about $860 per farm exclusive of indirect dairy support. This amount may not seem like a large sum, but to individual farmers at particular times it was enough to make the difference, especially in a diversified and self-sufficient agricultural county. Then, too, the AAA programs gradually gave farmers higher prices on the produce that went on the open market.

Parity was, of course, the major goal of America's farmers, but the need for credit to carry on day-to-day work and to stay on the land was critical to many. Government-sanctioned credit for farmers began in 1916 with the Federal Farm Loan Act. "Farmers . . . have occupied, hitherto, a singular position of disadvantage," President Woodrow Wilson declared as he signed the act on July 17. "They have not had the same freedom to get credit on their real estate as others have had who were in manufacturing and commercial enterprises."[44] The act established twelve regional Federal Land Banks, largely controlled by national farmer-owned loan associations. The Federal Land Bank system provided loans to purchase and expand farms. By November 30, 1917, eighteen thousand farmers had obtained $30 million in loans. In 1922 a record seventy-four thousand borrowed $234 million. But after that as the agricultural depression engulfed the countryside, loan delinquencies and farm abandonments increased each year.[45] In Minnesota farmers could also turn to the Minnesota Rural Credit Bureau, which the legislature established in 1923 to stimulate the agricultural sector of the state's economy. The bureau became a prime source of mortgage money for Otter Tail County farmers during the 1920s. By 1928 it held 421 mortgages of $2,262,900 in the county.[46]

Operating loans and short-term credit became increasingly difficult to obtain as small rural banks folded during the 1920s. In eight of the years between 1921 and 1932 Congress authorized emergency funds for crop production and seed loans for farmers through the secretary of agriculture. The loans, however, were often too small to help much, averaging $126 in 1932. The Reconstruction Finance Corporation (RFC) began in 1932 to deal with emergency credit problems through its twelve regional agricultural credit corporations, with operating loans going to farmers and particularly to ranchers.[47]

The New Deal faced two immediate farm-credit problems: the need to bring the various credit programs of the several governmental agencies into coordination and the need to provide more credit immediately to assist farmers with operating and refinancing loans. In March 1933 Roosevelt acted swiftly to solve the first problem, and by an executive order effective in May he merged existing credit programs under one agency — the Farm Credit Administration (FCA). The order transferred these powers and functions to the FCA: supervision of the Federal Land Bank, the National Farm Loan Association, the Federal Intermediate Credit Bank, the Regional Agricultural Credit Corporations, and the Crop Production and Seed Loan Offices (later the Emergency Feed and Seed Loan Offices); loans to cooperatives from the Agricultural Marketing Revolving Fund; and the Fund for Investments in Stock of the Agricultural Credit Corporations.[48] The New Deal attacked the second problem when Congress passed the Emergency Farm Mortgage Act in May and the Farm Credit Act (FCA) in June. The Emergency Farm Mortgage Act provided government funds to the FCA's land-bank system so that farmers could refinance their mortgages at a reduced interest rate of 4 1/2 percent. By the end of 1935 about 14 percent of the nation's mortgaged farms had been refinanced, saving thousands of farmers from foreclosure.[49] The Farm Credit Act finished the organization of a permanent cooperative farm-credit system, with twelve Production Credit Corporations that capitalized, supervised, and trained staff for local Production Credit Associations (PCA). By April 1934 more than six hun-

Lawrence Chesborough of Girard Township stood next to a tractor that had been converted from a car. Such measures were necessary when credit was short.

dred PCAs were operating in all the states and Puerto Rico, providing close and accessible loan services.[50]

In Otter Tail County the spotty drought of 1932–33 and the more general drought of 1934 created an urgent need for feed. Both Minnesota and the federal government developed feed-loan programs that helped dairy farmers immensely. The drought of 1932–33 left the Battle Lake area (Girard, Everts, Amor, and Otter Tail townships) with almost no feed for livestock. That part of Otter Tail County, as well as Chippewa, Lac qui Parle, Yellow Medicine, Swift, Big Stone, Traverse, Douglas, Pope, Stearns, Wright, and Sherburne counties, were earmarked as drought areas by the president. The state Executive Council authorized twenty-five thousand dollars, and the legislature appropriated an additional thirty-five hundred dollars in March 1933 for the distribution of feed in stricken areas.[51] Under the state's emergency feed plan local committees approved or disapproved farmers' applications for feed relief, to be given in the form of hay or grain. If granted feed relief, the farmer had to sign a note promising to pay back the value of the feed if possible. Between 175 and 200 farmers applied for relief and received loans that averaged twenty-five dollars, an amount the committee calculated would "tide each individual over for about two weeks."[52]

In March 1933, twenty-five hundred to three thousand dollars worth of feed, mostly hay, was slated to be distributed throughout the Battle

Lake area. By September the figure had risen to seven thousand dollars, largely in Amor, Everts, Girard, and Otter Tail townships.[53] In all, the state provided more than sixteen hundred tons of hay as well as fifteen carloads of wheat and corn.[54] In late 1933 the state Executive Council made several changes in its feed-loan scheme, making it more difficult to get state help. County agent John Grathwol told a meeting of farmers at Perham:

> The purpose of this relief is to help farmers carry on who would otherwise have to give up or to sacrifice their foundation stock of milch cows and brood sows. It will not be given to those who can get help by the use of their credit, nor will it be given even to the needy for the purpose of feeding or fattening surplus stock. To those who do not have and cannot get feed for such stock, the state will give both hay and grain, free of charge, in such amount as may be allot[t]ed by the county committee and approved by this Council. Herds must be cut down to a reasonable amount of breeding stock.
>
> The relief extended will be in the nature of a gift and will be made only to those who are destitute or nearly so. The Supreme Court has held that relief can be extended only to those who are only one step from becoming paupers. The State cannot help anyone whose lands or chattels are clear or so lightly mortgaged that he should have credit or can get increased loan from the government.[55]

Since most farmers could not repay their feed loans, the program became a direct-relief program for those who were on the verge of pauperism.

By the spring of 1934 the drought was becoming more severe in the county. "The feed situation in Otter Tail County is extremely acute, and it has been generally estimated that the amount of feed available in the county is between one-third and one-half of the amount necessary," Grathwol observed painfully.[56] The problem had become too large for the state of Minnesota to handle. The FERA came to the rescue when in early 1934 it began an emergency seed- and feed-loan program allocating seven hundred thousand dollars to Minnesota. The loans, however, were to be paid off through work. Under the state-run FERA plan, farmers received emergency seed and feed, but in return they had to "work off" the purchase price of the feed and seed, generally on local road-improvement projects.[57] During the spring and summer of 1934 seed and feed shipments moved into the county. For example, in early June the SERA announced that forty-five thousand pounds of sweet clover seed would be available to needy farmers.[58] At New York Mills five carloads of oats, corn, and wheat went to farmers who needed emergency feed. The lineup of trucks and wagons at local elevators became a common sight around the county.[59]

In early 1935 the feed plan adopted a more formal structure. Farmers could still "work off" the loans, but a rigid allotment system emerged. Farms up to 40 acres and "four units" of livestock would receive amounts up to $29 a month; 40 to 80 acres with 9 units, up to $40; 160 to 240 acres with 15 units, up to $80; farms over 240 acres with 20 units, up to $90.[60] During 1934 and 1935 about half of the county's farms took advantage of the emergency seed- and feed-loan program.[61]

Most farmers "worked off" their emergency feed-seed relief loans and appreciated the government's efforts to help Otter Tail County's farmers. "[It] helped alot," recalled Emma Richter who, with her husband Otto, farmed near Vergas in Hobart Township. "At least we could keep our cattle . . . there was just nothing . . . well, I shouldn't say nothing, we had 119 acres of oats and we threshed 151 bushel[s] out of that." Otto worked off the loan on a road project because "There was no cash to pay."[62]

Verner A. Anderson of Otto Township was not happy over the quality of the relief hay: "I said that it was good hay because you only fed it once and it was still there a week later." Anderson later recalled that "I think I was there with a team of horses with a dirt scraper" to work off the relief feed loan. As he put it, "there wasn't anything else we could do . . . we had alot of time so we worked it off. . . . It didn't bother me any. I wasn't getting much of a crop anyway."[63]

Everett Johnson, who was a teen-ager living on the farm of his parents Victor and Lottie Johnson in Erhards Grove Township, recalled that he and his father went to nearby Pelican Rapids to pick up their relief hay and feed. They spent time in the summer working on road projects to pay off the feed loan. "I didn't feel badly about that at all," he stated. "I was just glad that we had feed to feed the animals. And the return of work was not that difficult, although we stood in gravel pits . . . and filled the wagons by hand." The task was not all drudgery. According to Johnson the work became a "neighborhood thing . . . because everyone was in the same situation, and all the neighbors returned their . . . work at the same time so we had a good time."[64] Martha Hegge of Dent agreed that paying off the loans could be rather agreeable. Her husband Oscar "kind of enjoyed it. He had to get up real early, in the dark, and harness the horses and drive out to this place and they used scrapers [to fill in a sinkhole]," she explained. "After a while they found out that he could play the violin so at the noon hour . . . he'd take his fiddle along and play."[65]

The state and FERA feed and seed loans were emergency credit programs that were outside the normal channels that the New Deal had reorganized or established. Within the framework of the FCA, Otter Tail County farmers benefited from crop and feed loans, Federal Land Bank refinancing, and Production Credit Corporation services. The FCA's short-term seed and feed loans could be obtained only by farmers who could not qualify for private-bank or production-credit loans. Throughout the 1930s the FCA viewed this type of loan as "emergency credit" secured by a first lien on the crop or livestock that was financed.[66] In 1934–35 farmers took out about twenty-six hundred FCA emergency loans. In West Otter Tail County the loans totaled $110,000, an average of $122 each.[67] With better times in 1937 only 190 West Otter Tail County farmers needed FCA loans.[68]

Two Production Credit Associations were established for Otter Tail County. The Fergus Falls PCA, organized in 1933, included West Otter Tail and Wilkin counties; the PCA in Wadena served Wadena, northern Todd, and East Otter Tail counties. "These associations are not emergency loaning agencies. Only sound loans will be accepted in this new set-up. . . . In order for farmers to be eligible . . . they must be able to produce evidence that they are co-operative with the Agricultural Adjustment Administration," the secretary of the Wadena PCA explained when it opened in 1934. "It is not the purpose of these associations to make loans to farmers for the purpose of increasing production."[69] The destruction of PCA records makes an analysis of loan activity impossible, but an obscure news item reported that the Fergus Falls PCA approved more than ninety-seven hundred dollars in loans for twenty-four farmer-members in June 1936. The loans largely helped farmers with equipment purchases and operating expenses.[70]

Two governmental farm-loan agencies operated outside the FCA: the Minnesota Rural Credit Bureau and the Resettlement Administration (RA), which in 1937 was reorganized into the Farm Security Administration (FSA). Only in Polk County did the Rural Credit Bureau hold more mortgage paper than it did in Otter Tail County. When the bureau could not redeem its bonds because of the diminished capacity of farmers to pay on their loans, the 1933 legislature ordered its loaning activities to cease, abolished the bureau, and made its affairs the responsibility of the Department of Rural Credit. The department foreclosed on more than three hundred farms in Otter Tail County and began the process of selling them off at "a very reasonable price and on easy terms."[71] The lion's share of sales came after 1937 when the AAA and nature combined to give the county's farmers better times. In 1938, 180 farms were sold, and in 1939, another 99 found buyers.[72] By 1942 the department still held 26 farms.[73] In 1940 more than 65 percent were cash purchases while the state financed the rest. Tenants purchased about one-third of the farms, and former owners accounted for one in four transactions.[74] Even in liquidation the Department of Rural Credit acted as a positive agency in establishing farmers on the land.

The RA was the New Deal's response to rural poverty. Created by executive order in 1935, the RA had three major objectives: to resettle destitute rural and urban families, to initiate conservation-type projects, and to help farmers, farm tenants, sharecroppers, and farm laborers in the repurchase of land and machinery through loans. This program of rural rehabilitation, however, ran into political trouble when some charged that certain resettlement projects were too communal in nature, and others argued that some functions contradicted or duplicated policies of the AAA, the CCC, and the FCA. Through complicated political maneuvering RA programs were transformed into the FSA.[75] Otter Tail County did not experience the RA's resettlement or conservation activities, but between 1937 and 1940 the FSA assisted 130 farmers and tenants in becoming farm owners through low-interest, long-term loans.[76]

Certainly the New Deal's credit policies helped some to stay on the land and others to begin farming careers. Harry Burau, a charter member of the Fergus Falls PCA, pointed out the broader implications when he observed, "I think it stimulated business a great deal . . . every business in town [was] helped by the fact that . . . farmers could get the credit that they needed."[77]

The New Deal era created a system of credit that quite often was confusing to those in search of and those contracted for loans. The extension agent's office sponsored special days when farmers could come in and talk with credit experts who could explain the many detailed facets of available loan programs. Representatives of the FCA, the RA/FSA, and the Department of Rural Credit regularly sent field workers into Otter Tail County to hold public meetings. In order to avoid grass-roots discontent when debtor-creditor disagreements arose, the FCA organized an Agricultural Advisory Credit Committee in each extension district. In 1935 the two Otter Tail County committees took shape. Each had five members whom the governor appointed. The FCA charged the committees with the "equitable settlement of difficult debtor-creditor problems" that arose in their district. The committees met in different communities on a monthly basis, providing local people with a free and confidential hearing. "They have rendered a type of service which has been very helpful," the New York Mills newspaper commented, "and which could not have been given, in many instances, except by committees, the members of which have the confidence of the citizens of their local communi-

Lillie, Jorolf, Hans, and Myrtle Ronnevik in about 1940

ties."[78] Most of the time local folks could settle local disputes, avoiding litigation or the bureaucratic hierarchy.

The experience of Hans Ronnevik illustrates the role of government programs in the life of a county farmer. He came to Otter Tail County in 1919 and bought a 160-acre farm in Carlisle Township. Ronnevik sold the farm at a profit and with the help of the Minnesota Rural Credit Bureau purchased another 158-acre farm at $135 an acre in the same township near the village of Carlisle. It was a typical diversified, self-sufficient Otter Tail County farm in a prosperous agricultural community where farmers, most of whom were second-generation Germans and Norwegians, enjoyed relatively mortgage-free status. The 1920s, while not as profitable as the years during and before World War I, produced a reasonable income for the established area. Ronnevik and his wife raised a son Jorolf and a daughter Myrtle and made their tax and mortgage payments on time. He belonged to the Farm Bureau and was the only Democrat in the township.[79]

Ronnevik, who carried a sizeable mortgage, had a "terrible time" when the depression hit, especially 1932–35. He found it difficult to cope with low farm prices, but it was the 1934 drought that ruined him. "It was 1934; it was frightfully dry and so very hot in the spring," recalled Jorolf, who was a senior in high school at the time. "Our crops were stunted from the start."[80] Two nearby lakes dried up, the cottonwoods in the grove died, the lawn, including even the crabgrass, disappeared. Ronnevik grazed his cows in the road ditches and fed them Russian thistle.[81] He jumped at the opportunity to participate in the AAA's corn-hog program and in 1934 and 1935 received $431.10 in government payments. The AAA could not keep Ronnevik as a farm owner; the drought was too much. He lost his farm through foreclosure in 1935.[82]

Ronnevik remained on the same farm as a tenant for two years. In 1937 he took advantage of the Minnesota Rural Credit Department's liberal repurchase terms and joined the one in four farmers who repurchased their farms. The price was $8,000; the mortgage was almost $6,500; yearly payments stood at about $350 with very little on the principal. The tide turned after 1937. Normal rainfall, higher crop prices, and AAA programs combined to improve Ronnevik's position. Astute management made possible the purchase of an additional eighty acres for $1,600 in April 1938 with a loan from a neighbor. In the fall of 1939 he bought another 137 acres for $3,000 with $500 down and the remainder carried by the seller. That same year Ronnevik traded his old Dodge automobile for a newer Plymouth and a year later bought his first tractor.[83] His net cash income (after expenses) jumped from $113.88 in 1937 to $1,203.38 in 1938. It fell to $187.45 in 1939 because of land, machinery, and automobile purchases as well as long-needed building repairs. The additional acres doubled Ronnevik's crop land and allowed him to expand his operation into beef cattle.[84]

The New Deal credit programs played no role in the farm's maintenance and growth. Ronnevik used Minnesota's Rural Credit Department and private loans to buy and expand his farm. For short-term operating credit, usually under three hundred dollars, he went to the bank in Carlisle and later to the Fergus Falls National Bank. The AAA, however, was an important factor in Ronnevik's road to better times. He participated in the soil-conservation program, receiving an average annual payment of $176 in 1937–39. The 1938 wheat-loan program provided $136. In 1939 the wheat-loan plan guaranteed him $444.02, and his allotment check was $33.74. His work for the AAA as a committeeman and compliance inspector, however, had a great deal to do with Ronnevik's economic comeback. This employment accounted for 12 percent of total farm income in 1937; 13 percent in 1938; and 17 percent in 1939.[85] That provided a significant source of income for a farmer who was battling the depression.

The New Deal's credit program and the AAA eased the sting of the depression. During 1941 farm prices began to approach predepression levels and had climbed to a nearly equal position with prices farmers had to pay for goods.[86] Although it was World War II that ended the depression and ushered in unprecedented farm prosperity, most Otter Tail County farmers would have agreed with Ed Hintsala of New York Mills when he summarized the idea of the New Deal's farm programs simply and pointedly as "a good thing for the farmers."[87]

9

REA
"The Same as Getting God There"

DURING his campaign for the presidency in 1932 Franklin Roosevelt exclaimed, "Electricity is no longer a luxury. It is a definite necessity."[1] His words struck a responsive chord with the people on nine out of every ten farms who were tied to lives of dreariness and drudgery in a nonelectric world. Twenty-seven million rural Americans still depended upon kerosene lamps for light and hands or gasoline engines for power. To these people, electricity offered a transformation of both technology and their way of life.[2]

Electric companies moved slowly into the countryside. In 1921 Grover Neff of the Wisconsin Power and Light Company admonished the National Electric Light Association to heed increasing farm demands for electricity. "Rural business is very important to the utility," he declared. "The farmers are rapidly learning the value to them of electric service and are demanding it. . . . The utilities . . . should take steps to develop a practical plan for financing farm lines and to ascertain the fundamental factors upon which to base a proper rate."[3] That year the association formed its committee on the Relation of Electricity to Agriculture, which brought together utility officials, farm groups, and agricultural experts to study the uses of electricity on farms.

The 1920s was essentially a decade of study as the power companies opted for cautious experimentation before plunging into unproven territory. Northern States Power Company, for instance, built a 6.3 mile rural electric line to supply eleven farm consumers near Red Wing, Goodhue County, and collected data for 1923 to 1927 upon which to plan rural service. Wisconsin Power and Light conducted a similar study, connecting six farms along a 5.5 mile line near Ripon, Wisconsin. Near the end of the decade some companies stepped up their service to rural areas, but mostly to farms located close to existing power sources. As much as the utilities talked about expansion into rural America, profit lay with their lines in heavily populated places. Electrification of farms was an expensive proposition. And, with the onslaught of the depression,

134

The Otter Tail Power Company plant in Fergus Falls shortly after it opened in 1920

the utilities had to curtail corporate investment in rural lines.[4] Harry Burau, long-time Otter Tail County Farm Bureau leader, cut to the heart of the matter: "You can't blame the power companies because they didn't have the finances to go out . . . like the Otter Tail Power here, they just didn't have the money to go out and build lines out in the rural areas."[5]

Otter Tail Power Company, which in 1909 began to supply Fergus Falls and the Northern Light Electric Company in Wahpeton, North Dakota, is a case in point. In 1915, when it served twenty-two towns in Minnesota, North Dakota, and South Dakota, the company had eight farm customers. Four years later it supplied electricity to forty-four towns and seventeen farms. By 1929 Otter Tail Power provided electricity to 314 towns as far west as the Missouri River and as far north as the Canadian border but counted only 534 farm customers.[6] Otter Tail Power Company's financial formula for rural service was generous by utility standards. The company would extend lines to any farm and be responsible for the cost up to three times the estimated gross annual revenue that the account would produce. The farmer paid the rest. "In 1927, with a drop cord in each room as the only load we were serving," an informal company report explained in 1961, "we were lucky to get $4 a month from each customer, and applying the formula, 12 times the $4 would amount to $48 a year and that times three years would amount to $144. As you can readily see, this would not build much line even in those days when prices for both material and labor were way down. [Using the same formula to calculate the cost,] the line can be built to a farm today with no charge to the customer whereas in 1927 this was not possible."[7]

According to the 1929 Minnesota farm census, 16,879 (9.6 percent) of the total 175,056 state respondents answered "Yes" to the question "Is electric power or lights used on Farm?" In Otter Tail County, 428 (6.8 percent) out of the 6,257 respondents replied affirmatively. Only four townships had twenty or more farmers using electricity, and five townships had none. On the average, there were 6.9 farmers using electrical power in a township.[8]

Of the few respondents who could answer "Yes" to the census question concerning electric power or lights, some had their own light plants. "Well, the Delco light plants were sold starting back in the late 20s on a limited basis," recalled Roy Hintgen, whose family's electric appliance shop opened in Fergus Falls in 1926. "There again it was a matter of quite an investment because the battery which was 32 volt required the use of batteries; it took 16 batteries because each battery was 2 volts and the capacity that they had was usually 400 watts (of the plant) and that was only enough for about four 100 watt bulbs."[9] Most farmers could not afford a Delco system, which cost about seven or eight hundred dollars. Hintgen estimated that only 1 or 2 percent of the farmers "around here" owned their own plants. The Delco plants did not produce enough energy to run milking machines or household appliances. With the wattage held down one could use an iron for short periods of time. Essentially, however, the Delco plant was only for lighting.[10]

Lack of electricity did not mean lack of power. Some dairy farmers had gasoline-driven milking machines. Some farm families owned gasoline-engine washing machines and gasoline-heated irons, although the latter were dangerous. "Most farmers that I knew of had some sort of gas engine around," Hintgen observed, "but it would be primarily . . . located underneath the windmill and when there wasn't enough wind to pump water for the cattle they would have to crank up the gas engine."[11] As helpful as the gasoline engine was in an emergency, it did little to ease the burden of farm work and nothing to erase the darkness of Otter Tail County's countryside.

Roosevelt, of course, had this in mind as he charted the New Deal's policies on electric power. In 1933 the Tennessee Valley Authority (TVA) went into operation, providing inexpensive public power, among other services, to a large part of the middle border. The government was erecting huge dams in the West, and large dynamos were being prepared to discharge vast quantities of electricity. The climate was favorable for a rural electrification program, and Morris Llewellyn Cooke, a consulting engineer and an expert on utilities and rural electrification, knew it. In 1933 Roosevelt asked Cooke to chair the Mississippi Valley Committee of the PWA with an eye to using current conditions as a means of inaugurating a rural electrification program. As a result of Cooke's energy and his own sympathy, the president placed a rural electrification program in the Emergency Relief Appropriation Act of 1935. On May 11 Roosevelt signed Executive Order 7037, establishing the Rural Electrification Administration (REA). Cooke, the REA's first administrator, soon discovered that it was easier to draw up a plan than to carry it out. Of the problems that the new agency faced, the most difficult was how to bring electricity to 3.5 million farms in a short span of time. Of the three ways to accomplish the job — private power companies, municipalities with publicly owned plants, and nonprofit cooperatives — Cooke favored working with the power companies that already had the expertise, the organization, and the equipment. A joint venture between the REA and the power companies, however, never reached fruition, largely because the companies were increasingly hostile to the New Deal's public-power policy. Farmer-owned cooperatives moved into a dominant position in the REA loan program.

Between May 1935 and June 1936 the REA allocated about $14 million in loans for projects, mostly to cooperatives. Cooke and Senator George W. Norris of Nebraska believed that the REA needed a status that was independent of the relief program if it were to succeed. Cooke found it difficult to operate under relief guidelines that demanded that 25 percent of the funds be spent for labor and 90 percent of the workers be taken from relief rolls. On May 20, 1936, President Roosevelt signed the Rural Electrification Act (the Norris-Rayburn Bill), establishing the REA as an independent government agency. The act provided $40 million annually in loans to finance construction and operation of generating plants and transmission lines. The act also offered loans to assist farmers in the purchase of electrical equipment, which included wiring their houses, buying household appliances, and installing water systems. The self-liquidating loans, which were to be for twenty-five years, carried a low interest rate that ranged between 2 and 3 percent. The REA was now preprared to wage the government's battle against rural darkness.[12]

Farmers began to discuss what the REA would mean to them. During the fall of 1935 Otter Tail County buzzed with talk about the establishment of a cooperative under the REA program. On November 20, a group of sixty-five farmers met with the state commissioner of agriculture at the village of Erhard to talk about a cooperative for West Otter Tail County. Out of that meeting came an elected, temporary board of directors with a president, Albert R. Knutson, who emerged as the driving force behind the movement to organize an electric cooperative.[13]

Knutson was a determined and energetic person who understood that electricity would revolutionize farming. Born in Erhards Grove Township in 1884, he went to high school in Pelican Rapids and was graduated from the School of Agriculture at the University of Minnesota in 1912. He worked as an agricultural extension agent for the Great Northern Railway, as agricultural agent for Polk County from 1914 to 1915, and later as a teacher at the Northwest School of Agriculture in Crookston, before returning to Otter Tail County to manage his family's farm. Knutson's Clovercrest Dairy Farm at Pelican Rapids earned a reputation as one of the state's premier Holstein operations; along with Henry G. Page of Fergus Falls he operated the Pelican Valley Stock Farm. He organized the Pelican Livestock Shipping Association and was active in Holstein associations.[14]

As an agricultural agent Knutson had learned the value of cooperation among farmers. In 1929 he was looking into the feasibility of a member-owned electric light and power company. He discussed rates with Otter Tail Power Company, sought suggestions from the state Department of Agriculture, and garnered some information from reading correspondence between the department and the Hawk Creek Light and Power Company, a small operation near Granite Falls in southwestern Minnesota. During that year Knutson and several other farmers laid plans for Pelican River Electric Light and Power Company, which would generate or buy electric current for its members. They decided to investigate the possibility of damming the Pelican River at a point known as the Davis Rapids. Although the venture never moved out of the planning stage, it indicated that Knutson would be an agressive promoter in any attempt to organize an electric cooperative.[15] Chester Rosengren, who served as an attorney for Lake Region Co-op. Electrical Association, captured the essence of Knutson: "He was a one man dynamo."[16]

At a meeting on November 29, 1935, in Fergus Falls the leaders of the cooperative decided to hold informational meetings in every town-

Albert R. Knutson

ship in West Otter Tail County.[17] During the first two weeks of December farmers attended those township meetings, which drew between sixty and two hundred people each, to learn about the REA and the cooperative idea. The keen interest demonstrated during township discussions prompted Knutson and his colleagues to schedule a meeting that they hoped would organize a cooperative. On December 27, six hundred farmers crowded into the Fergus Falls High School auditorium to hear J. Howard Hay, deputy commissioner of the state Department of Agriculture, Dairy and Food, explain the procedures for forming an electric cooperative. When Hay finished speaking, Knutson told the audience that the time was right for action.[18] The farmers agreed, and the Lake Region Cooperative Electrical Association (later renamed Lake Region Co-op. Electrical Association) was born. Knutson was chosen to head the association; the amount of capital stock was set at six thousand dollars, two dollars per share. No stockholder could own more than one share.[19] The farmer-owned cooperative in West Otter Tail County was off the ground.

Organizers launched an intensive membership campaign throughout the western townships during January 1936. Agent Kelehan reported that "The R.E.A. project was really demanded by the farmers themselves which shows a very good sign."[20] By March 21, 1936, approximately three hundred shares had been sold.[21]

Knutson and the cooperative's board had hoped for stronger support and were caught in a bind. Farmers were reluctant to part with their hard-earned money until there was a guarantee that they would reap some benefit from an REA project. The REA, on the other hand, looked at membership as a barometer of local interest and as a sign of a cooperative's potential success. The board had to convince the farmers and the REA that the new cooperative would become a stable enterprise.

The formation of committees for East Otter Tail County gave the REA movement countywide support and organization. The board, which now represented farmers from all parts of the county, placed high priority on making loan applications to the REA. It hired a clerical worker and engaged Arnold Christopherson as its electrical engineer.[22] By early April the board members had a detailed plan to raise seven hundred miles of lines for nineteen hundred farms. In April they submitted a loan application to the REA, who found the plan "rather large," and recommended that only part of the program be requested. In July the association asked for a loan of $36,565 "as a part of our whole project for Otter Tail County, Minnesota and vicinity." A line of 35.5 miles would serve ninety-seven farms and twenty-eight cottages. The REA, however, suggested that the cooperative enlarge on this plan, so in September the association asked for aid in building 231.5 miles.[23] The board heard nothing definite until December when the REA reported that analysis of the Otter Tail project had "progressed," but two problems remained to be solved: the rate that the association would pay for its electricity and the economic status of the county.[24]

The source and rate for electricity became a complicated question for Lake Region. The loan application of July had listed the company that would supply the energy as "probably Otter Tail Power Co.," but no formal agreement had been arranged.[25] In June Otter Tail Power offered the cooperative a wholesale rate: a demand charge of $2.50 per kilowatt per month, plus an energy charge of 1.5 cents per kilowatt hour.[26]

Washington's opinion that the rate was "rather high" threw the cooperative's leadership into several months of frustrating negotiations that involved numerous meetings and reams of correspondence. The REA felt that Lake Region should negotiate further with Otter Tail Power and with the city of Detroit Lakes, which had a municipal power plant.[27] While Lake Region carried on negotiations, the REA kept in contact with officials at the two possible suppliers, perhaps playing one off against the other. By the time Knutson wrote to the REA in December, the delays had gotten under his skin. "Questions as to when our Project will be approved or rejected is a daily occurrence," he said. "An OK of out [sic] Project will be a real Christmas cheer to our 1300 members."[28]

The rate problem, however, dragged on until mid-February 1937, by which time Lake Region had signed a tentative contract with Otter Tail Power Company for electricity at two cents per kilowatt hour, including maintenance. The rate offered by Detroit Lakes was slightly lower, but accepting it would have required Lake Region to build and maintain a distribution line from that city to the association's district. "Everything taken into consideration," Knutson wrote, "we feel that the Otter Tail Power Company's rate is not very much different from the Detroit Lakes rate, considering the extra cost of the distribution system."[29] Chester Rosengren explained, "No one ever really thought it would be anyone except Otter Tail because Otter Tail was the only one that had plans for future capacity. . . . They were the only ones that we knew had enough guaranteed capacity."[30]

The REA still questioned the ability of the county's economy to sustain the cooperative, even though membership had topped thirteen hundred.[31] "We feel that their office is wrong in their statement regarding the economic situation," Knutson wrote to Senator Henrik Shipstead. "While we may not be as prosperous right now as ordinarilly [sic], this condition is unquestionably due to the drought situation and is not a normal condition." He asked the senator to explain the county's economic status to the REA.[32]

In late March an encouraging sign finally came from the REA: a suggestion to increase the loan request to between four and five hundred thousand dollars. "We immediately accepted this offer," Knutson recalled, "and our committeemen got busy and secured the necessary additional members although handicapped by terrible road and weather conditions." When the new plan reached the REA, the cooperative received notice that the proposal was out of the question, "on account of the economic condition existing at Washington." The REA would reconsider the earlier proposal of $250,000 to build 231.5 miles.[33]

That Knutson and the membership of the cooperatives were disheartened was understandable. In June 1937 Knutson once again turned to Senator Shipstead for assistance: "These continuous delays in getting our project through has caused considerable dissatisfaction among our members[,] and the officers of our Association are at a loss of what to say to inquiries about when our project will be accepted in Washington."

Congressional pressure on behalf of the association did not obtain an allotment from 1936–37 funds. On June 18 Louis C. Stephens, a REA administrative assistant, wrote a disappointing letter: "Funds available for REA loans during the current fiscal year ending June 30, have been exhausted." But Stephens held out a glimmer of hope: "I want to assure you that we shall give your project very careful and sympathetic consideration."[34] Knutson, of course, had heard that for some fourteen months.

The REA, however, responded quickly once the new fiscal year began. On July 13, 1937, the REA advised Richard T. Buckler, congressman from the Ninth District, that a partial allocation of $125,000 for Lake Region had been approved, allowing the cooperative to begin its long-awaited endeavor.[35]

One last obstacle delayed the completion of the loan contract. The association directors were informed that the contract could not be finished by the REA until the cooperative corrected "technical defects" in the articles of incorporation and bylaws. By late August it had reorganized with a new but similar name, the Lake Region Co-op. Electrical Association.[36] At their November 12 meeting stockholders authorized the board to "borrow additional sums of money from time to time not to exceed in the aggregate $875,000.00."[37] Sixteen months of hard work, laced with anxiety and sometimes anger, had paid dividends. "Members of the Otter Tail Association have been disappointed in that they have been unable to receive Rural Electrification service earlier," the Otter Tail County agent summarized, "but at the close of 1937 the project seemed to have met all requirements . . . and [they] are ready to take over the business of handling electric current in the very near future."[38]

With the struggle for initial funding behind them, Knutson and association members began the hard work necessary before the first poles could be raised: obtaining rights-of-way, staking out routes, convincing those along the lines who were not members to join, and holding educational meetings on the wiring of farmsteads. During the winter of 1937–38 the directors decided on the first routes: eighteen miles near Perham, sixty miles near Erhard, and thirty-six miles near Underwood. Signing up farmers for the cooperative was crucial and fell mostly to farmers in the areas where the lines were planned. "When we initiated [the cooperative] every farmer just begged to get on the line," Chester Rosengren recalled, "and they'd even pay a premium or make a contribution just to get on one of the lines."[39] But obtaining the necessary members was not always a cinch. Jeff Tikkanen, who farmed near New York Mills, wanted electricity to ease the work of dairying and canvassed the area north of New York Mills to convince farmers to join the cooperative. It was more of a challenge than he had anticipated. According to Tikkanen, "they were skeptical about it because it was hard for them to believe that all you pay is [a] five dollar share and you'd get it." He visited with many of the seventy farmers in the area several times and was about ready to give up. "Then I went and I told them that so-and-so had signed and so-and-so had signed," he related. "Then one Sunday evening just about all of them came to my place . . . and signed although I told some of them . . . that they already had signed."[40]

Homer Sem, who contacted farmers in Maine Township, encountered some, but not much, resistance. "We figured there was one feller . . . we'd never get. We talked about how we were going to get him for two days," Sem observed, "and after all our strategy we drove up to his place and he said, 'What you guys doin', going taking signers for electricity? We gonna take it.' All in one breath." Sem never convinced one farmer to join even though he had thirty cows on his place. The stubborn dairyman had once been stung in a share deal and preferred to rely on his "balky [gas] engine." Sem commented, "He wasn't gonna lose his farm on that. He didn't understand."[41] Russell Parta of New York Mills recalled a local farmer who, while against electrification at first, changed his mind:

> Somebody had said, "Well, you're not gonna put electricity — any electricity up to my farm, if you put any poles on my land I'm going to chop them down." "Well," they said, "fine, if that's the way you feel about it you don't have to have it. It's a free country you know." So the poles went up, on the other side of the road, and all the farmers had electricity but this one and he became very angry and he said, "How come I didn't [get] this?" Well, I guess he got things straightened out and eventually got his electricity.[42]

Not everyone shared Knutson's vision of an electrified countryside, but it was the rare farmer who did not eventually come around to his view. Some simply could not afford electricity. "The electricity was there but we didn't join up," recalled Conrad Toso. "We didn't have the cash to do it. . . . I wanted it in the worst way."[43]

In March 1938 the directors awarded the contract for the first project and after the spring thaw E. W. Wylie, Inc., of St. Paul began raising the poles.[44] On October 7, 1938, thirteen months after the negotiations for the loan had been ironed out with the REA, the first electric meter was set — on the farm of Herbert Romann near Perham.[45]

In 1937 and 1938 Lake Region received two allotments. The first, $125,000, built one hundred miles of lines; the second, $252,000, included a $10,000 allotment "for local financing of wiring and plumbing." By the end of the year, 240 farms were wired along 226 miles of power lines. Agent Kelehan observed that "Approximately 750 people along these energized lines will eventually be electrical users as many farms along these lines are just in the process of wiring and the farms being inspected by the local engineer." An additional loan of $400,000 allowed Lake Region to expand into adjacent counties. Of the 402 miles

E. W. Wylie, Inc., contracted to haul and distribute poles for the Lake Region Co-op. Electrical Association in the summer of 1938. Wylie raised some of these poles on Albert Knutson's farm in Erhards Grove Township.

of lines that the loan made possible, the county allocations were 204, Otter Tail; 75, Becker; 53, Hubbard; 30, Wilkin; 40, Norman.[46] A year later the REA announced an allotment of $175,000 for 140 miles of lines.[47] Knutson resigned as president of the cooperative in August 1938 to assume the duties of a full-time project superintendent, evidence that Lake Region was a growing operation.[48]

By the end of the decade the New Deal's program to electrify rural America was beginning to change life in Otter Tail County. In late 1939 electricity pulsed through 394 miles of lines, and about eight hundred members enjoyed the benefits of the REA. In August 1939 Otter Tail County farmers used 65,984 kilowatt hours.[49]

Although the East Otter Tail County agent reported that in 1940 the REA program had "gone forward by leaps and bounds," the war curtailed much further expansion, and most county farmers did not get on the line until after the war.[50] Change came slowly but surely. The kerosene lamp, the tired radio batteries, the sawdust for storing river or lake ice, the balky gasoline engine, and the fickle windmill were becoming relics of the past. Electricity, as Albert Knutson had predicted a decade earlier, was revolutionizing farm life.

No New Deal program was more popular with farmers than the REA, and nowhere was electricity more important than in a dairying county. "When we started selling milk, boy, that was where the bigger change was, because that was lots less work," recalled Leonard Hovland of Norwegian Grove Township. "I guess I used the gas engine on it [the separator] before, and . . . half of the time that gasoline engine wouldn't start. . . . It really was a lot of difference. For everybody."[51] Jeff Tikkanen graphically emphasized the value of electricity to dairy farmers when he observed, "I'd say that there would be no surplus of milk today if there was no electricity on the farm. People wouldn't do all that work."[52]

Most farms did not enjoy major appliances such as stoves and refrigerators until after the war when farm prices rose and the production of consumer goods resumed. Even without these conveniences farm women thrilled at the new advantages. Emma Tikkanen, who before her marriage in 1937 had had electricity in New York Mills, remembered, "The thing that struck me the worst was when evening began to come and then you had to light that kerosene light and you couldn't see anything."[53] Selma Kopperud of Norwegian Grove Township agreed: "Lights were the biggest change."[54] To Helen Sem of Maine Township electric lights were an improvement, but more important, she "didn't have to carry water, any more. I used to have to carry all the water for washing clothes and I'd heat it in the boiler on the cookstove."[55] No farmer would disagree with Emma Richter of Hobart Township who concluded that "it was almost too good to believe," or Emma Tikkanen who declared, "It was a transformation."[56] The praise for the REA and its impact on Otter Tail County was profuse. Perhaps Chester Rosengren captured it most vividly when he asserted, "At that time electricity was so wonderful to the people it was about the same as getting God there!"[57]

The formation of Lake Region Co-op. Electrical Association illustrates how a nonrelief New Deal program came to the grass roots and considerably altered the lives of its participants. Problems, both in Washington and in Otter Tail County, made the process of electrification painfully slow, and because of World War II, most farms did not get electricity until the late 1940s or early 1950s. But the glow of farmstead lights on the eve of the war symbolized the New Deal's and Albert Knutson's victory over rural darkness.

10

BANKING AND BUSINESS
"You People Must Have Faith"

OF THE PROBLEMS that confronted Franklin Roosevelt upon his inauguration as president, none was more severe than the banking crisis. During the 1920s more than five thousand banks had failed, and during the first three years of the 1930s another four thousand closed. Losses to depositors were staggering, and by March 1933 the people had lost confidence in the banking system. Roosevelt, placing top priority on the restoration of banking and public confidence in it, had mapped out his main line of attack: a bank holiday and a special session of Congress.[1]

On March 6, two days after taking the oath of office, Roosevelt closed the nation's banks. They were allowed to provide only minor services, such as making change, providing access to safe-deposit boxes, cashing checks drawn on the treasurer of the United States, accepting payment of obligations, and setting up trust accounts to receive new deposits. The next day the Department of the Treasury permitted banks to settle checks drawn before March 4 and to transact small withdrawals for the "necessities of life." On March 9 Congress passed the Emergency Banking Act of 1933, legislation that established a system for bank reopenings. The secretary of the treasury would issue reopening licenses to those banks that the Federal Reserve or state banking officials evaluated as sound. Other banks would be reorganized or closed. Since inspecting the banks would take a few days, no banks would open until March 13, a Monday.[2]

On the evening of March 12 Roosevelt spoke to an estimated sixty million Americans as he presented his first radio fireside chat. In his soothing voice he assured listeners that there was no need to panic over the bank closings. He explained how banks operated and why they were in trouble, promising a cautious plan that would open the nation's sound banks — those whose assets equaled deposits: "Confidence and courage are the essentials of success in carrying out our plan." He concluded, "You people must have faith."[3]

According to the *Fergus Falls Tribune*, the bank holiday caused no panic in its city. Under a bold headline, "Nation Wide Closing of Exchanges Finds Fergus Falls Serene," the newspaper reported that "The result locally has been a cheerful and optimistic outlook, with no excitement, and much good natured 'jollying.' "[4] The report, however, masked the reality of the crisis; the farm depression had already taken its toll of Otter Tail County banks. The Farmers State Bank in Deer Creek had become a victim of hard times — on January 19, 1925.[5] During the following eight years banks failed in Battle Lake, Elizabeth, Fergus Falls, Henning, New York Mills, Perham, Richville, Parkers Prairie, Pelican Rapids, Underwood, Vergas, and Vining.[6] The failures tied up hundreds of thousands of dollars as liquidators attempted to salvage people's deposits; often a liquidation took years.

The examples of Fergus Falls and Pelican Rapids indicate the chaos that confronted both the banks and their depositors. In late November 1927 the Farmers and Merchants State Bank in Fergus Falls did not open its doors for business. Not since 1897 when the Citizens National Bank folded had the city experienced the closing of a bank. When the Farmers and Merchants State Bank organized in 1915, it became the city's fifth bank, joining the First National Bank (1872), the Fergus Falls National Bank (1882), the First State Bank (1902), and the Scandia (later the American) State Bank (1902).[7] Ole C. Boyum, the bank's president, and Charles L. Alexander, the chairman of the board, struggled during 1927 to keep their bank open, using "every effort to make collections, but without sufficient success."[8]

Like many other banks, Farmers and Merchants had overextended its loan portfolio during the prosperous farm days of World War I. As the agricultural depression set in after 1921, land values and farm prices began to drop, making it difficult for borrowers to repay loans. When the bank closed, it had $457,000 (ten times its capital and surplus and more than the value of its deposits) in outstanding loans. Facing such an unfavorable balance sheet, the bank had no chance of survival.[9]

The *Fergus Falls Daily Journal* reported that "The closing of the Farmers & Merchants State Bank on Monday did not cause any flurry or excitement at any of the other banks in this city."[10] Depositors, who had almost four hundred thousand dollars in the bank, however, did not endorse the newspaper's calming comment. They had agreed to waive 15 percent of their deposits and to wait three years for the remainder of their money. But when the state Department of Banking officially locked the doors all agreements were canceled. The depositors were, of course, apprehensive.

The First National Bank of Fergus Falls in about 1940

A special bank examiner inventoried all assets and liabilities. The Department of Banking appointed H. E. Swenson as receiver to liquidate the bank's assets and to protect, as much as possible, the depositors. The *Fergus Falls Daily Journal* urged those who had loans with the bank to repay because "when a borrower beats the bank now he is beating the depositors whose money is in the bank."[11]

The frustration of the depositors surfaced at a meeting in late December when 150 people met with the bank's receiver. Swenson outlined the procedures for liquidation and asked the depositors to form a committee of representative and responsible people to assist him in his task. Although the group elected such a committee, it was in an angry mood. Depositors demanded that Boyum explain the bank's debacle. He told them that "personally he had lost everything he has made in the last thirty years" and that depositors had withdrawn $320,000 during the past few months, making it "impossible to continue." Some depositors wanted to hire an attorney and to go to court but cooler heads prevailed, giving Swenson a chance to handle the bank failure.[12]

With the backing of the depositors' committee, Swenson went to work. A year later the Department of Banking sent out checks that totaled thirty-seven thousand dollars (10 percent) to depositors. The largest check, twenty-two hundred dollars, went to the city of Fergus Falls, which had had twenty-two thousand dollars in the Farmers and Merchants State Bank.[13] "As is always the case in a closed bank there are rumors afloat about what has been done and what has not been done," a Fergus Falls reporter observed, "but it can be safely said that many of these are not correct."[14] The paper promised that another payment would be made after the first of the year.[15]

The saga of the Farmers and Merchants State Bank came to an end in March 1933 — more than five years after its closing. The bank's "uncollectable" paper came up for sale before the district court. In sealed bids the bank's remaining assets brought a bid of three hundred dollars. Judge Thompson opened the bidding to those in attendance. For $1,060 in cash an Owatonna, Steele County, businessman bought the remainder of the bank's portfolio. "Just think," declared Judge Thompson, "here we have $200,000 worth of paper and all I have been offered is one-half of one per cent of the face value."[16]

Two other Fergus Falls banks followed a similar pattern. In 1931 both the American State Bank and the First State Bank closed to face liquidation. Payments to depositors came slowly. By the end of 1939 the receiver for the American State Bank had repaid 83 percent of the deposits.[17] The First State Bank paid its depositors only sixty-five cents on the dollar. Searle Zimmerman, the bank's assistant cashier, blamed loans on western North Dakota farmland as a major factor in the demise of the First State Bank: "The bank carried a lot of paper on farmland

Searle A. Zimmerman

HAPPY PARTY
THE FERGUS FALLS NATIONAL BANK
SERVES LUNCH TO IT'S DEPOSITORS DEC. 4ᵗʰ 1931

The customers enjoyed the coffee and doughnuts, but the bank did not allow its money to be photographed.

that had really dropped in value — especially around Alexander, North Dakota. With bad conditions out there, there was no way to make the loans good."[18] The failures of three banks left Fergus Falls with two sound financial institutions: the First National Bank and the Fergus Falls National Bank. The latter had forestalled a run by placing bundles of money on a long table and inviting depositors in for a cup of coffee and a glimpse of its money supply.[19]

The banking situation in Pelican Rapids was typical of that found in many small towns. Before World War I the community had three banks: the First National Bank, the J. P. Wallace State Bank, and the Pelican Rapids State Bank. The First National, facing a crisis, reorganized and by 1930 was open for business as the Otter Tail County State Bank.[20] By 1926 the Pelican Rapids State Bank also was in dire trouble. It had loaned out $280,000 while deposits stood at $271,464 — a dangerous ratio. On November 19, 1926, the bank failed.[21] Over a period of six years its assets were liquidated, and the receiver made five payments to stockholders. Complicated by litigation, final payments were not made until February 1932.[22] In the end the stockholders recovered only 41.42 percent of their investment. The *Fergus Falls Weekly Journal* commented: "There are very few places where a man could have invested his money in the past two years without sustaining a larger percentage of loss than this."[23]

During the bank holiday Pelican Rapids's two remaining banks closed, but both were permitted to open within a few days — with restrictions. The J. P. Wallace State Bank and the Otter Tail County State Bank were required to place 40 percent of their deposits in a trust account while they were given time to collect outstanding loans to cover deposits. "You see, the people's ability to repay their loan was practically nill," recalled Clyde Thorstenson, who worked in the Wallace bank and later became its president.

> They couldn't even pay their taxes. They didn't have any income during those periods. . . . I remember in one particular instance we had a mortgage for $5000 on [a] 160 acre farm with a full set of buildings. . . . We could have foreclosed [but] he couldn't pay anything. I am real thankful that this Bank Holiday was set up and we could set up this trust fund so that we could collect that [the loans] gradually and then return the money [the 40 percent that was set aside] to the depositors."[24]

The J. P. Wallace State Bank paid off 100 percent, but the Otter Tail County State Bank had difficulty. "My dad . . . was in the farm implement business here, he did business with the other bank and they only repaid . . . I think it was 7% of the amount that was set aside," Thorstenson remembered.[25] When it was clear that the Otter Tail County State Bank could not recover, the J. P. Wallace State Bank bought it out, assuming its liability on May 12, 1938.[26] The economic woes of the 1920s and 1930s left Pelican Rapids with one bank — renamed the Pelican Valley State Bank in 1972.

The bank holiday accomplished in Otter Tail County what the president desired: a system in which the people were confident. "That was the objective," Searle Zimmerman observed. "The weak banks fell by the wayside. They were victims of the times. No one really blamed the bankers."[27] Fergus Falls businessman Roy Hintgen agreed: "As a general rule back in those days you knew the banker personally . . . and you knew just how he operated . . . it was largely laid to the fact that we had poor times and it was just one of those things."[28]

The holiday ended the crisis, and two federal programs strengthened financial institutions. The Reconstruction Finance Corporation (RFC), which had been established in 1932 as a lending agency to banks and other businesses, helped troubled, but liquid, banks to open after the holiday by extending them loans — usually in the form of preferred stock in the bank. A bank would gradually retire the RFC stock as outstanding loans were paid off and business improved. Between 1932 and 1936, for example, the RFC provided $264,649 for Otter Tail County, most of which took the form of loans to banks.[29]

The Federal Deposit Insurance Corporation (FDIC), also a government agency, did more than anything else to restore confidence in banks. "That's one good thing that the Roosevelt administration did. He started the insurance of deposits," exclaimed Clyde Thorstenson.[30] Beginning on January 1, 1934, the federal government insured deposits in subscribing banks up to five thousand dollars per depositor. When the Farmers and Merchants State Bank in New York Mills received its insurance signs, it was front-page news, and the newspaper explained the importance of the FDIC to the community:

> If by any unforeseen circumstance, an insured bank should suspend, the Insurance Corporation would begin paying off the depositors just as soon as a receiver was appointed for the closed institution. The depositors would receive their money in a few days instead of waiting months or years as was the case in the former method of liquidation. This is not only a benefit to the depositors, but it saves the community from a terrific economic and social blow. When the depositors receive their insured accounts they assign their claims to the Insurance Corporation. Thereafter liquidation proceeds on a business-like basis with the maximum chance of the Corporation and other creditors being paid in full.[31]

The county banks that subscribed to the FDIC insurance plan took out large newspaper advertisements to proclaim the banks' new security for depositors. The First National Bank in Battle Lake in a typical advertisement explained the workings of the FDIC, concluding, "Deposit insurance is for your protection."[32]

With the banking situation under control the New Deal attacked its thorniest problem — business recovery. Manufacturing production had decreased almost 50 percent from 1929 to 1932, and the total value of all finished commodities had dropped even more. Without the stimulation of industry the nation could not pull out of the economic dilemma. Many different voices advanced a multitude of ideas. Some who recalled the War Industries Board of World War I demanded strong-handed governmental intervention in the industrial sector of the economy. Business interests hoped to protect prices and profits with a minimum of government interference; trade unions advocated the maintenance of fair labor standards. Liberals wanted a system of creative national planning, socialists sought nationalization, and conservatives believed that industry could solve its own problems. Yet many people agreed with Alexander Sachs of the Lehman Corporation who argued that this was not a normal economic depression but *"economic nihilism, which, from a national point of view, cannot be permitted to go on."*[33]

The urgent need for a solution created a climate that was conducive to conciliation. After a period of debate the divergent views coalesced and took shape in the National Industrial Recovery Act (NIRA), which Roosevelt signed in June 1933. The NIRA represented an alliance of government, industry, and labor to bring about business recovery. The act allowed businesses to draft agreements that were exempt from antitrust action, provided for government liscensing of businesses, gave labor the right to bargain collectively, required codes establishing minimum wages and maximum hours, and granted $3.3 billion for public works. It also created the National Recovery Administration (NRA), headed by Hugh S. Johnson, to develop and carry out a system of fair practices concerning prices, labor relations, and production. Both large industries and small businesses were slow to respond; not until September had the last of the nation's largest industries agreed to comply with the codes.[34]

In order to gain support for his program Johnson, a businessman and a former brigadier general in the United States Army, turned the NRA into a national patriotic cause with symbols, slogans, and parades. Not since the Liberty Loan drives of World War I had Americans been exposed to such public pressure. The Blue Eagle symbol with the slogan "We Do Our Part" was soon displayed by employers who signed up with the NRA. The intent was clear: businesses that did not show the Blue Eagle were unpatriotic. Johnson's campaign worked.

By August the NRA's Blue Eagle had spread its wings over Otter Tail County. Although most employers were not quite sure what the NRA would mean to them, they joined the hundreds of thousands who were displaying the "bird of progress." On August 10 a Fergus Falls newspaper boasted that "Nearly 100 Business Firms" had joined the "NRA army." "Always a little conservative in getting under way, Fergus Falls rarely fails to come under the wire with a burst of speed in any public undertaking that distances most competitors," the *Fergus Falls Tribune* commented.[35] The county's other towns jumped on the NRA bandwagon. In a full-page advertisement in the *New York Mills Herald*, local

 DO YOURS BY

Patronizing the business places displaying
the Blue Eagle

HELP THE PRESIDENT		END THE DEPRESSION

Kela Brothers	N. Y. Mills Farmers Elev.	Vaughn's Chev. Service
New York Bottling Wks	Piilola-Kela-Mattson Co.	Atkinson Barber Shop
Bender Brothers	Lampert Lumber Co.	People's Cafe
Mills Meat Market	Mills Oil Company	John L. Karvonen
Denison & Lund	C. J. Kulla	Standard Oil Co.
Lauley's Store	Carl A. Ringdahl	Lakes Barber Shop
Merchants Hotel	The Bargain Store	Reynold's Cafe
Northwestern Pub. Co.	G. H. Kauppi	Jackson Feed & Flour
		Liberty Theatre

This advertisement sponsored by the merchants whose names appear on
this page.

businesses told the community in bold letters: "We Do Our Part, Do
Yours by Patronizing the Business Places Displaying the Blue Eagle."
Sporting three Blue Eagles, the ad urged readers to "Help the President"
and "End the Depression."[36]

Two examples illustrate the influence of the NRA in Otter Tail
County. At a meeting of the Civic and Commerce Association in Fergus

Falls, merchants decided to operate under the fair-competition code. As a newspaper article explained:

> These merchants of Fergus Falls have elected to operate under group "C" which provides that the establishment shall be open 63 hours or more per week and the employees of such an establishment shall work not more than 48 hours per week nor more than 10 hours per day.
>
> Therefore the . . . stores, if they so elect, will open at 8 a. m. and close at 6 p. m. except on Saturdays when they will open at 8 a. m. and close at 9 p. m. It is there [sic] intention to conform to the rules and regulations of the Code of Fair Competition for the Retail Trade as approved by President Roosevelt October 21, 1933.[37]

A special code, adopted October 3, 1933, regulated banks. The Farmers and Merchants State Bank in New York Mills informed its patrons that all the nation's banks would have to maintain a "uniform maximum number of banking hours," offer "uniform maximum interest rates," and follow "a uniform schedule of service charges."[38]

Otter Tail County joined the rest of the nation in hoping that the NRA would curtail the depression. It participated in the NRA education program for young people and even moved across the floor doing the "NRA dance." The New York Mills Q Q Club, after discussing what book should be given to the library that month, was treated to a demonstration of "the new NRA dance, in which each one does his part."[39]

The complexity of the NRA impressed one newspaper reporter, Genevieve F. Herrick, who asked readers, in an article reprinted in the *Fergus Falls Daily Journal,* "Were you at the tea party the Mad Hatter gave in Alice in Wonderland? Neither was I. But I feel as if I'd just left it. For I've spent the day at the NRA headquarters." [40] The NRA came under increasing attack, especially from small businesses that felt they had no control over their local operations. The United States Supreme Court, in part, agreed, and in 1935 it declared the NRA unconstitutional. The day of the Blue Eagle was over.

Roy Hintgen concluded that the NRA had little impact on the county's small retailers. "There was never much said about it," he recalled, "you had stickers that went onto an item and it gave the price . . . and you were not to exceed that. But whenever you make some kind of a rule, there's always someone [who] immediately starts to rig up something to abuse the rule or get around it and I think there was quite alot of that being done."[41] The NRA gave Otter Tail County the headache of government bureaucracy and paper work. "Relief" for merchants came indirectly through the employment of the county's people under the FERA, the CWA, the CCC, the WPA, and the PWA and through farm programs. Government checks trickled down into main-street cash registers.

The business climate in Otter Tail County was better than that found in many parts of the country. John Hartman, who as a young man worked with his father and older brother in the wholesale fruit and vegetable business in Perham, recalled, "I made several trips with our semi-trailer truck to Arkansas and Texas and Michigan. In Arkansas I bought cantalope . . . poverty in Arkansas was so bad, that it made Minnesota look like a state of wealth. The farmers who loaded our trucks were so poor, they asked what the wages were in Minnesota, and I told them 12, 15 dollars a week, they couldn't believe that the wages were that high. They were working for 10 dollars, 15 dollars a month."[42] Hartman also observed that, although business was slow, he usually collected his bills: "It was easy to sell the merchandise, but it was rather rough collecting for it, stores were in as bad shape as we were . . . we trusted them, and they didn't betray their trust, there was very little we lost from store keepers."[43]

Most businesses managed to survive even though bill collecting may have been "rough." The county newspapers were not filled with stories of business failures or advertisements for going-out-of-business sales. The examples of the Hintgen-Karst Electric Company in Fergus Falls and the business community in Battle Lake indicate that business was far from "bust."

Roy Hintgen and Ed Karst started their company in 1926. Hintgen handled the appliance sales and kept the books, while Karst supervised

Roy Hintgen

two (four by 1929) electricians, who did repair work and installed wiring in buildings. Although business was slow during the early 1930s, Hintgen and Karst never faced serious trouble even in 1932–33, which Hintgen termed "rock bottom."[44] "As a matter of fact," he remembered, "in 1936 even though the depression was still hanging on, we had sold a hundred refrigerators . . . most of them . . . for $119 [each]. . . . I was given a Hamilton watch by Frigidaire for selling . . . in 1936 that was considered quite a feat."[45] Hintgen saw few local businesses fail.

From August 1934 through April 1935 Battle Lake businesses made many improvements. During those nine months Hans Nelson and Sons began selling men's and boys' furnishings, including apparel and footwear, and the Peterson brothers opened a service station with two pumps, "one for Skelly and one for Super X gasoline."[46] Other businesses fixed up their facilities: Battle Lake Bakery installed an oven and a neon sign; Evert's Lumber Yard built a new lumber shed; Halverson Furniture Store renovated and redecorated; Martin's Meat Market and Gustafson's Grocery installed new vaporizers; Nelson's Grocery refinished its large counter; Corbett's Grocery and the drug store refurbished their interiors; Paulson's Hardware repaired and enlarged its display window; Peterson's Hotel and Cafe put in an illuminated clock; and

The main street of Battle Lake, looking toward the railroad tracks, in about 1940

Thomas C. Wright

Motor Inn remodeled its office and parts room.[47] The merchants of Battle Lake, like those throughout Otter Tail County, were able to make these changes, not because of the NRA, but because government farm and relief programs brought money into the county's economy.

At the other end of the business spectrum, Otter Tail Power Company of Fergus Falls employed about one hundred people within the county and was its largest corporation. Both the depression and New Deal programs influenced the company's development. "Territorial expansion came to a virtual standstill," and "depressed conditions had become very obvious, and with them the need for drastic retrenchment."[48] With those descriptive statements Thomas C. Wright (president of Otter Tail Power Company from 1933 to 1952 and then chairman of the board of directors or a board member until 1964) characterized the impact of the depression on the business that his family had controlled since its incorporation in 1907. Like other power companies, Otter Tail Power had expanded rapidly during the 1920s. In 1919 it had just under 400 miles of transmission lines that served 44 towns, 17 farm customers, and 6 wholesale consumers with 10,890,439 kilowatt hours generated. By 1930 almost 3,000 miles of transmission lines carried 69,284,000 kilowatt hours to 314 towns, 534 farm customers, 125 cottages, 19 wholesale consumers, and 6 interconnections. The company's service area expanded from Otter Tail County and locations in nearby Minnesota counties, northeastern South Dakota, and southeastern North Dakota to include more state counties and North Dakota towns as far west as Tuttle and Wilton and as far north as Hannah on the Canadian border. Plants were added to and rebuilt, and facilities were purchased from other businesses such as Midwest Power Company, Western Electric Company, and Harvey Electric Company.[49]

Otter Tail Power did not feel the economic pinch until 1931 when for the first time consumer demand declined somewhat; in 1932 and 1933 the kilowatt hours generated dropped slightly. From 1931 through 1938, the company added only thirty-six towns.[50] Yearly revenue grew slowly from $2.5 million in 1930 to $3 million in 1940. Profits, however, were down because of rate reductions.[51] In response to the difficult times the board of directors reduced common dividends in July 1932 and the following winter; between June 1933 and December 1938 no dividends were paid on common stock.[52] Fenwick Fetvedt of Fergus Falls, who joined Otter Tail Power as a clerk in 1922 and retired as manager of the rate department in 1968, recalled the impact of the depression on employees:

> It slowed it down and as far as employees were concerned, Otter Tail has always been a very careful company about spending their money. There was just one pay cut, 10% right across the board for everyone and some employees were let go and everybody took on more work, of course, but the employees actually were much better treated than in other businesses and firms around this part of the country at least. . . . I was making about $150 a month . . . and you were glad to have any kind of a job, any kind of a salary.[53]

By 1938, however, Otter Tail Power Company's business was on the upswing. "Dividends were resumed on the common stock on December 22, 1938, after a lapse of five years and nine months," Thomas Wright declared. "For the Company, the depression can be said to have ended on that date."[54] In 1941 the company added almost twice the number of towns as it had during 1931–38.[55]

The depression did more than retard the company's growth; it altered Otter Tail Power Company's operational system and corporate position. Of the New Deal reforms and programs that affected the company, two were especially important: the Public Utility Act of 1935 and the REA. The Public Utility Act imposed more stringent regulations on utilities, giving the Federal Power Commission authority over accounting practices and rates charged for power resold in interstate commerce. Since Minnesota had no public utility regulatory commission, the Federal Power Commission had jurisdiction over the issuing of securities by companies like Otter Tail Power.[56] The new controls complicated the company's life. "Obviously, the old, informal ways of doing business were a thing of the past," Wright lamented. "From here on, attorneys and accountants played a large and increasing part in all business operations."[57] Fetvedt, the rate department manager, agreed. "Everything had to have approval. . . . I remember whole books of statistics and, of course, lawyers' arguments being prepared and . . . auditors," he related, "it was bad enough to have to prepare all that work . . . and you don't know when it gets down to Washington if there is anybody who will read it or whether it will just be thrown in the corner." Fetvedt thought that most business insiders resented "all the regulations and all the red tape and management from Washington."[58]

The New Deal's approach to public power and rural electrification was especially disturbing to the utility companies, and Otter Tail Power Company was no exception. The TVA was a prime example. Its power operations were designed to serve as a "yardstick" to measure what would be reasonable rates for a private company to charge. Wright believed that to be extremely unfair: "Because of subsidies that it receives from the Federal and local treasuries (no interest on the money invested and a very small tax burden) TVA uses a very low rate schedule." The yardstick, however, was but a small part of a much larger question: how far would the New Deal go in public power? Talk of a similar program for the Missouri River valley, on the western fringe of the company's service area, understandably made Otter Tail Power Company officials uneasy, creating, according to Wright, "a feeling of uncertainty as to the future."[59]

The REA especially heightened anxiety among privately owned utility companies, and the management of Otter Tail Power groped for a tenable position in uncertain circumstances:

> With the passage of the National R.E.A. Act in 1936, and with R.E.A.-financed cooperatives coming into being in Otter Tail Power Company's service area in 1937 and later, Otter Tail's management was faced with a problem that was hard to resolve. Possible competition from an agency operating on a cooperative basis and receiving subsidies from the Federal government was in itself objectionable to Otter Tail. However, there was no way of knowing just how far the Government might go in its support of the R.E.A. program, even to the point of using R.E.A. as the forerunner of a gigantic public power program that might ultimately put Otter Tail out of business.[60]

Although Otter Tail Power Company was eligible for loans from the REA, it did not participate. "The original REA act provided for loans to utility companies for the purpose of building rural lines, if the companies would comply with the rules and regulations specified therein," Wright explained. "Most of the utility companies felt that the rules were too restrictive, so only a very few loans were made. It is unfortunate that no realistic program was worked out, because it could have saved a substantial amount through elimination of duplicate facilities."[61]

Otter Tail Power, however, came to supply REA cooperatives with wholesale electricity. It made its first REA contract with Douglas County Co-operative Light and Power Association in mid-December 1936.[62] Contracts followed with Baker Electric Co-operative Association of North Dakota in 1937 and Lake Region Co-op. Electric Association in 1938.[63] In 1945 REA cooperatives in Minnesota, North Dakota, and South Dakota accounted for nearly 8.6 percent of the company's sales.[64] The New Deal had forged a new partnership between Otter Tail Power Company and the farmer-owned electric cooperatives.

The New Deal's measures that related to the commercial community affected different businesses in different ways. Clearly banking reform placed the county's banks on a sound foundation. The closing of some banks, although painful to depositors, and the strengthening of others provided the county with the banking network that served residents for the generation after World War II. On the other hand, the NRA gave Otter Tail County little more than the patriotic displaying of the Blue Eagle. When the NRA died in early 1936 the county's small businesses did not mourn its passing. The relief agencies and farm programs that put money in people's pockets did far more for business than the NRA did. Otter Tail Power Company, unlike Hintgen-Karst Electric Company or Battle Lake Bakery, experienced considerable change because of New Deal programs. The REA and more stringent regulation altered its relationships with consumers and the federal government.

CONCLUSION

THE IMPLEMENTATION at the grass roots of programs devised in Washington was no easy task, especially for agencies that required immediate action. The FERA's decision to use state and local administrative machinery placed money in empty pockets much more quickly than if it had established federally controlled programs — such as the WPA became. Adopting essentially the same formula for local control of organization, the CWA was able to hire the county's unemployed two weeks after Roosevelt announced the plan. The complicated farm programs could not have been in place for the 1934 growing season had not the AAA engaged the Extension Service's agents as its local coordinators and employed farmers to oversee county operations. The agents and the farmers played monumental roles in bringing the New Deal's farm policy to the grass roots in a relatively short span of time. The PWA, which developed a reputation as a slow-moving and cautious agency, was working with New York Mills on its water system by fall 1933. Engineers working with the WPA assisted local governments with proposals as soon as the agency began operations in 1935. Although the county commissioners grumbled about delays, the WPA was able to approve most of the county's requests by November.

The CCC, the old-age assistance program, and the REA were quite different matters. Less than three weeks after the CCC received congressional approval, its first camp opened — on April 17, 1933. Ten days later a Fergus Falls newspaper reported that "quite a number" of the county's young men had asked about joining. They had to wait almost six months before the county received its first quota, and then the allocation of twenty-three openings was far short of expectations or demand. Residents faced the same situation with old-age assistance. The president signed the measure in August 1935, but not until March 1936 did Minnesota have the program in place, and not until October did qualified residents receive their first checks. Confusion at the grass roots accompanied the delay in implementation of the program. Most residents seemed to think that the program gave out automatic pensions, and a field worker had to be called in to explain that old-age assistance was a relief measure.

No New Deal program, however, was more fraught with local frustration than the REA. When the REA came into existence in 1935, the county's farmers immediately climbed on the rural electrification bandwagon, and before the year ran out Lake Region Cooperative Electrical Association was incorporated and set to bring electricity to area farmers. The REA administrative wheels turned painfully slowly in the eyes of the cooperative's leadership and members. Only after a year and a half of anxious negotiations did Lake Region obtain its first allotment. Not until October 7, 1938, did the cooperative set its first meter, more than three years from the inauguration of the REA program. In the case of the REA, as well as the CCC and old-age assistance, the people at the grass roots clearly expected swifter implementation of and participation in the New Deal programs.

Roosevelt and the New Deal leadership worried about the confusion that the multitude of complex new programs might, and often did, create. In an effort to coordinate the efforts of the many government agencies, the president created the National Emergency Council (NEC) in July 1933. Designed to supply information for cabinet members, advise officials, mediate conflicts between agencies, and eliminate needless duplication, the NEC faced a hopeless task. Its executive director for most of 1935, Frank C. Walker, recalled that while he was with the NEC he tried to "coordinate the uncoordinatable and unscrew the inscrutable."[1] Although the council had 175 people in Washington, D.C., and five hundred in the states, it did little to meet the president's expectations and after 1937 gradually faded into other government agencies.[2] The NEC's failure was rooted in the nature of the New Deal; each agency was independent and had its own purpose and objectives.

The New Deal made no concerted effort to coordinate its programs at the grass roots. Each program stood alone. Otter Tail County's agents gave a modicum of coordination to farm programs and were largely responsible for the interpretation of agricultural policies, but the AAA had little interaction with the FCA and the REA. The agencies that sponsored work-type programs (the FERA, the CWA, the WPA, the PWA, the NYA, and the CCC) suffered the same fate. With the exception of the relief committee's role in facilitating the FERA-CWA transitions, each went its own way, directed by its own independent objectives and leadership. Whether in Washington, St. Paul, or Fergus Falls, change occurred at a rapid pace, and coordination was less important than the more immediate demand to get things done.

In spite of the lack of coordination and frustrating delays in program implementation, the New Deal improved and sustained life. Small-town America could not have made the physical progress that it did in such a short time without the New Deal's programs that focused on the improvement and construction of public facilities. The FERA, the CWA, the PWA, and the WPA created a hothouse effect, providing an environment conducive to physical change. The people's quality of life was substantially upgraded, especially through the many recreational, educational, and health projects. It is doubtful that communities could have supplied new or improved schools, water and sewage systems, or parks and playgrounds for another decade without the support that the New Deal rendered. New York Mills had overwhelmingly rejected indebtedness for a water system in 1931, but two years later with the promise of a PWA grant and loan the people rallied to approve the construction of a water system. The new water system not only guaranteed residents a safe and steady supply but also assured them of more dependable fire protection and higher health standards.

Certainly the combined efforts of the New Deal work programs in the upgrading and construction of the county's road network were a boon to those on the farmstead. Except for the main highways, before the New Deal most farm-to-market roads were little more than wagon ruts. Going to town became much less of a chore. Without question the REA radically altered farm life, ending the farmers' position as second-class citizens to townspeople who had enjoyed the benefits of electricity for years. Labor-saving appliances and machines shortened the work day, taking much of the drudgery out of farmstead life. Electricity as a source for lighting ended the darkness, and as a steady power source for radios, and, much later, television sets, made leisure time more enjoyable. The REA brought a transformation to the farm. Whether one lived on main street or on a farmstead, the signs of physical progress were visible almost everywhere. The New Deal encouraged people at the grass roots to take advantage of its programs in order to enhance their own lives. Those programs allowed people to do those things which otherwise would or could not have been accomplished.

Physical progress was, however, the by-product of the New Deal's foremost objective — the alleviation of suffering and hardship. The relief and work programs (the FERA, the CWA, the PWA, the WPA, the CCC, and the NYA) did what they were intended to do — provide the jobless with the wherewithall to get through the difficult days of the depression. The FERA supplied emergency funding when local governments had lost or were losing the ability to give adequate relief to those who desperately needed it. Perham alone could not have supported the sixteen men who comprised its permanent FERA work force in 1934 and 1935. The CWA meant employment through the tough winter of 1933–34 for eighty-two-year-old Jacob Hatling of Dalton. The PWA gave work to all the unemployed men in New York Mills when it constructed the town water system in 1934. The monthly checks that the families of the CCC workers received "kept them going," as Clinton Thun put it. Roy Baker's employment with the WPA presents a graphic demonstration of the significance of one New Deal program to one family. Baker, because of his age and white-collar background, had almost no chance of finding employment in the private sector. With four children at home and with no means of support, he faced a bleak future. The WPA work sustained Baker and his family from 1935 into 1942. The assortment of jobs that he undertook provided the Bakers with the necessities of life, albeit at times barely so. The WPA, with no exaggeration, meant life to Roy Baker. The New Deal's work programs did indeed hold people's worlds together at a time when they easily could have been torn apart.

Even though the New Deal programs were the creatures of a new and massive Washington bureaucracy, grass-roots governments maintained a large measure of control over and responsibility for those programs. Town and township boards decided who was eligible to work on FERA, CWA, WPA, and NYA projects. That local certification was mandatory before one could participate in either direct or work relief. Indirectly the same was true of the CCC because the local governments had to ensure that the families of the workers qualified for government assistance. What those programs did, with the exception of the CCC, also rested on decisions made by the people within the county. The agencies encouraged but did not dictate participation. For instance, Battle Lake chose not to use WPA assistance to develop its water and sewage systems, while most of the other communities voted to undertake similar projects through the WPA program. The New Deal administrators understood that local people best knew what kinds of projects were most essential to the local community.

Agricultural programs, while more restrictive in their formulas, were completely voluntary. If farmers were philosophically disposed against the intrusion of federal regulations on the farmstead, they could fight it out in the free market, and some selected that course. Although forced to follow strict guidelines, farmers themselves through township and county boards administered and enforced the various AAA programs. Committees approved the production-reduction contracts, and farmer-inspectors saw to it that participants complied with their agreements. The AAA was a grass-roots program in an operational sense. The same was true of the emergency cattle-buying program. County and township committees organized and directed the purchasing procedures. The New Deal's desire to have local people handle local problems motivated the FCA to establish an Agricultural Advisory Credit Committee to conciliate debtor-creditor disputes in an effort to avoid litigation or the bureaucratic hierarchy. The successful organization of the PCA or the REA cooperatives lay solely on farmers at the local level. The federal agencies held out the promise, but only through farmstead action could that promise be realized.

In recognizing the legitimacy of grass-roots control and responsibility, the New Deal fostered a new sense of democracy and community. Never before had people on the main streets or on the farmsteads of Otter Tail County worked together so closely in organizing the present and planning the future, and never before had individuals and groups made such a variety of decisions that influenced the course of their separate and collective lives. The organization of REA and PCA cooperatives was a prime illustration of the self-determination process. If the farmers wanted farmer-controlled rural electrification or credit, they had to achieve those benefits with local effort. The federal agencies provided the guidelines and information, but only a collective and concerted grass-roots determination could turn that information into electricity or loans. Most New Deal programs enhanced the democratic process and promoted community cooperation.

The New Deal's emphasis on grass-roots planning, execution, and control worked to its advantage in small-town, rural America where the people cherished the virtues of self-reliance and self-determination. Otter Tail, a conservative and Republican county, took full advantage of the New Deal's programs. For example, Edward Barnard, a Republican businessman, doggedly pursued WPA grants for the Otter Tail County Historical Society. The Fergus Falls City Council and school board, dominated by Republicans, eagerly participated in FERA, PWA, CWA, and WPA programs and feverishly worked to gain a CCC camp. The rock-ribbed Republican *Fergus Falls Daily Journal* provided both explanations of and information about the various programs. Indeed, it and the county weeklies played key roles in what success New Deal programs brought to the county. The newspapers served as invaluable informational allies of the New Deal and more often than not lent praise to the improvements, both physical and personal, that the Roosevelt administration provided.

Otter Tail County suffered no penalty for its allegiance to the Republican party. The WPA spent about ninety-one dollars per person nationally, but in Otter Tail it expended almost ninety-eight dollars per county resident. And Fergus Falls, which gave Hoover a two-to-one margin over Roosevelt in the Democratic landslide of 1932, received more than its share of the county's work-project funds. The New Deal bureaucrats did not discriminate against the Republican stronghold.

Nor did the presence of New Deal programs alter the county's politics of conservatism. Liberals, especially the social planners, had hoped that the New Deal would create a liberal renaissance that would nurture a flourishing local progressivism. Such was not the case, as the Otter Tail County experience indicates. Only in the crisis of 1932 did the county abandon the Republican party. The emergency of the 1930s required only that Otter Tail County's people embrace New Deal programs, not its philosophy. Searle Zimmerman captured that sentiment when he observed in 1985, "The people around here were and are conservative. The depression pushed us into the New Deal programs. Sure those programs did a great deal for us. They gave us more security, but they didn't change our way of looking at things, not at all. We're still conservative."[3]

The New Deal may not have changed the county's political outlook, but its subsidized and regulated welfare capitalism has and does substantially influence the lives of Otter Tail County's people. The emergency work-relief agencies dissolved during the early years of World War II when unemployment ceased to be a vexing problem, but reform programs and policies have continued and have been expanded during the past fifty years. Social Security through its several programs has touched all families with its system of welfare delivery. Fears of old age and disability, anxious concerns in the 1930s, have been greatly minimized. The FDIC and more stringent regulation provided banks and their depositors with new-found security. No banks in the county failed during the postwar generation. Even though electricity did not reach some farms until long after the New Deal, no farm today depends upon a balky gasoline engine or kerosene lamps. Although the number of farms has been reduced by half since the 1930s (about thirty-two hundred with an average of 290 acres in 1987), participation in farm programs has remained at about the same level — 80 to 90 percent. As of July 1987, 122 farmers, mostly small operators who were nearing retirement or had low-producing herds, had taken part in the federal program and sold their dairy cattle to government buyers.[4] The New Deal charted a course that forged a new relationship between the federal government and the people of the nation's main streets and farmsteads.

REFERENCE NOTES

The following abbreviations have been used:
Otter Tail County Historical Society — OTCHS
Minnesota Historical Society — MHS
National Archives, Washington, D.C. — NA

INTRODUCTION

1. Bernard Sternsher, ed., *Hitting Home: The Great Depression in Town and Country* (Chicago: Quadrangle Books, 1970), 36–37. This book contains twelve previously published articles on the depression years in representative cities, counties, and states.

2. John Braeman, Robert H. Bremner, and David Brody, eds., *The New Deal: The State and Local Levels*, vol. 2 of *The New Deal*, Modern America, no. 4 (Columbus: Ohio State University Press, 1975), ix.

3. Braeman, Bremner, and Brody, *New Deal: State and Local Levels*, ix; James T. Patterson, *The New Deal and the States: Federalism in Transition* (Princeton, N.J.: Princeton University Press, 1969).

4. Theodore Saloutos, *The American Farmer and the New Deal* (Ames: Iowa State University Press, 1982); Susan Estabrook Kennedy, *The Banking Crisis of 1933* (Lexington: University of Kentucky Press, 1973); Francis W. Schruben, *Kansas in Turmoil, 1930–1936* (Columbia: University of Missouri Press, 1969); D. Jerome Tweton, *Depression: Minnesota in the Thirties* (Fargo: North Dakota Institute for Regional Studies, 1981).

5. Sternsher, *Hitting Home*, 3–4.

Chapter 1. OTTER TAIL COUNTY: The People, the Politics, the Place

1. Pope quoted in John W. Mason, ed., *History of Otter Tail County, Minnesota: Its People, Industries and Institutions*, 2 vols. (Indianapolis, Ind.: B. F. Bowen & Co., 1916), 1:80.

2. Mason, ed., *History of Otter Tail County*, 1:57–67; Jon Lyman Walstrom, "Ethnic Segregation in Otter Tail County, Minnesota: 1884 to 1912" (Master's thesis, University of Minnesota, 1974), 10–13.

3. *Fergus Falls Daily Journal*, Nov. 3, 1933, p. 3; Vic Spadaccini, ed., *Minnesota Pocket Data Book, 1985–1986* (St. Paul: Blue Sky Marketing, Inc., 1985), 187.

4. Mason, ed., *History of Otter Tail County*, 1:82–93. For more information about Old-Stock Americans in the state, see John G. Rice, "The Old-Stock Americans," in *They Chose Minnesota: A Survey of the State's Ethnic Groups*, ed. June Drenning Holmquist (St. Paul: Minnesota Historical Society Press, 1981), 55–72.

5. Rice, "Old-Stock Americans," in *They Chose Minnesota*, ed. Holmquist, 59–65. See also Walstrom, "Ethnic Segregation."

6. Carlton C. Qualey and Jon A. Gjerde, "The Norwegians," in *They Chose Minnesota*, ed. Holmquist, 223.

7. Hildegard Binder Johnson, "The Germans," in *They Chose Minnesota*, ed. Holmquist, 156, 159.

8. John G. Rice, "The Swedes," in *They Chose Minnesota*, ed. Holmquist, 251.

9. Timo Riippa, "The Finns and Swede-Finns," in *They Chose Minnesota*, ed. Holmquist, 300.

10. United States, *Census*, 1900, *Population*, 1:762–63; Ann Regan, "The Danes," in *They Chose Minnesota*, ed. Holmquist, 279. The Anglo-Canadian and British immigrants blended with the Old-Stock Americans and did not form identifiable communities.

11. Frank Renkiewicz, "The Poles," in *They Chose Minnesota*, ed. Holmquist, 364.

12. U.S., *Census*, 1930, *Population*, vol. 3, pt. 1, p. 1200, 1221, 1222.

13. Denomination membership statistics for 1936 are derived from U.S. Census Bureau, *Special Reports, Religious Bodies: 1936*, 1:232–35, 772, 774.

14. E. Clifford Nelson, ed., *The Lutherans in North America*, rev. ed. (Philadelphia: Fortress Press, 1980), 370–73.

15. Nelson, *Lutherans in North America*, 189–90, 337, 341–43.

16. Nelson, *Lutherans in North America*, 344; J. Gordon Melton, *The Encyclopedia of American Religions*, 2 vols. (Wilmington, N.C.: McGrath Pub. Co., 1978), 1:104–5; Jane Thompson, ed., *Fergus Falls, Minnesota, 1872–1972* (N.p.: Centennial Committee, 1972), [45–46, 62].

17. Erwin L. Lueker, ed., *Lutheran Cyclopedia* (St. Louis, Mo.: Concordia Publishing House, 1954), 606; Nelson, *Lutherans in North America*, 178–81, 377–81.

18. Nelson, *Lutherans in North America*, 191–93, 325–28.

19. Nelson, *Lutherans in North America*, 272–76; Lueker, ed., *Lutheran Cyclopedia*, 377–78.

20. Nelson, *Lutherans in North America*, 386.

21. Quoted in Nelson, *Lutherans in North America*, 387. The General Synod, formed in 1820, was a precursor of the United Lutheran Church in America; Nelson, 373–77.

22. Nelson, *Lutherans in North America*, 454; U.S. Census Bureau, *Special Reports, Religious Bodies: 1936*, 2:925.

23. Melton, *Encyclopedia of American Religions*, 1:24–25.

24. *Fergus Falls City Directory*, 1935–36; Centennial Book Committee, *New York Mills Centennial History, 1884–1984* (New York Mills: The Committee, 1984), 114.

25. Minnesota, *Legislative Manual*, 1921, p. 525.

26. Two other candidates were Frank F. Johns (Social Industrial party, 21 votes) and William Z. Foster (Workers party, 137 votes). Minnesota, *Legislative Manual*, 1925, p. 318 (following); Bruce M. White et al., comps., *Minnesota Votes: Election Returns by County for Presidents, Senators, Congressmen, and Governors, 1857–1977* (St. Paul: Minnesota Historical Society, 1977), 20.

27. Minnesota, *Legislative Manual*, 1929, p. 371.

28. Charles R. Lamb, "The Nonpartisan League and its Expansion into Minnesota," *North Dakota Quarterly* 49 (Summer 1981): 108–43. For a detailed study of the coalition,

see Millard L. Gieske, *Minnesota Farmer-Laborism: The Third-Party Alternative* (Minneapolis: University of Minnesota Press, 1979).

29. Minnesota, *Legislative Manual*, 1923, p. 386, 452 (following); 1925, p. 318 (following), 420.

30. Minnesota, *Legislative Manual*, 1921, p. 458, 459, 527; 1923, p. 386, 387, 453; 1925, p. 420, 421, 487; 1927, p. 286, 287, 351; 1929, p. 302, 303, 374; White et al., *Minnesota Votes*, 104, 105, 107, 108, 110.

31. *Fergus Falls Weekly Journal*, Oct. 6, 1927, p. 1, 9, 14.

32. *Annual Report of the County Agricultural Agent in East Otter Tail County Minnesota*, 1929, p. 13; *Annual Report of the County Agricultural Agent in West Otter Tail County Minnesota*, 1929, p. 5, copies in OTCHS.

33. *Annual Report East*, 1929, p. 52.

34. U.S., *Census*, 1940, *Agriculture*, vol. 2, pt. 1, p. 488–96; *Fergus Falls Weekly Journal*, Sept. 7, 1939, p. 4.

35. *Fergus Falls Weekly Journal*, Dec. 21, 1933, p. 1.

36. *Annual Report West*, 1932, p. 21.

37. U.S., *Census*, 1940, *Agriculture*, vol. 1, pt. 2, p. 44–45; *Fergus Falls Daily Journal*, June 13, 1931, p. 2.

38. U.S., *Census*, 1940, *Agriculture*, vol. 1, pt. 2, p. 16–23, 56, 63, vol. 2, pt. 1, p. 492–93.

39. U.S., *Census*, 1940, *Agriculture*, vol. 1, pt. 2, p. 56, 100, vol. 2, pt. 1, p. 502–3; *Fergus Falls Daily Journal*, June 13, 1931, p. 2.

40. Interview of Jorolf Ronnevik with author, Jan. 19, 1985, p. 2, notes in author's possession.

41. Ronnevik interview, 2–3.

42. U.S., *Census*, 1940, *Population*, 1:546.

43. *New York Mills Herald*, Jan. 7, 1936, p. 1, 4.

44. U.S., *Census*, 1930, *Distribution*, vol. 1, pt. 1, p. 546–47, pt. 2, p. 1325.

45. [Russell O. Parta, ed.], *New York Mills: "Seventy-five Years of Progress": 1884–1959* (New York Mills: Civic and Commerce Assn., 1959), 16.

46. Transcript of audio-tape interview of Roy Hintgen with author, Jan. 19, 1985, p. 5, OTCHS '30s Project Papers; *Fergus Falls City Directory*, 1931.

47. *A History of Vergas, Minnesota: Written during the Nation's Bicentennial Year of 1976* (Hawley, Minn.: Hawley Herald, 1976), 72–73.

48. *Historical Album and Centennial Book, 1871–1971, Perham, Minnesota* (N.p., 1971), [45].

49. Centennial Book Committee, *New York Mills Centennial History*, 131; [Frank Jacobs and E. L. Peterson], *Pelican Rapids Diamond Jubilee* (Pelican Rapids: Privately published, 1958), 29; *Pelican Rapids Press*, May 19, 1932, p. 8.

50. U.S., *Census*, 1930, *Agriculture*, vol. 2, pt. 1, p. 864–65.

51. History Book Committee, *Dent Diamond Jubilee, 1904–1979* (Dent: The Committee, 1979), 52–53.

52. "Summer Resorts, Otter Tail County," in Julian S. Ree and Thomas O. Nelson, comps., *Plat Book of Otter Tail County, Minnesota* (Fergus Falls: The Authors, 1933?).

53. Blair W. McNea, *Pelican Reflections: 50 Years — Pelican Lake Property Owners Association* ([Detroit Lakes, Minn.]: Lakes Pub. Co., 1983), 37–43.

54. Here and below, transcript based on notes of interview with Searle A. Zimmerman by author, Feb. 16, 1985, 2–3, OTCHS '30s Project Papers.

Chapter 2. OTTER TAIL COUNTY: The Economic Crisis and the Politics of Response

1. William E. Leuchtenburg, *Franklin D. Roosevelt and the New Deal: 1932-1940*, The New American Nation Series (New York: Harper & Row, 1963), 1; Broadus Mitchell, *Depression Decade: From New Era through New Deal: 1929-1941*, The Economic History of the United States, vol. 9 (New York: Rinehart & Co., 1947), 32-33.

2. Kennedy, *Banking Crisis of 1933*, 16-21; Helen M. Burns, *The American Banking Community and New Deal Banking Reforms: 1933-1935*, Contributions in Economics and Economic History, no. 11 (Westport, Conn.: Greenwood Press, 1974), 3-7.

3. Leuchtenburg, *Franklin D. Roosevelt*, 1-3.

4. For information on wartime production, see Maxcy Robson Dickson, *The Food Front in World War I* (Washington, D.C.: American Council on Public Affairs, 1944). For an analysis of the postwar farm problem, see James H. Shideler, *Farm Crisis: 1919-1923* (Berkeley and Los Angeles: University of California Press, 1957).

5. Saloutos, *American Farmer*, 5-9; Shideler, *Farm Crisis*, 13.

6. Analysis based on United States, Census Bureau, *Historical Statistics of the United States: Colonial Times to 1957* (Washington, D.C.: Government Printing Office, 1960), 289, 294, 295, 296-97.

7. Saloutos, *American Farmer*, 12-13.

8. Saloutos, *American Farmer*, 13.

9. U.S., Census Bureau, *Historical Statistics*, 283, 289, 294, 295, 296-97.

10. This analysis is based on U.S., Census Bureau, *Historical Statistics*, 289-97; *Fergus Falls Daily Journal*, June 13, 1931, p. 2.

11. U.S., *Census*, 1920, *Agriculture*, vol. 6, pt. 1, p. 520-21.

12. Transcript of audio-tape interview of Ed and Jeanette Hintsala with Roberta Klugman, New York Mills, June 18, 1980, p. 1, 12, OTCHS '30s Project Papers.

13. Ronnevik interview, 1.

14. *Annual Report East*, 1930, p. 21, 48, 50; *Annual Report West*, 1930, p. 7; CCC Camp Work Plan, Camp SCS-MN-21, Fergus Falls, Minnesota, photocopy of undated typescript, 7, OTCHS.

15. *Perham Enterprise-Bulletin*, June 23, 1932, p. 1.

16. Transcript of audio-tape interview of Martha Hegge with Roberta Klugman, n.d., p. 1-2, 4, 12, OTCHS '30s Project Papers.

17. Transcript of audio-tape interview with Conrad Toso, Dorothy Toso Williams, and Conrad E. ("Gene") Toso by Roberta Klugman, Fergus Falls, Sept. 22, 1980, p. 1-2, 3, 4, 6-7, 10, 17-18, 20, 22, OTCHS '30s Project Papers.

18. Transcript of audio-tape interview with Susie Dillon by Ruth Berg and Roberta Klugman, Fergus Falls, Sept. 11, 1980, p. 1-2, 3, 6, 10, OTCHS '30s Project Papers.

19. Tweton, *Depression*, 9.

20. *Annual Report West*, 1929, p. 6.

21. *Fergus Falls Daily Journal*, June 13, 1931, p. 2, percentage computed by author.

22. Analysis by author based on Ree and Nelson, comps., *Plat Book*.

23. George H. Mayer, *The Political Career of Floyd B. Olson* (Minneapolis: University of Minnesota Press, 1951; St. Paul: Minnesota Historical Society Press, Borealis Books, 1987), 107.

24. *Fergus Falls Tribune*, Nov. 5, 1936, p. 1, Dec. 17, 1936, p. 1.

25. Minnesota, *Legislative Manual*, 1933, p. 306, 375.

26. *Fergus Falls Daily Journal*, Nov. 11, 1932, p. 9; Minnesota, *Legislative Manual*, 1933, p. 304, 306, 374.

27. Here and below, see Minnesota, *Legislative Manual*, 1935, p. 310; 1937, p. 381; 1939, p. 320; 1941, p. 332, 399; *New York Mills Herald*, Oct. 29, 1936, p. 1; *Fergus Falls Daily Journal*, Nov. 6, 1940, p. 3.

28. Minnesota, *Legislative Manual*, 1933, p. 500; 1939, p. 532.

29. Transcript of audio-tape interview with John Hartman by Roberta Klugman, Detroit Lakes, Aug. 20, 1980, p. 1, 12, OTCHS '30s Project Papers.

30. *Fergus Falls Weekly Journal*, July 2, 1931, p. 1, July 16, 1931, p. 3, notes in OTCHS '30s Project Papers.

31. *Fergus Falls Daily Journal*, Mar. 12, 1935, p. 7.

32. White et al., *Minnesota Votes*, 21.

33. Lowell K. Dyson, *Red Harvest: The Communist Party and American Farmers* (Lincoln: University of Nebraska Press, 1982), 34-37, 48-49, 69; Harvey Klehr, *The Heyday of American Communism: The Depression Decade* (New York: Basic Books, 1984), 138.

34. See Carl Ross, *The Finn Factor in American Labor, Culture and Society* (New York Mills: Parta Printers, 1977), especially Chapters 4 and 7.

35. Tweton, *Depression*, 9, 11; Mayer, *Olson*, 103-7.

36. Lyndon Larry Johnson, "The Farmers' Holiday Association in Southwestern Minnesota, 1932-33" (Master's thesis, University of North Dakota, 1984), 48-53.

37. *Fergus Falls Daily Journal*, Sept. 22, 1932, p. 4, Sept. 23, 1932, p. 3.

38. *Fergus Falls Daily Journal*, Sept. 26, 1932, p. 7, Sept. 30, 1932, p. 9, Oct. 1, 1932, p. 2.

39. *Fergus Falls Daily Journal*, Oct. 5, 1932, p. 9.

40. *Fergus Falls Weekly Journal*, Feb. 16, 1933, p. 1.

41. *Fergus Falls Daily Journal*, May 2, 1933, p. 3.

42. *Fergus Falls Daily Journal*, Oct. 9, 1933, p. 1.

43. *Fergus Falls Daily Journal*, Apr. 6, 1935, p. 3; *New York Mills Herald*, Apr. 11, 1935, p. 1.

44. *Annual Report West*, 1939, p. 5; *New York Mills Herald*, Jan. 5, 1939, p. 1; Minnesota Farm Bureau Federation, "Proceedings of Twenty-first Annual Meeting, Jan. 15-18, 1940," bound copy in Reference Library, MHS; John L. Shover, *Cornbelt Rebellion: The Farmers' Holiday Association* (Urbana: University of Illinois Press, 1965), 212.

Chapter 3. DIRECT RELIEF: "In Dire Need of Help"

1. *Fergus Falls Weekly Journal*, June 23, 1927, p. 1.

2. *Fergus Falls Weekly Journal*, Oct. 27, 1927, p. 5.

3. *Fergus Falls Weekly Journal*, Oct. 6, 1927, p. 2.

4. *Fergus Falls Weekly Journal*, Dec. 18, 1930, p. 1.

5. See Frances Fox Piven and Richard A. Cloward, *Regulating the Poor: The Functions of Public Welfare* (New York: Random House, Vintage Books, 1972), 3-38.

6. Aurdal Township, Treasurer's Orders, 1928-33, notes in OTCHS '30s Project Papers.

7. Clitherall Township, Board Minutes, 1926-32, notes in OTCHS '30s Project Papers.

8. Western Township, Treasurer's Statement, 1927, 1931, Board Minutes, 1931, notes in OTCHS '30s Project Papers.

9. Otto Township, Treasurer's Statement, 1929, Register of Town Orders from Poor Fund, 1932, notes in OTCHS '30s Project Papers.

10. Ottertail Village, Minute Books, 1927–28, Finance Book, 1934, Underwood, Minute Books, 1928, 1932, Battle Lake, Minute Books, 1927, 1932, Vining, Minute Books, 1933, Elizabeth, Minute Books, 1928, 1933, Dent, Minute Books, 1929 — notes in OTCHS '30s Project Papers.

11. *Fergus Falls Daily Journal*, Mar. 20, 1928, p. 7.

12. *Fergus Falls Daily Journal*, Apr. 4, 1933, p. 5.

13. *Fergus Falls Weekly Journal*, Apr. 13, 1933, p. 3.

14. *New York Mills Herald*, Jan. 11, 1934, p. 1; *Fergus Falls Daily Journal*, Nov. 1, 1933, p. 4; *Fergus Falls Weekly Journal*, Mar. 15, 1934, p. 7.

15. *Fergus Falls Daily Journal*, Nov. 21, 1928, p. 7.

16. *Fergus Falls Weekly Journal*, Mar. 29, 1928, p. 1, Nov. 8, 1928, p. 11, Dec. 20, 1928, p. 1.

17. *Fergus Falls Daily Journal*, Oct. 31, 1933, p. 7, Nov. 9, 1933, p. 8, Nov. 17, 1933, p. 5.

18. *Fergus Falls Daily Journal*, Nov. 9, 1933, p. 8.

19. Arthur M. Schlesinger, Jr., *The Coming of the New Deal*, vol. 2 of *The Age of Roosevelt* (Boston: Houghton Mifflin Co., 1958), 263.

20. It is impossible to determine the exact figure because many township records are incomplete. The percentage is an estimate based on existing and complete township records and on the American Red Cross flour and clothing distribution information.

21. Schlesinger, *Coming of the New Deal*, 264–67.

22. "In the Matter of the Administration of State Emergency Relief Funds in Otter Tail County," Otter Tail County Commission, Proceedings, Nov. 14, 1933, p. 496–97, Otter Tail County Courthouse, Fergus Falls.

23. Lorena Hickok, *One Third of a Nation: Lorena Hickok Reports on the Great Depression*, ed. Richard Lowitt and Maurine Beasley (Urbana: University of Illinois Press, 1981), 55.

24. Hickok, *One Third of a Nation*, 126.

25. Hickok, *One Third of a Nation*, 127.

26. United States, Federal Emergency Relief Administration, *Final Statistical Report of the Federal Emergency Relief Administration* (Washington, D.C.: Government Printing Office, 1942), 270.

27. Minnesota, Board of Control of State Institutions, *A Report of the Minnesota State Board of Control as the State Emergency Relief Administration: September 29, 1932 to July 1, 1934*, prepared under the direction of Frank M. Rarig, Jr., executive secretary, State Emergency Relief Administration (St. Paul, 1934, Mimeographed), 248–51, copy in Reference Library, MHS; U.S., *Census*, 1930, *Population*, vol. 3, pt. 1, p. 1187, 1238, 1248, 1251, 1253.

28. *Fergus Falls Weekly Journal*, Apr. 18, 1935, p. 4.

29. "In the Matter of the Administration of County Emergency Relief Funds in Inman Township," Inman Township records, Aug. 18, 1934, notes in OTCHS '30s Project Papers.

30. Gorman Township, Board Minutes, Apr. 15, 1934, notes in OTCHS '30s Project Papers.

31. Analysis based on available village and township records. See Battle Lake, Council

Minutes, 1934–35, Ottertail, Council Minutes, 1934–35, notes in OTCHS '30s Project Papers.

32. Fergus Falls, Council Minutes, Apr. 16, 1934, notes in OTCHS '30s Project Papers.

33. Fergus Falls, Council Minutes, Apr. 24, 1934, notes in OTCHS '30s Project Papers.

34. FERA, *Final Statistical Report of the Federal Emergency Relief Administration*, 103–4. Some small amounts were subsequently given out to reimburse states and finish liquidation of activities.

35. Otter Tail County Relief Administration to Inman Township, Inman Township records, Mar. 16, 1936, notes in OTCHS '30s Project Papers.

36. *Battle Lake Review*, Mar. 12, 1936, p. 1.

37. *Fergus Falls Daily Journal*, Dec. 24, 1937, p. 3, Jan. 6, 1938, p. 2.

38. *Fergus Falls Daily Journal*, Dec. 24, 1937, p. 3.

39. OTC Relief Administration, Memorandum to All Relief Clients, Inman Township records, Apr. 13, 1937, notes in OTCHS '30s Project Papers.

40. *Fergus Falls Weekly Journal*, Mar. 19, 1936, p. 7.

41. 271 North Western 491.

42. Otter Tail County Commission, Proceedings, Dec. 14, 1937, p. 152, Jan. 6, 1938, p. 158.

43. Fergus Falls, Council Minutes, Dec. 20, 1937, July 18, Aug. 1, Sept. 6, 1938, notes in OTCHS '30s Project Papers; City of Fergus Falls v. County of Otter Tail, cases no. 19742 and 19743, Civil Case Files, 1871–1950, District Court, Otter Tail County, Minnesota State Archives, MHS.

44. Otter Tail County Commission, Proceedings, Feb. 10, 1938, p. 162–63.

45. Bluffton Township, Board Minutes, 1937, 1939, Aurdal Township, Treasurer's Orders, 1936, 1939, Elmo Township, Board Minutes, 1936, 1938, Gorman Township, Board Minutes, 1937, 1939, Sverdrup Township, Board Minutes, 1937, 1938, Parkers Prairie, Board Minutes, 1936, 1938, Battle Lake, Treasurer's Orders, 1940 – notes in OTCHS '30s Project Papers; *New York Mills Herald*, Dec. 1, 1938, p. 3; *Battle Lake Review*, Dec. 3, 1936, p. 4. See also *Fergus Falls Daily Journal*, Feb. 5, 1938, p. 3; *Fergus Falls Weekly Journal*, Mar. 30, 1939, p. 7.

46. Ethel McClure, *More Than a Roof: The Development of Minnesota Poor Farms and Homes for the Aged* (St. Paul: Minnesota Historical Society, 1968), 162–63.

47. *Battle Lake Review*, Jan. 9, 1936, p. 1.

48. *Fergus Falls Weekly Journal*, July 9, 1936, p. 3.

49. *Fergus Falls Weekly Journal*, Mar. 26, 1936, p. 3.

50. *Analysis and Report on Old Age Pension and Mothers' Allowance by Counties*, 6, 8, 17, 19, Reports, Emergency Relief Administration Papers, Minnesota State Archives, MHS.

51. *Fergus Falls Weekly Journal*, Nov. 5, 1936, p. 3.

52. *Fergus Falls Weekly Journal*, Jan. 26, 1939, p. 7.

53. Hartman interview, 6.

54. *Fergus Falls Weekly Journal*, July 26, 1934, p. 7, Jan. 17, 1935, p. 9.

55. American Public Welfare Association, *Minnesota State Public Welfare Study* (Chicago, 1940), [iii], mimeograph copy in Reference Library, MHS.

56. Otto Township, Board Minutes, June 11, 1934, notes in OTCHS '30s Project Papers.

57. Gorman Township, Board Minutes, Dec. 1, 10, 20, 30, 1933, notes in OTCHS '30s Project Papers.

58. Fergus Falls, Council Minutes, Nov. 4, 1935, notes in OTCHS '30s Project Papers.

59. Vining, Council Minutes, Feb. 1, Mar. 1, June 9, 11, 1937, Nov. 4, 1938, notes in OTCHS '30s Project Papers.

60. New York Mills, Council Minutes, Jan. 16, Feb. 20, 1939, notes in OTCHS '30s Project Papers.

61. Bluffton, Council Minutes, Feb. 8, 1938, notes in OTCHS '30s Project Papers.

62. Elizabeth, Council Minutes, June 8, 13, 1931, notes in OTCHS '30s Project Papers.

63. Vergas, Council Minutes, Jan. 5, 1937, Battle Lake, Council Minutes, May 6, 1941, notes in OTCHS '30s Project Papers.

64. Vergas, Council Minutes, Feb. 7, 1938, Jan. 6, 1939, Jan. 8, 1939, Perham Township, Board Minutes, Mar. 19, 1940, Treasurer's Orders, Sept. 11, 1935, Oct. 5, 1936, June 4, 1937, Mar. 15, 1938, Mar. 21, 1939, Mar. 19, 1940, Elmo Township, Board Minutes, Mar. 21, 1934, Folden Township, Board Minutes, July 27, 1933 — all notes in OTCHS '30s Project Papers.

65. Fergus Falls, Council Minutes, Feb. 1, 15, 1937, notes in OTCHS '30s Project Papers.

66. Fergus Falls Township, Board Minutes, Mar. 3, 16, 1937, notes in OTCHS '30s Project Papers.

67. Paddock Township, Board Minutes, Jan. 10, 1934, notes in OTCHS '30s Project Papers.

68. New York Mills, Council Minutes, Feb. 11, 1935, notes in OTCHS '30s Project Papers.

69. Ottertail, Council Minutes, Feb. 24, 28, 1941, notes in OTCHS '30s Project Papers.

70. Perham Township, Board Minutes, Dec. 2, 1939, notes in OTCHS '30s Project Papers.

71. Clitherall, Council Minutes, Mar. 2, 1942, copy in OTCHS '30s Project Papers.

72. Otter Tail County Commission, Proceedings, Jan. 1938.

73. Lida Township, Board Minutes, Mar. 1, May 2, 1938, notes in OTCHS '30s Project Papers.

74. Battle Lake, Council Minutes, June 2, 1931, Mar. 7, 1933, notes in OTCHS '30s Project Papers.

75. Battle Lake, Council Minutes, Aug. 4, 1931, notes in OTCHS '30s Project Papers.

76. Tordenskjold Township, Board Minutes, Nov. 6, 1933, notes in OTCHS '30s Project Papers.

77. Leaf Lake Township, Board Minutes, Apr. 7, 1934, copy in OTCHS '30s Project Papers.

78. Otter Tail County Commission, Proceedings, Nov. 1937.

79. *Fergus Falls Weekly Journal*, Mar. 3, 1938, p. 9.

80. *Fergus Falls Weekly Journal*, Feb. 9, 1939, p. 3.

Chapter 4. CWA, FERA, PWA: "Finding Jobs for the People"

1. Arthur E. Burns and Edward A. Williams, *Federal Work, Security, and Relief Programs*, Works Progress Administration, Division of Research, Research Monograph 24 (Washington, D.C.: Government Printing Office, 1941), 27–29, 32. For a detailed study of the CWA, see Bonnie Fox Schwartz, *The Civil Works Administration, 1933–1934: The*

Business of Emergency Employment in the New Deal (Princeton, N.J.: Princeton University Press, 1984).

2. *New York Mills Herald*, Nov. 23, 1933, p. 1.

3. Minnesota, State Emergency Relief Administration, *Minnesota Work Relief History: During the Period from April 1, 1934 to June 30, 1935* (St. Paul, 1935), 12–14, copy in Reference Library, MHS.

4. Otter Tail County Commission, Proceedings, Feb. 14, 1934, p. 513.

5. *Fergus Falls Daily Journal*, Nov. 25, 1933, p. 3.

6. *New York Mills Herald*, Nov. 30, 1933, p. 1, Jan. 11, 1934, p. 1.

7. *Fergus Falls Weekly Journal*, Jan. 4, 1934, p. 8.

8. *Fergus Falls Weekly Journal*, Jan. 11, 1934, p. 14.

9. *Fergus Falls Weekly Journal*, Feb. 15, 1934, p. 11.

10. *Fergus Falls Weekly Journal*, Jan. 11, 1934, p. 7.

11. *Fergus Falls Weekly Journal*, Jan. 18, 1934, p. 3.

12. Transcript of audio-tape interview with Paul Schroeder by Roberta Klugman, Aug. 15, 1980, p. 3, OTCHS.

13. *Fergus Falls Daily Journal*, Mar. 14, 1934, p. 9.

14. *Minnesota Emergency Relief Administration: Statistical Report No. 5: June 17, 1934*, [34], Reports, Emergency Relief Administration Papers.

15. Zimmerman interview, 4.

16. *New York Mills Herald*, Jan. 4, 1934, p. 4; *Fergus Falls Daily Journal*, Dec. 23, 1933, p. 3, Dec. 27, 1933, p. 7.

17. Minnesota, SERA, *Minnesota Work Relief History*, 14–15; *Fergus Falls Daily Journal*, Mar. 14, 1934, p. 9.

18. *Fergus Falls Weekly Journal*, Mar. 29, 1934, p. 4.

19. *Fergus Falls Weekly Journal*, Apr. 19, 1934, p. 1. See Doris Carothers, *Chronology of the Federal Emergency Relief Administration: May 12, 1933, to December 31, 1935*, Works Progress Administration, Division of Social Research, Research Monograph 6 (Washington, D.C.: Government Printing Office, 1937), 49–52, for the transition between the CWA and the FERA.

20. Minnesota, SERA, *Minnesota Work Relief History*, 13–17, 21; *Fergus Falls Weekly Journal*, Apr. 26, 1934, p. 9.

21. Minnesota, SERA, *Minnesota Work Relief History*, 23–25.

22. Here and below, W. L. Potter to All ERA Foremen, Mar. 18, 1935; Otter Tail County ERA, Works Division, "Instructions to Foremen," undated carbon; Otter Tail County Relief Administration, Works Division, "To All ERA Foremen and Timekeepers," undated carbon — all OTCHS '30s Project Papers.

23. Time Sheets, Projects 56-B2-24, 56-B7-25, 56-B1-32, 56-D3-38, OTCHS '30s Project Papers.

24. Minnesota, SERA, *Minnesota Work Relief History*, 49.

25. Minnesota, SERA, *Minnesota Work Relief History*, 90.

26. Minnesota, SERA, *Minnesota Work Relief History*, 186.

27. Minnesota, SERA, *Minnesota Work Relief History*, 165–67.

28. *Fergus Falls Weekly Journal*, July 12, 1934, p. 11; *New York Mills Herald*, Apr. 26, 1934, p. 1; *Fergus Falls Daily Journal*, May 2, 1934, p. 3, May 10, 1934, p. 3, July 19, 1934, p. 6.

29. Otter Tail County Commission, Proceedings, Jan. 1935, copy in OTCHS '30s Project Papers; *Battle Lake Review*, Nov. 1, 1934, p. 1.

30. *New York Mills Herald*, Apr. 19, 1934, p. 4.

31. *New York Mills Herald*, Apr. 26, 1934, p. 4.

32. *New York Mills Herald*, May 31, 1934, p. 2, June 7, 1934, p. 1.

33. *Fergus Falls Weekly Journal*, Mar. 14, 1935, p. 3.

34. *Fergus Falls Weekly Journal*, Jan. 17, 1935, p. 9.

35. Otter Tail County Commission, Proceedings, Jan. 1935, copy in OTCHS '30s Project Papers.

36. *Battle Lake Review*, Nov. 29, 1934, p. 1.

37. Otter Tail County Commission, Proceedings, Dec. 1934, copy in OTCHS '30s Project Papers.

38. Zimmerman interview, 6.

39. U.S., Public Works Administration, *America Builds: The Record of PWA* (Washington, D.C.: Government Printing Office, 1939), 7.

40. PWA, *America Builds*, 37-39; Schlesinger, *Coming of the New Deal*, 282-87.

41. PWA, *America Builds*, 8.

42. *New York Mills Herald*, Apr. 30, 1931, p. 1.

43. *New York Mills Herald*, July 20, 1933, p. 4.

44. *New York Mills Herald*, July 13, 1933, p. 5.

45. *New York Mills Herald*, Dec. 14, 1933, p. 1.

46. *New York Mills Herald*, Feb. 22, 1934, p. 1.

47. *New York Mills Herald*, June 14, 1934, p. 1, July 5, 1934, p. 1, July 19, 1934, p. 1, Aug. 16, 1934, p. 1.

48. *New York Mills Herald*, Nov. 29, 1934, p. 2.

49. *New York Mills Herald*, July 5, 1934, p. 1.

50. *Fergus Falls Weekly Journal*, Jan. 19, 1939, p. 1, Dec. 21, 1939, p. 9; Jane Thompson, ed., *1872-1972: Fergus Falls, Minnesota* (Fergus Falls: [Centennial Committee?], 1972), [32-42].

51. *New York Mills Herald*, Mar. 9, 1939, p. 2, notes in OTCHS '30s Project Papers.

52. *Fergus Falls Weekly Journal*, Apr. 13, 1939, p. 7.

53. *Fergus Falls Weekly Journal*, July 27, 1939, p. 1, Dec. 21, 1939, p. 9.

54. *Fergus Falls Weekly Journal*, Dec. 21, 1939, p. 9.

55. *Fergus Falls Weekly Journal*, Nov. 30, 1939, p. 3.

56. *Battle Lake Review*, July 26, 1934, p. 1.

57. *Fergus Falls Daily Journal*, Mar. 15, 1939, p. 3; Otter Tail County Commission, Proceedings, Oct. and Nov. 1938, notes in OTCHS '30s Project Papers.

58. *Fergus Falls Daily Journal*, Mar. 14, 1934, p. 9.

Chapter 5. WPA: "To Keep Body and Soul Together"

1. "Boondoggles," Relief, *Time*, Apr. 15, 1935, p. 14-16.

2. Leuchtenburg, *Franklin D. Roosevelt*, 124-30; Arthur W. Macmahon, John D. Millett, and Gladys Ogden, *The Administration of Federal Work Relief*, Studies in Administration, vol. 12 (Chicago: Published for the Committee on Public Administration of the Social Science Research Council by Public Administration Service, 1941), 17-66.

3. OP #165-71-463, OP #165-71-2277, A30, WPA Records, NA, microfilm 30.

4. Transcript of audio-tape interview with Jim Daly by Roberta Klugman, July 5, 1979, p. 1, OTCHS.

5. FWA, WPA, Application of the Schedule of Monthly Earnings to Counties and Metropolitan Districts, State of Minnesota, State Administrator's Order No. W-306, Oct.

14, 1939; WPA, Schedule of Hourly Wage Rates, Hours of Work, and Monthly Earnings, Form 405, for Otter Tail County, Sept. 1, 1938 — both Edward T. Barnard Papers, OTCHS.

6. WPA, Time Report for Personal Services — Work Projects: Form 502, June 25, 1937–Sept. 7, 1939, Barnard Papers. See Chapter 6, below, for a discussion of the project.

7. See Administrative field bulletins and Operations field letters, Administrative Files, Works Projects Administration Papers, MHS.

8. WPA, District 7, *Timekeepers Manual*, Bulletin 1, Aug. 28, 1936, Barnard Papers.

9. WPA, District 7, *Timekeepers Manual*, Bulletins 1–27, Aug. 28, 1936-June 30, 1937, Barnard Papers.

10. WPA, District 7, *Timekeepers Manual*, Bulletin 1, Aug. 28, 1936, Barnard Papers.

11. WPA, District 7, *Timekeepers Manual*, Bulletin 27, June 29, 1937, Barnard Papers.

12. *Fergus Falls Tribune*, Sept. 19, 1935, p. 1.

13. The statistics and project activities have been calculated from the list of approved applications, A30, WPA Records, NA, microfilm 30.

14. Leuchtenburg, *Franklin D. Roosevelt*, 244.

15. OP #165-71-21 — , OP #465-71-3-98, WPA Records, NA, microfilm 30.

16. A7, WPA Records, NA, microfilm 7.

17. A5234, WPA Records, NA, microfilm 8.

18. A5234, WPA Records, NA, microfilm 8.

19. OP #265-1-71-271, OP #165-1-71-343, WPA Records, NA, microfilm 30.

20. *Battle Lake Review*, June 27, 1935, p. 4.

21. *Fergus Falls Tribune*, Sept. 19, 1935, p. 1.

22. *Fergus Falls Weekly Journal*, Jan. 2, 1936, p. 1.

23. *Fergus Falls Weekly Journal*, June 18, 1936, p. 3, Oct. 22, 1936, p. 3.

24. *New York Mills Herald*, July 16, 1936, p. 1.

25. *Fergus Falls Weekly Journal*, July 23, 1936, p. 3.

26. "Resolution," Otter Tail County Commission, Proceedings, Oct. 14, 1936.

27. *Fergus Falls Weekly Journal*, July 2, 1936, p. 11, Oct. 22, 1936, p. 3, Oct. 29, 1936, p. 7, Nov. 19, 1936, p. 3; *Battle Lake Review*, Aug. 13, 1936, p. 1, Nov. 19, 1936, p. 1.

28. *Fergus Falls Weekly Journal*, Feb. 2, 1939, p. 1.

29. *New York Mills Herald*, Sept. 8, 1938, p. 3.

30. *New York Mills Herald*, Oct. 28, 1937, p. 2.

31. *New York Mills Herald*, Sept. 8, 1938, p. 3; *WPA Status Report*, Jan. 1, 1938, Department of Conservation, State of Minnesota, 3-4.

32. Analysis based on WPA records, A7, microfilm 7, A5234, microfilm 8, A30, microfilm 30, NA.

33. Quoted in *New York Mills Herald*, Aug. 10, 1939, p. 1. See also *Fergus Falls Weekly Journal*, Feb. 9, 1939, p. 1.

34. Transcript of interview of Adeline F. Karst with author, Feb. 16, 1985, p. 2, OTCHS '30s Project Papers.

35. Karst interview, 1-2.

36. Karst interview, 7.

37. Karst interview, 4.

38. Karst interview, 5.

39. *Fergus Falls Daily Journal*, Mar. 6, 1939, p. 4.

40. Analysis based on WPA records, A7, microfilm 7, A5234, microfilm 8, A30, microfilm 30, NA.

41. See William F. McDonald, *Federal Relief Administration and the Arts: The Origins and Administrative History of the Arts Projects of the Works Progress Administration* (Columbus: Ohio State University Press, 1969).

42. *New York Mills Herald*, Jan. 12, 1939, p. 1.

43. Clement Haupers, State Director of Federal Art Project, Minnesota, to E. T. Barnard, Apr. 13, 21, May 15, June 3, 13, 1936, photocopies; Barnard to Haupers, Apr. 17, 25, May 17, June 11, 1936, photocopies of carbons, Barnard Papers.

44. WPA, FAP, Form 10221, July 25, 1938, carbon (an oil by Arthur A. Allie of St. Paul was also received), WPA of Minnesota, FAP, Form 9950-D, Apr. 29, 1939, photocopy of carbon, Mar. 15, 1940, carbon, WPA Art Program, A608 DPS Form 13, May 29, July 2, Sept. 10, Nov. 28, 1940, carbons, E. T. Barnard to Clement Haupers, Nov. 8, 1938, carbon, Haupers to Barnard, Nov. 14, 1938 — all in Barnard Papers; *Fergus Falls Daily Journal*, July 30, 1938, p. 7; *Minneapolis City Directory*, 1939; *St. Paul City Directory*, 1939.

45. E. T. Barnard to Clement Haupers, Nov. 16, 1938, May 26, 1939, carbons, Barnard Papers.

46. "The Index of American Design in Minnesota," undated memo by Clement Haupers, Jeanne Taylor to E. T. Barnard, Dec. 24, 1937, Mar. 21, 1938, photocopies — all in Barnard Papers; *New York Mills Herald*, Feb. 4, 1937, p. 1.

47. *Fergus Falls Tribune*, Dec. 17, 1936, p. 1.

48. *Fergus Falls Weekly Journal*, Oct. 29, 1936, p. 7, Nov. 26, 1936, p. 7; *New York Mills Herald*, Jan. 21, 1937, p. 1.

49. *Fergus Falls Tribune*, Nov. 5, 1936, p. 1.

50. *New York Mills Herald*, Aug. 5, 1937, p. 1.

51. *New York Mills Herald*, July 6, 1939, p. 5; calculation based on U.S., *Census*, 1940, *Census of Business*, vol. 1, pt. 3, p. 340-41.

52. OP #465-71-2-321, OP #465-71-2-520, A30, WPA Records, NA, microfilm 30.

53. Transcript of interview with Henry Holmgren, Henning, n.d., p. 1, 2, OTCHS '30s Project Papers.

54. [Harvey D.] Smalley, [Sr.], to E. T. Barnard, Apr. 14, 1936, Barnard Papers.

55. E. T. Barnard to Bena Johnson, Sept. 22, 1938, carbon, Barnard Papers.

56. Alex Freedland to Mr. C. Goodroad, June 24, 1937, Inman Township records, typed copy in OTCHS '30s Project Papers.

57. J. B. Marek to Alex Freedland, no date, Inman Township records, typed copy in OTCHS '30s Project Papers.

58. Toso and Williams interview, 4.

59. Transcript of audio-tape interview with Russell Parta by Roberta Klugman and Jennie Mills, New York Mills, Sept. 4, 1980, p. 3, OTCHS '30s Project Papers; *Fergus Falls Weekly Journal*, Sept. 19, 1935, p. 4.

60. Transcript of audio-tape interview with Laura Dunlap by Marian Kohlmeyer, July 11, 1980, p. 2-3, 14, 16, 21, OTCHS '30s Project Papers.

61. Hartman interview, 6.

Chapter 6. A WPA PROJECT AND ITS
PEOPLE: "The Boys Down at the Courthouse"

1. Time Report for Personal Services — Work Projects, Feb. 25–Mar. 10, 1941. Correspondence and reports cited in notes for this chapter are in the Barnard Papers unless otherwise indicated.

2. *New York Mills Herald*, Oct. 28, 1937, p. 2.

3. [E. T. Barnard] to Theodore C. Blegen, Sept. 2, 1935, carbon.

4. E. T. Barnard to Theodore Blegen, Sept. 4, 1935, carbon.

5. A. C. Godward to Anton Thompson, Dec. 18, 1935; Willoughby M. Babcock to Thompson, Dec. 27, 1935.

6. A. C. Godward to Anton Thompson, Dec. 28, 1935.

7. Alma B. Kerr to Anton Thompson, Feb. 4, 1936.

8. E. T. Barnard to H. D. Smalley[,Sr.], Mar. 30, Apr. 8, 1936, carbons.

9. [H. D.] Smalley[,Sr.] to E. T. Barnard, Apr. 14, 1936.

10. E. T. Barnard to H. D. Smalley[,Sr.], Apr. 15, 1936, carbon.

11. Ralph D. Brown to E. T. Barnard, July 30, 1937; Willoughby M. Babcock and Richard Sackett, "Statement Regarding the Attached Mimeographed Subjects and the Use of Local Historical Projects," July 14, 1937, copy.

12. E. T. Barnard to Cecil Sherin, Apr. 3, 1937, photocopy of carbon; Barnard to Anton Thompson, Apr. 2, 1937, carbon.

13. Babcock and Sackett, "Statement."

14. Time Reports for Personal Services, June 25, 1937–Jan. 7, 1940; R[oy] A. Baker to Jacob Hodnefield, June 30, 1939, carbon.

15. Physical Progress Report for Clerical and Professional Type Projects, MWPA Form 223, Mar. 1939.

16. R[oy] A. Baker to Jacob Hodnefield, June 30, 1939, carbon.

17. E. T. Barnard to Beatrice Mertens, Aug. 16, 1937, carbon; Mertens to Barnard, Aug. 24, 1937.

18. Beatrice E. Mertens to E. T. Barnard, Sept. 10, 1937.

19. E. T. Barnard to Bena Johnson, Sept. 22, 1938, carbon; Time Reports for Personal Services, Sept. 17, 1938–Feb. 1, 1939.

20. Figures based on monthly Physical Progress Reports for Clerical and Professional Type Projects, MWPA Form 223, May 1937–Nov. 1939; memo, Nov. 3 or 4, 1942?, photocopy; Minnesota, Historical Records Survey, *Inventory of the County Archives of Minnesota: No. 56: Otter Tail County (Fergus Falls)* (St. Paul: The Minnesota Historical Records Survey Project, Nov. 1940, Mimeographed), copy in Reference Library, MHS; *New York Mills Herald*, Dec. 19, 1940, p. 8.

21. Time Reports for Personal Services, July 17, 1937–Jan. 7, 1940; Physical Progress Report for Clerical and Professional Type Projects, May 1939.

22. [Roy A. Baker] to Dorothy L. Stander, Dec. 7, 21, 1939, carbons; Jacob Hodnefield to Al. G. Muske, Dec. 27, 1939.

23. Time Report for Personal Services, Dec. 23, 1939–Jan. 7, 1940.

24. Richard R. Sackett for Jacob Hodnefield to Al[.] G. Muske, Apr. 10, 1940.

25. Richard R. Sackett to Mr. [Albert G.] Muske, Apr. 24, 1940; Jacob Hodnefield to Al. Muske, Aug. 14, 1940; *Fergus Falls Daily Journal*, Apr. 24, 1940, p. 11.

26. Jacob Hodnefield to Al. G. Muske, Aug. 2, 1940.

27. [Albert G. Muske] to [Jacob Hodnefield], Aug. 10, 1940, carbon.

28. Jacob Hodnefield to Al. Muske, Aug. 14, 1940.

29. Jacob Hodnefield to Albert Muske, Aug. 28, 1940.

30. Jacob Hodnefield to A. G. Muske, Oct. 2, 1940.

31. Jacob Hodnefield to Al Muske, Oct. 9, 1940.

32. Al. G. Muske to Merle Merwin, Dec. 13, 1940, carbon.

33. Jacob Hodnefield to Al. G. Muske, Dec. 19, 1940.

34. Minnesota Work Projects Administration, Local Worker's Daily and Weekly Service Reports for Albert G. Muske, Jan. 7–Feb. 28, 1941.

35. Al. G. Muske to M. Merwin, Jan. 15, 1941, carbon.

36. Jacob Hodnefield to Al Muske, Jan. 22, 1941.

37. [Albert G. Muske] to M. Merwin, Jan. 23, 24, 1941, carbons.

38. Jacob Hodnefield to Al Muske, Jan. 29, 1941.

39. Jacob Hodnefield to Albert Muske, Mar. 5, 1941.

40. Jacob Hodnefield to Albert Muske, Apr. 9, 1941.

41. Al. G. Muske to Mr. [Merle] Merwin, Apr. 14, 1941, carbon.

42. Jacob Hodnefield to Retained Field Workers, July 2, 1941, mimeograph.

43. Jacob Hodnefield to Albert Muske, July 23, 1941.

44. Helene Michell to A. O. [G.] Muske, Mar. 19, 1942.

45. Jacob Hodnefield to Albert Muske, Apr. 8, 1942. The story of Muske's subsequent life is not known to this author.

46. R[oy] A. Baker to Jacob Hodnefield, June 30, 1939, carbon; *Fergus Falls Daily Journal*, Aug. 20, 1943, p. 9.

47. R[oy] A. Baker to Jacob Hodnefield, June 30, 1939, carbon; Roy A. Baker, *History of Fergus Falls to January 1, 1893* ([Fergus Falls]: Otter Tail County Historical Society, 1935).

48. E. T. Barnard to Theodore C. Blegen, July 27, 1939, carbon; Time Reports for Personal Services, Feb. 8–July 7, 1939.

49. E. T. Barnard to Jacob Hodnefield, Aug. 9, 1939.

50. [Roy A. Baker] to Dorothy L. Stander, Sept. 25, 1939, carbon.

51. Dorothy L. Stander to Roy A. Baker, Sept. 26, 1939.

52. Time Reports for Personal Services, Feb. 8, 1939–Jan. 7, 1940; R[oy] A. Baker to Jacob Hodnefield, June 30, 1939, carbon.

53. [Roy A. Baker] to Dorothy L. Stander, Dec. 21, 1939, carbon; Jacob Hodnefield to Baker, Dec. 27, 1939.

54. R[oy] A. Baker to Jacob Hodnefield, Jan. 12, 1940, carbon.

55. [Roy A. Baker] to Dorothy L. Stander, June 17, 1940, carbon.

56. [Roy A. Baker] to Dorothy L. Stander, June 28, 1940, carbon.

57. [Roy A. Baker] to Dorothy L. Stander, June 28, 1940, carbon.

58. [Roy A. Baker] to Dorothy L. Stander, June 28, 1940, carbon.

59. E. T. Barnard to Arthur J. Lars[e]n, June 19, 1940, carbon.

60. Arthur J. Larsen to E. T. Barnard, June 28, 1940.

61. Dorothy L. Stander to E. T. Barnard, July 15, 1940.

62. E. T. Barnard to Dorothy Stander, July 17, 1940, carbon.

63. Works Progress Administration Project Proposal, WPA form 301, transmitted to Washington on Oct. 9, 1940; *Fergus Falls Daily Journal*, Dec. 2, 1940, p. 5; Physical Progress Report for Clerical and Professional Type Projects, Feb. 1941.

64. Roy A. Baker to S. P. Roach, Apr. 25, 1941, carbon.

65. E. T. Barnard to Dorothy L. Stander, Apr. 17, 1941, carbon; Time Report for Personal Services, June 3–16, 1941.

66. Richard R. Sackett to Roy A. Baker, Aug. 27, 1941; [Roy A. Baker] to Edward T. [F.] Landin, Aug. 29, 1941.

67. R[oy] A. Baker to Richard R. Sackett, Sept. 19, 1941, carbon.
68. R[oy] A. Baker to Edward F. Landin, Sept. 12, 1941, carbon.
69. R[oy] A. Baker to Edward T. [F.] Landin, Oct. 24, 1941, carbon.
70. E. T. Barnard to Ethel Gronner, Dec. 17, 1941, carbon.

Chapter 7. CCC AND NYA: "Youth Must Rebuild What Has Been Destroyed"

1. Aubrey Williams, "A Crisis for Our Youth: A Task for the Nation," in *The New Deal*, ed. Carl N. Degler (Chicago: Quadrangle Books, New York Times Books, 1970), 112.
2. John A. Salmond, *The Civilian Conservation Corps, 1933–1942: A New Deal Case Study* (Durham, N.C.: Duke University Press, 1967), 4.
3. Salmond, *Civilian Conservation Corps*, 7–8.
4. Roosevelt quoted in Frank Freidel, *Franklin D. Roosevelt: Launching the New Deal*, vol. 4 of *Franklin D. Roosevelt* (Boston: Little, Brown, 1973), 260.
5. Salmond, *Civilian Conservation Corps*, 29–30, 84–85, 121.
6. Salmond, *Civilian Conservation Corps*, 30–31.
7. Salmond, *Civilian Conservation Corps*, 37, 56, 63, 84.
8. Salmond, *Civilian Conservation Corps*, 200.
9. *Fergus Falls Weekly Journal*, Apr. 27, 1933, p. 11.
10. *Fergus Falls Daily Journal*, Oct. 3, 1933, p. 7.
11. *Fergus Falls Weekly Journal*, Apr. 19, 1934, p. 4, June 28, 1934, p. 1, July 26, 1934, p. 4, Jan. 10, 1935, p. 1, Apr. 25, 1935, p. 1, June 27, 1935, p. 11, Oct. 10, 1935, p. 2. Total number of Otter Tail County enrollees computed from C. N. Alleger, *Civilian Conservation Corps: Minnesota District* (N.p.: The Author, [1935?]).
12. *Fergus Falls Weekly Journal*, Apr. 16, 1936, p. 1, May 21, 1936, p. 1, July 9, 1936, p. 1, Oct. 15, 1936, p. 1.
13. *Fergus Falls Weekly Journal*, July 13, 1939, p. 7, Oct. 12, 1939, p. 9. Some of the Otter Tail enrollees listed addresses as rural mail routes originating in towns that were close to the Otter Tail County border.
14. Harold R. Davis, "The Civilian Conservation Corps," transcript of slide presentation given at Park Region History Conference, Fergus Falls Community College, Oct. 25, 1980, p. 1; transcript of audio-tape interview with Leonard Hovland by Roberta Klugman, Norwegian Grove Township, Aug. 10, 1979, p. 1, 4, 15; transcript of audio-tape interview with Clinton Thun and Alex Klimek by Roberta Klugman, Moorhead, Aug. 16, 1979, p. 1 — all in OTCHS '30s Project Papers.
15. Hovland interview, 1.
16. Thun and Klimek interview, 3.
17. Hovland interview, 1.
18. Thun and Klimek interview, 2; Alleger, *Civilian Conservation Corps*, 57, 74.
19. Salmond, *Civilian Conservation Corps*, 135–36.
20. Davis, "Civilian Conservation Corps," 2.
21. Alleger, *Civilian Conservation Corps*, 74; Davis, "Civilian Conservation Corps," 3.
22. Davis, "Civilian Conservation Corps," 3, 4, 5.
23. Hovland interview, 1, 2.
24. Thun and Klimek interview, 2–3.

25. Thun and Klimek interview, 6.
26. Davis, "Civilian Conservation Corps," 3, 7; Thun and Klimek interview, 4.
27. Davis, "Civilian Conservation Corps," 3.
28. Hovland interview, 18.
29. Hovland interview, 1, 2, 18.
30. Davis, "Civilian Conservation Corps," 3.
31. Thun and Klimek interview, 4.
32. Davis, "Civilian Conservation Corps," 5; Thun and Klimek interview, 5.
33. Hovland interview, 3.
34. Thun and Klimek interview, 3.
35. Hovland interview, 3.
36. Thun and Klimek interview, 3.
37. Hovland interview, 4.
38. Fergus Falls, Council Minutes, July 6, 1934, notes in OTCHS '30s Project Papers.
39. Fergus Falls, Council Minutes, July 16, 1934, notes in OTCHS '30s Project Papers; *Fergus Falls Weekly Journal*, July 19, 1934, p. 1.
40. *Fergus Falls Weekly Journal*, Aug. 2, 1934, p. 3, Aug. 9, 1934, p. 1.
41. *Fergus Falls Weekly Journal*, Aug. 16, 1934, p. 1.
42. Fergus Falls, Council Minutes, Aug. 20, 1934, notes in OTCHS '30s Project Papers.
43. *New York Mills Herald*, Sept. 20, 1934, p. 1.
44. *Fergus Falls Weekly Journal*, Jan. 31, 1935, p. 1.
45. Fergus Falls, Council Minutes, Feb. 4, 1935, notes in OTCHS '30s Project Papers.
46. *Fergus Falls Weekly Journal*, Feb. 7, 1935, p. 3.
47. CCC Camp Work Plan, 1.
48. *Fergus Falls Daily Journal*, June 5, 1941, p. 5, July 10, 1941, p. 3.
49. *Fergus Falls Daily Journal*, July 15, 1941, p. 9, July 25, 1941, p. 7.
50. CCC Camp Work Plan, 16.
51. *Fergus Falls Daily Journal*, Apr. 24, 1941, p. 3.
52. *Fergus Falls Daily Journal*, Aug. 21, 1941, p. 9.
53. CCC Camp Work Plan, 20–23, 11.
54. CCC Camp Work Plan, 10.
55. Transcript of audio-tape interview with Harry Burau by Roberta Klugman, n.d., p. 2, OTCHS '30s Project Papers.
56. "Critics Keep Their Hands Off the CCC," *Literary Digest*, Aug. 18, 1934, Topics of the Day sec., p. 8.
57. U.S., National Youth Administration, *Final Report of the National Youth Administration: Fiscal Years 1936–1943*, Federal Security Agency, War Manpower Commission (Washington, D.C.: Government Printing Office, 1944), 23–24. For the history of the first years of the NYA, see Betty Lindley and Ernest K. Lindley, *A New Deal for Youth: The Story of the National Youth Administration* (New York: Viking Press, 1938).
58. U.S., NYA, *Final Report*, 57.
59. U.S., NYA, *Final Report*, 113, 135–46, 170–71, 177.
60. U.S., NYA, *Final Report*, 234, 242; Fergus Falls, Council Minutes, Jan. 6, 1936, notes in OTCHS '30s Project Papers.
61. Williams, "Crisis for Our Youth," in *New Deal*, ed. Degler, 119.
62. See, for example, *Fergus Falls Weekly Journal*, Oct. 12, 1939, p. 9, for list of CCC enrollees and Nov. 26, 1936, p. 10, for brief notice given NYA.
63. Fergus Falls, Council Minutes, Jan. 6, 1936, notes in OTCHS '30s Project Papers.
64. Fergus Falls, Council Minutes, Jan. 20, 1936, Apr. 17, 1939, June 26, 1939, Nov. 6, 1939, notes in OTCHS '30s Project Papers.

65. Gladys Bauman, "Fergus Falls Playgrounds," 1937 Report, carbon typescript, 11 unnumbered pages, OTCHS; Fergus Falls, Council Minutes, Jan. 20, 1936, notes in OTCHS '30s Project Papers.

66. E. T. Barnard to Arthur J. Larson [Larsen], June 19, 1940, carbon, WPA Records, Barnard Papers; [Barnard] to Henry Hoff, July 1, 1940, photocopy of carbon, OTCHS '30s Project Papers; *Fergus Falls Daily Journal*, July 1, 1940, p. 3.

67. OTCHS, "Expense Account for the Tordenskjold Meeting, Sunday, June 30, 1940," photocopy of carbon, OTCHS '30s Project Papers.

68. Gerry M. Houg to Anton Thompson, Feb. 7, 1941, E. T. Barnard to Haug [Houg], Feb. 17, 20, 1941, Houg to Barnard, Feb. 18, 1941, [Barnard] to Arthur J. Larsen, May 19, 1941 — all photocopies of carbons, OTCHS '30s Project Papers; *Fergus Falls Daily Journal*, June 30, 1941, p. 3. See also Richard S. Prosser, *Rails to the North Star* (Minneapolis: Dillon Press, 1966), 154.

69. Interview with Lorna Anderson Olson by author, Mar. 15, 1985, p. 1, 2, notes in OTCHS '30s Project Papers.

Chapter 8. FARM PROGRAMS: "A Good Thing for the Farmers"

1. Van L. Perkins, *Crisis in Agriculture: The Agricultural Adjustment Act and the New Deal, 1933*, University of California Publications in History, vol. 81 (Berkeley and Los Angeles: University of California Press, 1969), 21–23; Saloutos, *American Farmer*, 20–23.

2. Perkins, *Crisis in Agriculture*, 25–26; Saloutos, *American Farmer*, 28–29.

3. Wallace quoted in Perkins, *Crisis in Agriculture*, 37.

4. Richard S. Kirkendall, "The New Deal and Agriculture," in *The New Deal: The National Level*, ed. Braeman, Bremner, and Brody, vol. 1 of *The New Deal*, 88; Perkins, *Crisis in Agriculture*, 41–46; Saloutos, *American Farmer*, 47–48.

5. Perkins, *Crisis in Agriculture*, 97–98; *New York Mills Herald*, July 20, 1933, p. 1.

6. *New York Mills Herald*, Aug. 3, 1933, p. 1, July 20, 1933, p. 1, Aug. 24, 1933, p. 1.

7. Quoted in *New York Mills Herald*, Aug. 17, 1933, p. 1.

8. *Annual Report East*, 1933, p. 7; *Annual Report West*, 1933, p. 19; *Fergus Falls Weekly Journal*, Oct. 19, 1933, p. 1.

9. *Battle Lake Review*, June 6, 1935, p. 1.

10. *Fergus Falls Daily Journal*, Feb. 11, 1936, p. 2.

11. *Annual Report West*, 1934, p. 6.

12. Edwin G. Nourse, Joseph S. Davis, and John D. Black, *Three Years of the Agricultural Adjustment Administration*, Institute of Economics, Publication no. 73 (Washington, D.C.: Brookings Institute, 1937), 102–3.

13. Nourse, Davis, and Black, *Three Years*, 103–4; *New York Mills Herald*, Nov. 9, 1933, p. 1, Dec. 28, 1933, p. 4, Feb. 1, 1934, p. 1, Feb. 8, 1934, p. 1, Jan. 3, 1935, p. 1.

14. *New York Mills Herald*, Jan. 4, 1934, p. 3.

15. *New York Mills Herald*, Jan. 18, 1934, p. 1, Feb. 8, 1934, p. 4, Mar. 22, 1934, p. 1.

16. *Annual Report East*, 1935, p. 22–23, 25–26; *Annual Report West*, 1934, p. 7, 8; *Annual Report West*, 1935, p. 6, 27, 28. See also *New York Mills Herald*, Dec. 14, 1933, p. 1, Jan. 11, 1934, p. 1.

17. *Annual Report East*, 1934, p. 7; *Annual Report East*, 1935, p. 13; *Annual Report West*, 1934, p. 7–8, 18; *Annual Report West*, 1935, p. 3, 6, 7.

18. Corn-Hog Reduction Contract, 1934, Hans Ronnevik Papers, OTCHS.

19. Corn-Hog Reduction Contract, 1935, Ronnevik Papers.

20. Saloutos, *American Farmer*, 78–83.

21. *Battle Lake Review*, July 11, 1935, p. 1.

22. Burau interview, 19.

23. Toso and Williams interview, 3.

24. *Annual Report East*, 1934, p. 6–7; *Annual Report West*, 1934, p. 3, 9; *Fergus Falls Weekly Journal*, June 7, 1934, p. 3.

25. *Annual Report West*, 1934, p. 9.

26. Wayne D. Rasmussen, Gladys L. Baker, and James S. Ward, *A Short History of Agricultural Adjustment, 1933–75*, Agriculture Information Bulletin no. 391 (Washington, D.C.: U.S. Department of Agriculture, Economic Research Service, 1976), 4.

27. Rasmussen, Baker, and Ward, *Short History*, 4–5; Saloutos, *American Farmer*, 237–39.

28. *Annual Report West*, 1937, p. 15.

29. *New York Mills Herald*, Aug. 5, 1937, p. 1, Jan. 21, 1937, p. 1.

30. *New York Mills Herald*, Apr. 7, 1938, p. 3.

31. *Annual Report West*, 1937, p. 15.

32. *Annual Report West*, 1937, p. 12; *Fergus Falls Weekly Journal*, Sept. 7, 1939, p. 2.

33. Farm Record Book, 1938, Ronnevik Papers.

34. Saloutos, *American Farmer*, 242–44; Mitchell, *Depression Decade*, 205–7.

35. *Fergus Falls Weekly Journal*, Feb. 9, 1939, p. 3.

36. *Annual Report West*, 1939, p. 5.

37. See, for example, *Fergus Falls Daily Journal*, July 14, 1938, p. 1.

38. *New York Mills Herald*, Aug. 18, 1938, p. 1.

39. *New York Mills Herald*, Aug. 10, 1939, p. 1, Nov. 30, 1939, p. 1.

40. Rasmussen, Baker, and Ward, *Short History*, 5; *New York Mills Herald*, July 3, 1938, p. 2; Murray R. Benedict, *Farm Policies of the United States, 1790–1950: A Study of Their Origins and Development* (New York: Twentieth Century Fund, 1953), 380–81.

41. *New York Mills Herald*, Feb. 9, 1939, p. 3.

42. *New York Mills Herald*, Aug. 24, 1939, p. 1, Aug. 1, 1940, p. 1.

43. *New York Mills Herald*, Jan. 15, 1942, p. 1.

44. Wilson quoted in W. Gifford Hoag, *The Farm Credit System . . . A History of Financial Self-Help* (Danville, Ill.: Interstate Printers & Publishers, 1976?), 213–14.

45. Hoag, *Farm Credit System*, 213–16, 219.

46. *Fergus Falls Weekly Journal*, Feb. 23, 1928, p. 6; Minnesota, *Legislative Manual*, 1925, p. 243.

47. Hoag, *Farm Credit System*, 232–33; Benedict, *Farm Policies*, 280–83.

48. Hoag, *Farm Credit System*, 233–34.

49. Hoag, *Farm Credit System*, 234–37.

50. Hoag, *Farm Credit System*, 237–38.

51. *Fergus Falls Weekly Journal*, Mar. 2, 1933, p. 1.

52. *Fergus Falls Weekly Journal*, Mar. 2, 1933, p. 3, Mar. 16, 1933, p. 1, Mar. 23, 1933, p. 9.

53. *New York Mills Herald*, Sept. 26, 1933, p. 1; *Fergus Falls Weekly Journal*, Mar. 2, 1933, p. 3.

54. *Annual Report East*, 1933, p. 7; *Annual Report West*, 1934, p. 3.

55. *New York Mills Herald*, Nov. 23, 1933, p. 1.

56. *Annual Report East*, 1934, p. 4.

57. *New York Mills Herald*, Apr. 12, 1934, p. 4, July 5, 1934, p. 1.

58. *Battle Lake Review*, June 21, 1934, p. 1.
59. *New York Mills Herald*, July 5, 1934, p. 1.
60. *New York Mills Herald*, Mar. 7, 1935, p. 1.
61. *New York Mills Herald*, Mar. 7, 1935, p. 1.
62. Transcript of audio-tape interview with Otto and Emma Richter by Roberta Klugman and Connie Nelson, Hobart Township, Aug. 16, 1979, p. 1–2, 4, OTCHS '30s Project Papers.
63. Transcript of audio-tape interview with Verner A. Anderson, Melvin J. Reynolds, and Anna Reynolds by Roberta Klugman, Otto Township, July 15, 1980, p. 7, 8, OTCHS '30s Project Papers.
64. Transcript of audio-tape interview with Everett Johnson by Roberta Klugman and Marilyn Stromberg, Pelican Rapids, Oct. 16, 1980, p. 1, 7, 10, OTCHS '30s Project Papers.
65. Hegge interview, 1.
66. *Fergus Falls Weekly Journal*, Feb. 16, 1939, p. 7.
67. *Annual Report East*, 1934, p. 4; *Annual Report East*, 1935, p. 9–10; *Annual Report West*, 1934, p. 4; *Annual Report West*, 1935, p. 3, 15.
68. *Annual Report West*, 1937, p. 38.
69. *New York Mills Herald*, Feb. 22, 1934, p. 1.
70. *Fergus Falls Weekly Journal*, July 23, 1936, p. 3.
71. *New York Mills Herald*, July 18, 1940, p. 1; Minnesota, *Legislative Manual*, 1939, p. 166.
72. *New York Mills Herald*, July 18, 1940, p. 1.
73. *New York Mills Herald*, Jan. 22, 1942, p. 3.
74. *New York Mills Herald*, July 18, 1940, p. 1.
75. Saloutos, *American Farmer*, 157–58, 160–63, 176–78.
76. *Fergus Falls Daily Journal*, Mar. 2, 1937, p. 1; *New York Mills Herald*, Feb. 29, 1940, p. 4.
77. Burau interview, 30–31.
78. *New York Mills Herald*, May 30, 1935, p. 3.
79. Ronnevik interview, 1–3, 6.
80. Ronnevik interview, 3.
81. Ronnevik interview, 4, 9–10.
82. Ronnevik interview, 5, 1; Hog-Corn Reduction Contracts, 1934, 1935, Ronnevik Papers.
83. Ronnevik interview, 7, 11–12; Farm Record Books, 1937, 1938, and 1939, Ronnevik Papers.
84. Farm Record Books, 1937, 1938, and 1939, Ronnevik Papers.
85. Farm Record Books, 1937, 1938, and 1939, Ronnevik Papers.
86. Mitchell, *Depression Decade*, 448.
87. Hintsala interview, 7.

Chapter 9. REA: "The Same as Getting God There"

1. Roosevelt, *The Public Papers and Addresses of Franklin D. Roosevelt* (New York: Random House, 1938), 1:733.

2. Arthur M. Schlesinger, Jr., *The Politics of Upheaval*, vol. 3 of *The Age of Roosevelt* (Boston: Houghton Mifflin Co., 1960), 379-80.

3. Neff quoted in Otter Tail Power Company, "R.E.A. Relationships," photocopy of typescript, Oct. 4, 1961, p. 3, OTCHS '30s Project Papers.

4. E. A. Stewart, J. M. Larson, and J. Romness, *The Red Wing Project on Utilization of Electricity in Agriculture* (St. Paul: University of Minnesota, Agricultural Experiment Station, 1928?), 1-4; Otter Tail Power Co., "R.E.A. Relationships," 3-5.

5. Burau interview, 33.

6. Caroline Bale, comp., *Otter Tail Power Company Historical Data: Generating Plants, Cities and Villages Served Retail and Wholesale, Also Large Power Users Listed by Year as Connected* (Fergus Falls: Otter Tail Power Co.?, 1956?), 1, 7-19, 63, 65, copy in OTCHS '30s Project Papers.

7. Otter Tail Power Co., "R.E.A. Relationships," 11-12.

8. "Acres of Crops Planted or to be Planted for Harvest in 1929, Etc.," Farm Census Township Summaries, Minnesota Department of Agriculture, Minnesota State Archives, MHS. Aurdal, Buse, Effington, and Leaf Lake townships each had twenty or more farmers with electric power or lights; Blowers, Butler, Candor, Homestead, and Leaf Mountain townships had none.

9. Hintgen interview, 1, 8.

10. Hintgen interview, 7-8.

11. Hintgen interview, 7.

12. Marquis Childs, *The Farmer Takes a Hand: The Electric Power Revolution in Rural America* (Garden City, N.Y.: Doubleday & Co., 1953), 38-72; D. Clayton Brown, *Electricity for Rural America: The Fight for the REA*, Contributions in Economics and Economic History, no. 29, ed. Robert Sabel (Westport, Conn.: Greenwood Press, 1980), 35-67.

13. *Lake Region Co-op. Electrical Association, Pelican Rapids, Minnesota* (Pelican Rapids?: Lake Region Co-op. Electrical Association, 1962?), 7-8.

14. *Lake Region Co-op. Electrical Association*, 15-16; *Pelican Rapids Press*, Dec. 7, 1950, p. 1; Minutes, Pelican River Electric Light and Power Co., Mar. 7, 1929, photocopy in OTCHS '30s Project Papers.

15. Minutes, Pelican River Electric Light and Power Co., Mar. 7, July 30, 1929, J. H[oward] Hay to Albert R. Knutson, Jan. 16, 1929, O. A. Anderson to Hay, Dec. 24, 1928 — all photocopies, OTCHS '30s Project Papers.

16. Transcript of audio-tape interview with Chester Rosengren by Roberta Klugman, Fergus Falls, July 26, 1979, p. 1, OTCHS '30s Project Papers.

17. *Annual Report West*, 1936, p. 15.

18. *Fergus Falls Weekly Journal*, Jan. 2, 1936, p. 3; *Annual Report West*, 1936, p. 15.

19. *Lake Region Co-op. Electrical Association*, 9; "Articles of Incorporation of the Lake Region Cooperative Electrical Association of Fergus Falls, Minnesota," Dec. 27, 1935, photocopy of typescript, OTCHS '30s Project Papers; *Annual Report West*, 1936, p. 5.

20. *Annual Report West*, 1935, p. 24.

21. *Annual Report West*, 1936, p. 16.

22. *Lake Region Co-op. Electrical Association*, 12; *Annual Report West*, 1936, p. 16.

23. Arnold J. Christopherson to Morris Llewellyn Cooke, April 6, July 15, 1936, Albert R. Knutson to Henrik Shipstead, June 15, 1937 — all photocopies of carbons, OTCHS '30s Project Papers; *Annual Report West*, 1936, p. 37.

24. Albert R. Knutson to Henrik Shipstead, June 15, 1937, photocopy of carbon, OTCHS '30s Project Papers.

25. "Information Desired in Application for Rural Electrification Loan," photocopy of form accompanying Arnold J. Christopherson to Morris Llewellyn Cooke, July 15, 1936, OTCHS '30s Project Papers.

26. C[.] S[.] Kennedy to Lake Region Cooperative Electrical Association, June 12, 1936, photocopy, OTCHS '30s Project Papers.

27. Albert R. Knutson to Henrik Shipstead, June 15, 1937, Knutson to H. Zinder, Oct. 6, 1936, photocopies of carbons, H. Zinder to Knutson, Sept. 22, 1936, photocopy, OTCHS '30s Project Papers.

28. Albert R. Knutson to H. Zinder, Oct. 6, Dec. 19, 1936, photocopies of carbons, Zinder to Knutson, Oct. 20, 1936, photocopy, OTCHS '30s Project Papers.

29. Albert R. Knutson to Henrick [sic] Shipstead, Feb. 13, 1937, photocopy of carbon, OTCHS '30s Project Papers. For details of the rate problem, see E. J. Bestick to Knudson [sic], Aug. 11, photocopy of copy, Knutson to Bestik [sic], Oct. 27, photocopy of carbon, H. Zinder to Knutson, Aug. 24, Sept. 22, Oct. 20, Nov. 19, Dec. 9, photocopies, Knutson to Zinder, Sept. 3, Oct. 10, 21, Nov. 13, 27, Dec. 19, photocopies of carbons — all 1936, OTCHS '30s Project Papers.

30. Rosengren interview, 10.

31. Lake Region Co-op. Electrical Association, 3.

32. Albert R. Knutson to Henrick [sic] Shipstead, Feb. 13, 1937, photocopy of carbon, OTCHS '30s Project Papers.

33. Here and below, Albert R. Knutson to Henrik Shipstead, June 15, 1937, photocopy of carbon, OTCHS '30s Project Papers.

34. Louis C. Stephens to Albert R. Knutson, June 18, 1937, photocopy, OTCHS '30s Project Papers.

35. R[ichard] T. Buckler to Albert R. Knutson, July 13, 1937, photocopy, OTCHS '30s Project Papers.

36. Lake Region Co-op. Electrical Association, 13.

37. Annual Report West, 1937, p. 31.

38. Annual Report West, 1937, p. 31.

39. Rosengren interview, 2.

40. Transcript of audio-tape interview with Jeff Tikkanen, Emma Tikkanen, and Arnold Virnala by Roberta Klugman and Einar Saarela, New York Mills, n.d., p. 7, OTCHS '30s Project Papers.

41. Transcript of audio-tape interview with Homer and Helen Sem by Roberta Klugman and Jeffrey A. Hess, Amor Township, Oct. 2, 1980, p. 11, 12, OTCHS '30s Project Papers.

42. Parta interview, 9.

43. Toso and Williams interview, 6, 7.

44. Pelican Rapids Press, Mar. 10, 1938, p. 1; Minnesota Electric Farmer (Perham), Oct. 1938, p. 12, copy in OTCHS '30s Project Papers; St. Paul City Directory, 1938.

45. Fergus Falls Weekly Journal, Oct. 12, 1939, p. 2.

46. Minnesota Electric Farmer, July 1938, p. 5; Annual Report West, 1938, p. 55–56.

47. Fergus Falls Weekly Journal, Oct. 12, 1939, p. 2.

48. Fergus Falls Daily Journal, Aug. 27, 1938, p. 2.

49. Fergus Falls Weekly Journal, Oct. 12, 1939, p. 2.

50. Annual Report East, 1940, p. 40.

51. Hovland interview, 9.

52. Tikkanen and Virnala interview, 10.

53. Tikkanen and Virnala interview, 4.

54. Transcript of audio-tape interview with Selma and Calmer Kopperud by Roberta Klugman, Norwegian Grove Township, Aug. 10, 1979, p. 3, OTCHS '30s Project Papers.

55. Sem interview, 12.

56. Richter interview, 8; Tikkanen and Virnala interview, 10.

57. Rosengren interview, 8.

Chapter 10. BANKING AND BUSINESS: "You People Must Have Faith"

1. For the most comprehensive studies of the New Deal and the banking crisis and reform, see Helen Burns, *American Banking Community*, and Kennedy, *Banking Crisis of 1933*. Conditions in Minnesota, North Dakota, South Dakota, and Montana are discussed in Curtis L. Mosher, *The Causes of Banking Failure in the Northwestern States* (Minneapolis: Federal Reserve Bank, 1930).

2. For a concise review of the banking crisis, see Mitchell, *Depression Decade*, 120–33.

3. Roosevelt, *Public Papers and Addresses*, 2:65; Freidel, *Roosevelt: Launching the New Deal*, 231; Leuchtenburg, *Franklin D. Roosevelt*, 44–45.

4. *Fergus Falls Tribune*, Mar. 9, 1933, p. 1.

5. *Fergus Falls Daily Journal*, Nov. 21, 1927, p. 5.

6. Information drawn from *Fergus Falls Weekly Journal*, which carried a column headed "Condition of Closed Banks."

7. Mason, ed., *History of Otter Tail County*, 1:310, 311.

8. *Fergus Falls Weekly Journal*, Dec. 1, 1927, p. 2.

9. *Fergus Falls Weekly Journal*, Dec. 1, 1927, p. 2.

10. *Fergus Falls Daily Journal*, Nov. 29, 1927, p. 3.

11. *Fergus Falls Daily Journal*, Nov. 29, 1927, p. 3; *Fergus Falls Weekly Journal*, Dec. 22, 1927, p. 6.

12. *Fergus Falls Weekly Journal*, Dec. 22, 1927, p. 6.

13. *Fergus Falls Daily Journal*, Nov. 14, 1928, p. 4, Nov. 15, 1928, p. 3.

14. *Fergus Falls Daily Journal*, Nov. 15, 1928, p. 3.

15. *Fergus Falls Daily Journal*, Nov. 15, 1928, p. 3.

16. *Fergus Falls Daily Journal*, Mar. 20, 1933, p. 3.

17. *Fergus Falls Daily Journal*, Dec. 2, 1931, p. 2, Dec. 3, 1931, p. 2; *Fergus Falls Weekly Journal*, July 25, 1935, p. 1, Oct. 12, 1939, p. 1.

18. Zimmerman interview, 5.

19. Zimmerman interview, 5.

20. Mason, ed., *History of Otter Tail County*, 1:318; *Polk's Bankers Encyclopedia*, 1925, p. 1161, 1930, p. 1204.

21. *Fergus Falls Weekly Journal*, Aug. 18, 1927, p. 7.

22. *Fergus Falls Weekly Journal*, Jan. 12, 1928, p. 2, Feb. 18, 1932, p. 3.

23. *Fergus Falls Weekly Journal*, Feb. 18, 1932, p. 3.

24. Transcript of audio-tape interview with Clyde Thorstenson by Edith Trygstad, July 19, 1979, p. 1–2, 3, OTCHS '30s Project Papers.

25. Thorstenson interview, 3.

26. Thorstenson interview, 3; *Polk's Bankers Encyclopedia*, 1940, p. 947.

27. Zimmerman interview, 5.

28. Hintgen interview, 5.

29. *New York Mills Herald*, Oct. 15, 1936, p. 2.

30. Thorstenson interview, 8.
31. *New York Mills Herald*, Sept. 6, 1934, p. 1.
32. *Battle Lake Review*, Aug. 29, 1935, p. 5.
33. Quoted in Schlesinger, *Coming of the New Deal*, 87–95 (Sachs's italics).
34. Leuchtenburg, *Franklin D. Roosevelt*, 57–58, 64–67.
35. Leuchtenburg, *Franklin D. Roosevelt*, 64–67; *Fergus Falls Tribune*, Aug. 10, 1933, p. 1.
36. *New York Mills Herald*, Sept. 14, 1933, p. 5.
37. *Fergus Falls Daily Journal*, Nov. 9, 1933, p. 9.
38. *New York Mills Herald*, Dec. 21, 1933, p. 5.
39. *New York Mills Herald*, Sept. 7, 1933, p. 1, Nov. 30, 1933, p. 3.
40. *Fergus Falls Daily Journal*, Nov. 3, 1933, p. 2, reprinted from *Minneapolis Journal*, Nov. 1, 1933, p. 15, 17.
41. Hintgen interview, 9.
42. Hartman interview, 8.
43. Hartman interview, 7.
44. Hintgen interview, 1–3.
45. Hintgen interview, 4.
46. *Battle Lake Review*, Aug. 23, 1934, p. 1, Nov. 11, 1934, p. 1, Apr. 17, 1947, p. 1.
47. *Battle Lake Review*, Sept. 13, 1934, p. 1, Apr. 4, 1935, p. 1, Apr. 11, 1935, p. 1.
48. Thomas C. Wright, *Otter Tail Power Company: From Its Origin Through 1954* (Fergus Falls: The Company, 1955), 43, 44, 45.
49. Bale, *Otter Tail Power Company*, 7–19, 51, 83; Wright, *Otter Tail Power Company*, 32–34; *Fergus Falls Daily Journal*, May 2, 1966, p. 1, 2.
50. Bale, *Otter Tail Power Company*, 63, 65, 67.
51. Bale, *Otter Tail Power Company*, 51; Wright, *Otter Tail Power Company*, 51–52.
52. Wright, *Otter Tail Power Company*, 45, 46.
53. Transcript of audio-tape interview with Fenwick Fetvedt by author, Jan. 16, 1985, p. 1–2, 3, OTCHS '30s Project Papers; Fenwick Fetvedt, "Life with Otter Tail Power," *Otter Tail Record* (Otter Tail County Historical Society) 6 (Spring 1985): 1–3.
54. Wright, *Otter Tail Power Company*, 59.
55. Bale, *Otter Tail Power Company*, 69.
56. Wright, *Otter Tail Power Company*, 53.
57. Wright, *Otter Tail Power Company*, 55.
58. Fetvedt interview, 2, 6.
59. Wright, *Otter Tail Power Company*, 73–74.
60. Otter Tail Power Company, "R.E.A. Relationships," 12.
61. Wright, *Otter Tail Power Company*, 74.
62. Bale, *Otter Tail Power Company*, 22; Wright, *Otter Tail Power Company*, 57.
63. Bale, *Otter Tail Power Company*, 22; Wright, *Otter Tail Power Company*, 57–58.
64. Wright, *Otter Tail Power Company*, 76.

Chapter 11. CONCLUSION

1. Walker quoted in Patterson, *New Deal and the States*, 105.
2. Patterson, *New Deal and the States*, 106, 111.
3. Thun and Klimek interview, 3; Zimmerman interview, 3.

4. Farms in the western half of Otter Tail County were considerably larger than those in the eastern half. The selling of cattle in 1987 caused a 10 percent reduction in the county's dairy herds. Dairying was prohibited on the sellers' farms for five years following the time of the sale. Otter Tail County Extension, "1987 Comprehensive Situational Statement," copy in OTCHS; telephone conversation with Kenneth R. Rose, Otter Tail County Extension Agent, by Pamela Brunfelt, OTCHS, April 21, 1988.

BIBLIOGRAPHIC ESSAY

Rather than relist the information that is available in the complete notes, I have chosen to discuss those sources that were most useful to me in this effort to probe the New Deal at the grass roots.

Oral History Interviews

In the preface to his *The American Farmer and the New Deal*, Theodore Saloutos lamented the fact that few farmers left diaries and "thus materials needed to bring out the human aspects have not been readily available." He went on to raise questions about oral history as a "trustworthy" source, "especially when the information has been gathered by persons untrained for the assignment and insufficiently knowledgeable in the field to ask the right kinds of questions" (p. xii). Saloutos made an extremely important point. The success of an oral interview depends upon the knowledge and skill of the interviewer. Asking the right questions in the proper way is indeed critical. Over the last ten years I have logged hundreds of hours conducting oral history interviews and have researched over a hundred interviews that others have generated. One of the great frustrations is discovering a crucial interview in which the wrong questions were asked or in which the questions were asked in such a manner as to render the response invalid.

For this study I have relied on many interviews, the majority of which I did not personally conduct or supervise. The interviewers with the Otter Tail County Historical Society, however, were knowledgeable persons who asked sound questions. I have been particularly careful not to use responses that interviewers, including myself, forced in a certain direction or employed what now appear as leading questions.

Oral histories do, to use Saloutos's words, "bring out the human aspects." They have been as invaluable to this study of federal programs at the grass roots as FERA reports or WPA records in the National Archives. No one knew more about the women's projects that the WPA operated in Otter Tail County than Adeline Karst, for she supervised them. No one had a better grasp of the general business and specific banking problems in Fergus Falls of the depression years than Searle A. Zimmerman, who worked in a failed bank. These two and the others who participated in oral histories have left important grass-roots memoirs.

Otter Tail County Historical Society Manuscript Collections

Of the collections that the Otter Tail County Historical Society has gathered and preserved, two are particularly outstanding and contributory to this study. The WPA Collection is a treasure trove of material that brings the human dimension to federal work. It contains a complete file of directives to foremen and timekeepers, correspondence of the district office in Detroit Lakes, reports on playground programs, timesheets for workers, and the records of the county's extensive involvement in WPA historical projects. Fortunately, because Roy Baker and Albert Muske worked so intensively with WPA projects, their letters have survived to provide a unique glimpse into the role of federal programs in people's everyday lives. Not many WPA workers left that kind of complete record. Secondly, the combined collection of the Lake Region Co-op. Electrical Association and Otter Tail Power Company present splendid material through which to explore the formation of a REA cooperative and the relationship between private and public power. That these two organizations allowed the society to photocopy pertinent records and correspondence is indeed gratifying.

Newspapers

Otter Tail County newspapers were especially useful in many ways. They provided in-depth reports on federal programs, and, as the papers became informational outlets for the federal agencies, their pages were filled with program details and announcements. In one case, between July 1933 and August 1934 the *New York Mills Herald* included lengthy weekly reports on PWA involvement in constructing the city's water system. The *Fergus Falls Daily Journal* and the *Fergus Falls Weekly Journal* presented far more information on the county's banking crisis (1927–33) than was available from the Minnesota Department of Banking. The newspapers carried financial statements on all the closed banks and reported on depositors' meetings and the process of liquidation. Because the surviving records of the Farmers' Holiday Association are skimpy, the story of that movement in the county could not have been told without the coverage that the *Fergus Falls Daily Journal* gave it between 1932 and 1935.

The newspapers also provided a glimpse of what was happening on main street and how the depression was affecting individuals. The newspapers gave me a sense of place, bringing the towns to life. For examples, business activity along Battle Lake's main street in 1934 and 1935 was thoroughly described through a series of stories in the *Battle Lake Review*. The treatment that the Fergus Falls City Council gave a poverty-stricken, lame itinerant was not entered into that body's official minutes. Only because a reporter deemed the affair to be newsworthy has the incident become part of the historical record. Similarly the *Fergus Falls Weekly Journal* elaborated with quotations upon a mere mention in the minute book of the Workers' Alliance meetings with the Fergus Falls City Council in 1938 and 1939. For an understanding of the depression and the operation of New Deal programs, the newspaper is an invaluable source. Rarely did editors allow their political bias to interfere with "New Deal news."

Local Records

Grass-roots history cannot be written without grass-roots records. In piecing together the relationship between the federal government and local governments, three record sets are indispensible. The minute books and the subject files of the county commission laid out the fiscal problems that the depression caused, the unfolding story of the New Deal's direct- and work-relief programs (the FERA, the PWA, the WPA, and the CWA), the development and progress of county-sponsored projects, and the question of county and township poor relief. The council minutes of the villages and the city of Fergus Falls are especially useful for finding what assistance was given to the unemployed, the applications for and organization of federal projects, and locally sponsored work-relief programs. Although township records were poorly kept and haphazardly preserved, those that have survived provide the clearest picture of the administration of grass-roots relief and the problems attendant on it. Nowhere did I find a more detailed statement of federal-local relations or a more ringing denunciation of the WPA than in the Inman Township records.

Of special significance for the study of a rural county are the annual reports of the county agricultural agents. (Otter Tail County had one agent, who oversaw the west half of the county, and an assistant agent, who looked after the east half.) These documents, often seventy or eighty pages in length, are gold mines of information. In addition to supplying important statistical, farm-organization, and weather data, the agents left an almost day-to-day log concerning the development of farm-related programs such as the AAA, the FCA, the emergency cattle-purchase program, drought federal seed programs, and the REA. The agents' observations, at times similar to editorials, create memoirs of the depression on the county's farmsteads. These reports are essential to an understanding of farm programs. The agents' files also held the only surviving document on the county's CCC camp. CCC Camp Work Plan, Camp SCS-MN-21, proved to be a key source on camp activity.

Federal and State Records

Because most federal agencies organized their statistical information along county as well as state lines, the reports of the FERA, the WPA, the CWA, and the PWA provide the data to place a county in perspective. Like the census, they are bare but essential. Of special significance was the microform edition of WPA records that are relevant to the county. Each project, large and small, is listed as to material matching and federal expenditure, illustrating the physical side of WPA. Four reports housed with the Minnesota Historical Society were extremely useful in the statistical data that they provided. *A Report of the Minnesota State Board of Control as the State Emergency Relief Administration: September 29, 1932 to July 1, 1934* by the Minnesota Board of Control of State Institutions discusses the nature of some of the county's projects and analyzes the financial impact on the county. *Minnesota Work Relief History: During the Period from April 1, 1934 to June 30, 1935* carries the above-mentioned report down to the end of FERA. Together, the two reports present as clear a picture as is possible of the FERA in Otter Tail County. The "Summary of Approved Projects, CWA Payroll, November 15, 1933-March 31, 1934" gives a complete breakdown of that agency's work. The Minnesota Department of Agriculture's annual manuscript census, cited as "Acres of Crops Planted or to be Planted for Harvest," contains complete data pertaining to farms.

INDEX

Aastad Township, settlers, 6
Adams, Elmer E., career, 29
Adams School, Fergus Falls, depicted, 65; built, 66
Agricultural Adjustment Act, *1933*, provisions, 114–15
Agricultural Adjustment Act, *1938*, provisions, 121
Agricultural Adjustment Administration (AAA), organization, 115; programs, 116–18, 122, 132; terminated, 119
Agricultural Advisory Credit Committee, 130
Agricultural Marketing Act, *1937*, 114, 123
Agriculture, farm acreage, 14; diversified, 14, 17, 23; income, 14, 22–24, 116–19, 121–24, 132; rural-urban ties, 15; onset of depression, 21; soil conservation, 110, 120–24, 132. *See also* various crops
American Farm Bureau Federation, policies, 12, 13; members, 36
American Legion, Fergus Falls, relief work, 41
American Legion Auxiliary, Fergus Falls, relief work, 37, 41
American Public Welfare Assn., on relief administration, 50
American Red Cross, relief work, 41
American State Bank, Fergus Falls, 148, 150
Anderson, C. Arthur, depicted, 60
Anderson, Verner A., reminiscences, 128
Art, federal project, 82
Assembly of God church, membership, 10
Associated Charities, Fergus Falls, organized, 41
Aurdal Township, settlers, 6; poor fund, 40, 47; electricity, 188n8

Baker, Roy A., WPA worker, 88, 90–93, 95–99; depicted, 97

Banks and banking, failures, 20, 125, 148–52; land holdings, 27; bank holiday, 147; regulated, 153, 156
Baptist church, membership, 10
Barley, market, 22
Barnard, Edward T., historical society secretary, 82, 85, 88–89, 91, 96, 98, 167; depicted, 90
Battle Lake, depicted, 11, 158; population, 16; poor fund, 41, 45–46, 48; relief cases, 51–52; recreation, 62; school, 74; bank, 148; businesses, 158; water and sewage systems, 166
Battle Lake Bakery, Battle Lake, 158
Baumgartner, Florence, depicted, 60
Becker County, electric service, 145
Beef, consumption, 21; as surplus commodity, 50. *See also* Cattle
Benevolent and Protective Order of Elks, Fergus Falls, relief work, 41
Benson, Elmer, governor, 28; U.S. Senator, 76
Bierman, Bernard W. ("Bernie"), coach, 87
Blake, George, political activist, 53
Blanche Lake, conservation, 78
Blowers Township, settlers, 6; electricity, 188n8
Blue Eagle, as symbol, 154–55
Bluffton, population, 16; relief cases, 51
Bluffton Township, poor fund, 47
Boen, Robert, student, 41
Bookbinding, WPA project, 81, 98
Bosch, John H., political activist, 31, 32
Boy Scouts of America, 62
Boyum, Ole C., banker, 148, 149
Breen, Inez, depicted, 60
Brown, Earle, candidate, 28
Brunson, Capt. Frank W., 109
Buckler, Richard T., congressman, 142
Budack, Edward C., depicted, 90; WPA worker, 90

Burau, Harry, reminiscences, 110, 119, 130, 135; depicted, 120
Buse Township, electricity, 188n8
Business, retail trade, 16; recovery, 153–54, 157–60
Butler, Steve, poor commissioner, 37, 41
Butler Township, electricity, 188n8
Butter, as surplus commodity, 39, 50. *See also* Dairy industry

Camp Fire Girls, 62
Camp Kabetogama Lake, CCC camp, 103–6, 107; depicted, 104, 105
Candor Township, electricity, 188n8
Carlisle, schools, 56
Catholic church, membership, 10
Cattle, sales, 14; prices, 22–23; government buy out, 59–60, 119. *See also* Beef
Cemeteries, inventoried, 94–95
Challenge Co., Batavia, Ill., contractor, 65
Charlson, Maybelle, depicted, 60
Chesborough, Lawrence, depicted, 126
Chesborough, Virginia, depicted, 13
Children, campers, 30. *See also* Civilian Conservation Corps, National Youth Administration
Christgau, Victor A., administrator, 76
Christian church, membership, 10
Christianson, Dorothy, depicted, 60
Christianson, Theodore, governor, 12
Christopherson, Arnold, engineer, 140
Christopherson, Tilford, farmer, 110
Citizens' Alliance, policies, 11
Civic and Commerce Assn., Fergus Falls, 155–56
Civil Works Administration (CWA), program, 55–56; terminated, 57
Civilian Conservation Corps (CCC), enrollment, 47, 102–3, 109; administration, 101; camp life, 103, 107; camps described, 104; projects, 104, 106, 108–10; assessed, 108, 110
Clitherall, population, 16; relief cases, 52
Clitherall Township, poor fund, 40
Clothing, dresses depicted, 13, 80; homemade, 27; as direct relief, 41, 45; sewing project, 78–81; boots, 106; sales, 158
Cloverleaf Creamery Assn., Heinola, 17
Commodity Credit Corporation, makes loans, 117, 122, 123
Communist party, activities, 29–31, 33, 35–36, 53

Community Chest, Fergus Falls, 41, 42
Congregational church, membership, 10
Conservation, water projects, 78; soil, 110, 120–24, 132. *See also* Civilian Conservation Corps: projects
Construction, federal programs, 63
Cooke, Morris Llewellyn, engineer, 137
Coolidge, Calvin, president, 11, 114
Cooperatives, dairy, 17; meat packing, 59–60; electric, 137–42, 162
Corbett's Grocery, Battle Lake, 158
Corliss Township, settlers, 6
Corn, consumption, 21; prices, 22–23; harvested, 44; production controlled, 116–18; loan program, 123
Courts, lawsuits, 47, 51–52

Dairy industry, production, 13–14, 17; income, 22, 23, 27; production controlled, 118–19; prices supported, 123; impact of electricity, 145. *See also* Butter
Dalton, population, 16; recreation, 62
Daly, Michael James ("Jim"), lawyer, 70
Dams, built, 78
Dane Prairie Township, settlers, 6
Danes, settlers, 5, 6
Davis, Harold R., CCC camper, 103, 104, 106, 107; depicted, 104, 107
Davis, John W., candidate, 11
Deer Creek, population, 16; roads, 66
Deer Creek Township, settlers, 6
Democratic party, campaigns, 12
Dent, population, 16; poor fund, 41
Dillon, Josephine, farmer, 27
Dillon, Robert Elton, 27
Dillon, Robert F., farmer, 27
Dillon, Susie, farmer, 27
Direct relief, case histories, 37–38; funded, 40–42, 45; administered, 40, 43, 46, 47, 52, 53, 61; percentages of persons receiving, 42; eligibility of recipients, 47, 49–51; for the elderly, 48–49; program, 127
Dreught, ———, depicted, 60
Drought, impact, 24, 78, 103, 119, 121, 126–27, 131–32; cattle buy out, 59; work-relief project, 76
Duddles, ———, depicted, 13
Duddles, Kitty, depicted, 13
Dunlap, Laura, reminiscences, 87

Eastern Township, settlers, 6
Eckstrom, Violet, depicted, 60
Edna Township, settlers, 6

Education, courses, 56, 61–62; financed, 111. *See also* Schools

Effington Township, settlers, 6; electricity, 188n8

Eggs, consumption, 21; prices, 23. *See also* Poultry

Electricity, in rural areas, 134, 136, 137, 145; costs, 135–36; rates, 140–41; companies, 159–62

Elizabeth, population, 16; poor fund, 41; relief cases, 51; schools, 56; roads, 66; bank, 148

Elizabethan Poor Laws, origin, 40

Elmo Township, relief cases, 38, 51; poor fund, 47–48

Emergency Banking Act, *1933*, 147

Emergency Farm Mortgage Act, *1933*, 125

Emergency Relief Appropriation Act, *1935*, 70, 137

Episcopal church, membership, 10

Estlick, Mildred, depicted, 60

Evangelical and Reformed church, membership, 10

Evangelical church, membership, 10

Extension Service, agents used, 115

Fargeland, Gus, depicted, 60

Farm Bureau, *see* American Farm Bureau Federation

Farm Credit Act (FCA), *1933*, provisions, 125; loans, 129

Farm Credit Administration (FCA), functions, 125

Farm Security Administration (FSA), operations, 129–30

Farmer-Labor party, organized, 12; platform, 28

Farmers and Merchants State Bank, Fergus Falls, fails, 148–50

Farmers and Merchants State Bank, New York Mills, 156

Farmers' Co-Operative Creamery Co., Pelican Rapids, 17

Farmers' Holiday Assn., activities, 31–34, 36

Farmers State Bank, Deer Creek, 148

Farmers Union, membership, 12; policies, 13

Farms, *see* Agriculture

Federal Art Project, 82

Federal Crop Insurance Corporation (FCIC), operations, 124

Federal Deposit Insurance Corporation (FDIC), created, 153

Federal Emergency Relief Administration (FERA), created, 42; funds, 45, 57; terminated, 46, 63; projects, 59, 127; employees depicted, 60

Federal Farm Loan Act, *1916*, 124

Federal Land Bank, 125; land holdings, 27; operations, 124

Federal Music Project, 82

Federal Power Commission, 160

Federal Surplus Relief Corporation, created, 49

Federal Theatre Project, 82

Federal Writers' Project, 82

Feed, loan programs, 126–29

Fergus Falls, depicted, 15, 74; population, 16; poor fund, 41, 48; finances direct relief, 46; lawsuit, 47; relief clients, 47, 51–52; relief policies, 53–54; civic improvements, 56, 57, 58, 75, 111; recreation, 62, 112; schools, 65, 66; water supply, 108–9; banks, 148–51

Fergus Falls Cooperative Packing Co., operations, 59–60

Fergus Falls National Bank, 148; customers, 151; depicted, 151

Fergus Falls State Hospital, remodeled, 74

Fergus Falls Township, relief cases, 51

Fetvedt, Ethel, depicted, 60

Fetvedt, Fenwick, reminiscences, 160, 161

Finns, settlers, 5, 6; religion, 7, 10; politics, 31

First National Bank, Fergus Falls, 148, 151; depicted, 149

First National Bank, Pelican Rapids, 151

First National Bank of Battle Lake, 34

First State Bank, Fergus Falls, 148, 150

Flax, raised, 14, 23

Flint, John, pastor, 32, 34

Flowers, Jim, political activist, 34; depicted, 35

Folden Township, relief cases, 51

Food, raised, 14; diets, 21, 27; prices, 39; as direct relief, 41, 45; for relief workers, 61; funds expended, 83; in CCC camps, 107. *See also* Gardens, Surplus commodities

Forestry, federal projects, 78. *See also* Civilian Conservation Corps

Foster, William Z., candidate, 30

Franklin, Edward, manufacturer, 16

Franklin Fence Co., Vergas, factory, 16

Freedland, Alex, opposes WPA, 85
Funerals, costs controlled, 51

Galena and Sons, Fergus Falls, contractors, 66
Gardens, products, 14; as relief projects, 61. *See also* Food
Gasoline, used on farms, 136
Gedney, M. A., Co., Dent, factory, 17
Germans, settlers, 5, 6; religion, 7
Girard Go-For 4-H Club, Perham, depicted, 13
Girard Township, relief cases, 51
Glorvigen, Afton, depicted, 60
Glotzbach, Linus C., administrator, 79
Gorman Township, settlers, 6; poor fund, 48; relief cases, 51
Grant, Charles J., artist, 82
Grapefruit, as surplus commodity, 49
Grasshoppers, infestations, 24–25
Grathwol, John, county agent, 24, 117, 118, 127
Gray, Mary, depicted, 60
Gustafson's Grocery, Battle Lake, 158

Halverson Furniture Store, Battle Lake, 158
Hanson, Stella, depicted, 60
Harding, Warren G., president, 11
Harju, Rudolph, political activist, 30
Hartman, John, 49; reminiscences, 29, 87, 157
Hatling, Jacob O., carpenter, 57
Haut, Gust W., farmer, 36
Hay, J. Howard, commissioner, 139
Hay, raised, 14
Hegge, Martha, farmer, 24, 26; reminiscences, 128
Hegge, Oscar, farmer, 24, 26; worker on roads, 128
Helleckson, Corrine, depicted, 60
Henderson, John M., superintendent, 81–82
Henning, population, 16; civic improvements, 56, 75; recreation, 62; roads, 66; monument, 112, 113; bank, 148
Henrikson, Solveig, depicted, 60
Herrick, Genevieve F., reporter, 156
Hickok, Lorena, journalist, 43
Highways, *see* Roads and highways
Hintgen, Roy, reminiscences, 136, 152, 156; depicted, 157; businessman, 157, 158
Hintsala, Ed, manager, 23; reminiscences, 133

Historical Records Survey (HRS), 82, 83; project, 73; described, 88–99; program, 89; assessed, 92
Hodnefield, Jacob J., supervisor, 93, 94, 95
Holmgren, Henry, mayor, 84; depicted, 112
Homestead Township, education, 61; recreation, 62; electricity, 188n8
Hoover, Herbert C., president, 11, 28
Hopkins, Harry, administrator, 42, 55, 70, 75, 76
Horses, used, 14, 68, 76
Hotchkiss, June, depicted, 13
Houg, Gerry M., supervisor, 112
Hovland, Leonard, CCC camper, 103, 106, 107, 108; reminiscences, 145
Hubbard County, electric service, 145
Hyde, Arthur M., secretary of agriculture, 22

Ickes, Harold L., secretary of the interior, 63
Immigrants, *see* individual ethnic groups
Index of American Design, research project, 82
Inman Township, opposes WPA, 86
Insurance, on crops, 124
Iverson, Carl M., politician, 32, 34

Jacobs Brothers, Bird Island, contractors, 64
Jefferson School, Fergus Falls, depicted, 65; built, 66
Jensen, George A., political activist, 32–33
Johnson, Everett, reminiscences, 128
Johnson, Hugh S., administrator, 154
Johnson, Lottie, farmer, 128
Johnson, Magnus, U.S. Senator, 12
Johnson, Victor, farmer, 128

Karst, Adeline F., depicted, 79; supervisor, 79, 81
Karst, Edward N. ("Ed"), businessman, 79, 157, 158
Kelehan, Charles M., county agent, 27, 109, 121, 122, 139, 143
Kellogg, Frank B., U.S. Senator, 12
Kerr, Alma B., administrator, 89
Kimber, Ben, administrator, 12, 13
Klimek, Alex, CCC camper, 103, 106, 108
Knutson, Albert R., 144; career, 138;

depicted, 139; leads cooperative, 139,
140, 141, 142, 145
Kopperud, Selma, reminiscences, 145

La Follette, Robert M., Sr., candidate,
11
Lake Region Co-op. Electrical Assn., or-
ganized, 139; recruits members, 139,
142–43; finances, 140–43; builds lines,
143–45
Landon, Alfred M., candidate, 28
Larsen, Arthur J., administrator, 98
Leaf Lake Township, settlers, 6; politics,
30; relief cases, 53; electricity, 188n8
Leaf Mountain Township, roads, 59;
electricity, 188n8
Liberty Garment Manufacturing Co.,
Fergus Falls, factory, 16
Lida Township, relief cases, 52
Loans, to farmers, 116–17, 122–30, 132;
for electrification, 137, 140–43; from
banks, 148–50; to banks, 153
Long Lake, conservation, 78
Lutheran church, membership, 6, 7; and
social reform, 10

Machinery, used on farms, 23
McKinley School, Fergus Falls, 66
Maier, Walter A., preacher, 10
Malmstrom, Alice, depicted, 60
Maplewood Township, relief cases, 51;
roads, 77
Mark, John, mayor, 64, 87
Martin's Meat Market, Battle Lake, 158
Mattson, Abraham, farmer, 33
Mattson, Anna, farmer, 33
Medical care, treatment for poor, 37–38;
for relief clients, 45, 51, 52; funds ex-
pended, 83; in CCC camp, 106
Methodist Episcopal church, member-
ship, 10
Milk, consumption, 22; prices, 23. See
also Dairy industry
Miller, George, political activist, 34
Minneapolis, politics, 30
Minnesota Board of Control, administers
relief funds, 43, 48–49; activities, 57
Minnesota Department of Banking, liqui-
dator, 36
Minnesota Department of Conservation,
project, 78
Minnesota Department of Rural Credit,
farm holdings, 129; loans, 132
Minnesota Division of Forestry, projects,
78, 106

Minnesota Farmers' Nonpartisan League,
12
Minnesota Historical Society, sponsors
projects, 89–90
Minnesota Rural Credit Bureau, land
holdings, 27; makes loans, 125, 131;
operations, 129
Minnesota Statewide Archaeological and
Historical Research Survey Project, 99
Minnesota Supreme Court, decisions, 47,
51
Moe, Thor, depicted, 60
Monson, Philip R., mayor, 53–54
Mortgages, on farms, 23, 27, 125, 129,
132; foreclosures, 33–36
Motor Inn, Battle Lake, 159
Muchow, Minnie, depicted, 26
Music, programs, 62; federal project, 82
Muske, Albert G., WPA worker, 90,
92–95

National Emergency Council (NEC),
created, 164
National Industrial Recovery Act
(NIRA), 1933, provisions, 63, 154
National Recovery Administration
(NRA), business compliance, 154–56;
impact, 156
National Re-Employment Service, 56, 68
National Youth Administration (NYA),
created, 110–11; projects, 111–12; as-
sessed, 113
Neff, Grover, businessman, 134
Neilsen, Neils C., depicted, 60
Nelson, E. Clifford, historian, 10
Nelson, Hans, and Sons, Battle Lake,
store, 158
Nelson, John C., farmer, 34
Nelson, Martin A., candidate, 28
Nelson's Grocery, Battle Lake, 158
New Deal, programs assessed, 163–68.
See also individual programs
New York Mills, settlers, 6; described,
15; population, 16; politics, 30; poor
fund, 48; relief cases, 51–52; civic im-
provements, 56, 75, 87; recreation, 62;
waterworks, 64, 165; high school
band, 82; bank, 148
New York Mills Q Q Club, 156
Newspapers, indexed, 91
Newton Township, settlers, 6
Nonpartisan League, supported, 11–12
Noren, Louise, depicted, 60
Norman County, electric service, 145
Norris, George W., U.S. Senator, 137

North Dakota, politics, 11
Northern Light Electric Co., Wahpeton, N.Dak., 135
Northern Pacific Railroad Co., 18
Northern States Power Co., 134
Northwestern Sash and Door Co., Fergus Falls, 16; depicted, 18
Norwegian Grove Township, settlers, 6
Norwegians, settlers, 5, 6; religion, 6, 7

Oak Valley Township, opposes WPA, 85
Oelslager, Elsie, depicted, 60
Old-age assistance, programs, 48–49
Old-Stock Americans, settlers, 5
Olson, Floyd, governor, 28, 44, 55
Olson, Lorna Anderson, reminiscences, 113
Olson, Walter S., administrator, 108
Oscar Township, settlers, 6
Otter Tail County, described, 5; population, 15–16; relief funds, 45; relief policies, 53; courthouse, 57; electric service, 145
Otter Tail County Emergency Relief Committee, activities, 45, 55
Otter Tail County Historical Society, 82, 88, 89, 97; collections, 90–91; depicted, 92; sponsors projects, 112
Otter Tail County Relief Administration, activities, 46
Otter Tail County State Bank, Pelican Rapids, 151, 152
Otter Tail County Welfare Board, activities, 47
Otter Tail Lake, conservation, 78
Otter Tail Power Co., Fergus Falls, 16; customers, 135; plant depicted, 135; rates, 140–41; discussed, 159–62
Otter Tail River, cleaned up, 76, 108–9
Ottertail, population, 16; poor fund, 41, 46; relief cases, 52
Otto Township, poor fund, 40–41; relief cases, 51

Paddock Township, settlers, 6; relief cases, 51–52
Page, Henry G., farmer, 138
Parity, principle adopted, 115, 122; payments, 122–23
Park Region Luther College, Fergus Falls, as CCC camp, 108–9
Parkers Prairie, population, 16; recreation, 62; roads, 68; waterworks, 70; projects, 75, 84; school depicted, 85; bank, 148

Parkers Prairie Township, poor fund, 48
Parta, Russell, reminiscences, 143
Paulson's Hardware, Battle Lake, 158
Pelant, ———, depicted, 60
Pelican Lake, resort, 18; conservation, 78
Pelican Rapids, population, 16; depicted, 17; civic improvements, 59, 75; recreation, 62; banks, 148, 151–52
Pelican Rapids State Bank, Pelican Rapids, 151–52
Pelican River, conservation, 78
Pelican Township, settlers, 6
"Penny auction", occurances, 33, 34–36
Perham, population, 16; recreation, 62; streets improved, 67; projects, 75, 84; sewage plant depicted, 84; bank, 148
Perham Township, settlers, 6; relief cases, 51–52
Peterson, P. C., farmer, 32
Peterson brothers, Battle Lake, service station, 158
Peterson's Hotel and Cafe, Battle Lake, 158
Pine Lake, conservation, 78
Pine Lake Township, settlers, 6
Poles, settlers, 5, 6
Poor, funds, 40–41, 45–48; case histories, 44
Poor farm, closed, 49; used as threat, 53
Pope, Capt. John, engineer, 5
Population, of ethnic groups, 6; census figures, 15–16
Pork, consumption, 22
Potatoes, raised, 14; loan program, 123
Potter, Bill, depicted, 60
Poultry, income, 14; prices, 22; production, 23. See also Eggs
Presbyterian church, membership, 10
Preus, Jacob A. O., governor, 12
Prices, of farm products, 22; of farmland, 24; for food, 39; for wood, 61; for cattle, 119; for wheat, 121
Prince, William I., Jr., depicted, 60
Production Credit Associations (PCA), established, 125; operations, 129
Prohibition, impact, 22
Public Utility Act, 1935, provisions, 160
Public Works Administration (PWA), projects, 63–68, 137; finances, 64

Quick, Gail, depicted, 13
Quick, Phoebe, depicted, 13

Rarig, Frank, administrator, 43

Reconstruction Finance Corporation (RFC), makes loans, 125, 153
Recreation, dances, 26, 41; programs, 62; facilities, 75, 112; in CCC camps, 107–8
Regan, John E. candidate, 28
Relief, *see* Direct relief, Work relief
Relief Work Administration (RWA), created, 57
Religion, churches surveyed, 93–94, 95. *See also* individual religious denominations
Reno, Milo, political activist, 31
Republican party, campaigns, 10, 11, 12, 28; poster, 29; politics, 167
Resettlement Administration (RA), operations, 129–30
Resorts, development, 17–18
Rice, as surplus commodity, 50
Richter, Emma, reminiscences, 128, 146
Richter, Otto, reminiscences, 128
Richville, population, 16; recreation, 62; bank, 148
Roads and highways, improved, 59, 75–78, 128; built, 66, 68, 165
Romann, Herbert, farmer, 143
Ronnevik, Hans, farmer, 14, 24, 117–18, 121, 131; depicted, 131
Ronnevik, Jorolf, reminiscences, 14, 131; depicted, 131
Ronnevik, Lillie, depicted, 131
Ronnevik, Myrtle, depicted, 131
Roosevelt, Franklin, president, 28, 42, 46, 55, 63, 70, 111, 114, 125, 134, 137, 154; conservation efforts, 101; closes banks, 147
Rosengren, Chester, attorney, 138; reminiscences, 141, 142, 146
Rosholt, Gertrude, depicted, 60
Rural Electrification Act, *1936*, 137
Rural Electrification Administration (REA), operations, 137; and cooperatives, 138–42, 145, 162; impact, 161
Rush Lake, conservation, 78
Rye, raised, 14; loan program, 123

Sachs, Alexander, economist, 154
St. Louis County, Communist voters, 30
St. Olaf Township, settlers, 6; relief cases, 51
St. Paul, politics, 30
Salvation Army, membership, 10; direct relief, 38
Sandin, Herlin L., engineer, 57–58, 68, 76; depicted, 60

Scambler Township, settlers, 6
Scanlon, ———, depicted, 60
Schall, Thomas D., U.S. Senator, 12
Schmidt, L. H. D., blacksmith, 17
Schmidt Wagon Factory, Perham, 16, 17
Schools, hold essay contest, 41–42; repaired, 56–57, 74–75, 84; built, 65–66; depicted, 65, 85; bands, 82. *See also* Education
Schroeder, Paul, reminiscences, 56
Seed, loan program, 127–29
Sem, Helen, reminiscences, 145
Sem, Homer, reminiscences, 143
Sewage systems, improved, 57–59, 84; built, 75; plant depicted, 84
Shaw, J. A., contractor, 65
Shipstead, Henrik, U.S. Senator, 12
Sieling, Louis O., administrator, 123
Silver Lake, conservation, 78
Smalley, Harvey D., Sr., editor, 85, 89
Smith, Alfred E., candidate, 11
Snowberg, Carl A., journalist, 38
Social life, *see* Recreation
Social Security Act, *1935*, provisions, 48
Soil Conservation and Domestic Allotment Act (SCDAA), *1936*, provisions, 120–21
Soil Conservation Service, work with CCC, 109–10
Sports, *see* Recreation
Stabnow, Fay, depicted, 13
Stabnow, Marvel, depicted, 13
Stai, Ed, deputy sheriff, 34
Stalker Lake, conservation, 78
Stassen, Harold E., governor, 28
State Bank of Perham, 36
State Emergency Relief Administration (SERA), created, 43; administers relief funds, 45; organization, 57; projects, 58–62, 127
Stephens, Louis C., administrator, 141
Stock, Elmer, farmer, 110
Streets, improved, 56, 59, 75, 84; project depicted, 67
Surplus commodities, produced, 22; dairy, 39, 118; distributed, 49, 50, 60; depicted, 50; crops stored, 122; government purchases, 123. *See also* Food
Svendsgaard, John, farmer, 110
Sverdrup Township, settlers, 6; poor fund, 48
Swedberg, Carl, contractor, 66, 68
Swedes, settlers, 5, 6; religion, 7
Swenson, H. E., receiver, 149

Swine, income produced, 14; raised, 21; prices, 22–23; production controlled, 116–18

Taxes, increased, 22; for direct relief, 47; poor-fund levies, 48; delinquent, 76
Tenants, on farms, 27
Tennessee Valley Authority (TVA), 137
Theater, plays produced, 61; federal project, 82
Thein, P. G., contractor, 64
Thompson, Anton, judge, 89, 150; depicted, 112
Thorstenson, Clyde, reminiscences, 152, 153
Thun, Clinton, CCC camper, 103, 106, 107, 108
Tikkanen, Emma, reminiscences, 145, 146
Tikkanen, Jeff, reminiscences, 142, 145
Tordenskjold Township, settlers, 6; relief cases, 52–53; marker, 112
Torgerson, Onan, farmer, 110
Toso, C. Eugene, depicted, 26; reminiscences, 27
Toso, Conrad, farmer, 26; depicted, 26, 44; reminiscences, 27, 87, 119, 143
Toso, Donald, depicted, 26, 86
Toso, Dorothy, depicted, 26. See also Williams, Dorothy
Toso, Elizabeth, depicted, 26; homemaker, 26, 27
Toso, Harvey Richard ("Dickie"), depicted, 26, 86
Toso, Kenneth, depicted, 26
Toso, Lorraine, depicted, 26
Toso, Luella, depicted, 26
Toso, Mildred, depicted, 26
Toso, Norman, depicted, 26, 44
Trondhjem Township, settlers, 6
Tumuli Township, settlers, 6

Underwood, church, 10; population, 16; poor fund, 41; civic improvements, 56, 70, 75; recreation, 62; bank, 148
Unemployment, numbers, 27–28; projects to remedy, 64, 68; among youths, 101
Unitarian church, membership, 10
United Farmers Educational League, 30, 31
United Farmers League, members, 30
United States Army, work with CCC, 106

United States Supreme Court, decisions, 119, 156

Vanderslius, Bette, depicted, 60
Vaughn, F. F., depicted, 60
Vergas, population, 16; relief cases, 51; roads, 68; bank, 148
Vining, population, 16; poor fund, 41; recreation, 62; roads, 68; bank, 148
Vining Township, relief cases, 51
Voran, Margaret, student, 42

Wages, for unskilled labor, 52, 59; rates protested, 53; for CWA work, 56; of foremen, 58; of teachers, 62; for PWA work, 68; for WPA work, 71–73, 99; for historical work, 90, 93, 96, 98; for CCC work, 101; for NYA work, 111; comparative, 157
Walker, Frank C., administrator, 164
Wallace, Henry A., secretary of agriculture, 114, 118
Wallace, J. P., State Bank, Pelican Rapids, 151, 152
Wangness, Charlotte, depicted, 60
Waterworks, improved, 56, 75, 84; built, 64, 70
Weather, conditions, 5; annual rainfall, 24
Wefald, Knud, congressman, 12
West, John K., entrepreneur, 18
Western Township, poor fund, 40–41; recreation, 62
Wheat, raised, 14, 121; consumption, 21; prices, 22–23; production controlled, 23, 116; loan program, 122–23, 132; insured, 124
Wilkin County, churches, 94; electricity, 145
Willard, E. Victor, administrator, 109
Williams, Aubrey Willis, administrator, 111
Williams, Dorothy Toso, reminiscences, 27. See also Toso, Dorothy
Willkie, Wendell L., candidate, 28
Wilson, Woodrow, president, 124
Winters, P. E., farmer, 110
Wisconsin Power and Light Co., 134
Wold, Edwin J., farmer, 110
Women, on work relief, 56, 62, 78–81; WPA workers depicted, 80
Woodcutting, projects, 59, 61
Work Promoters' Assn., activities, 53
Work relief, to repay loans, 52, 127, 128; programs, 55, 70–71; guidelines, 137

Workers' Alliance, activities, 53
Working People's Nonpartisan Political
    League, 11
Works Progress Administration (WPA),
    workers depicted, 25, 74, 77, 80;
    created, 63, 70; funds, 70–71, 74–75,
    78; administration, 70, 73; civic im-
    provement projects, 73–75, 84;
    drought-relief project, 76; sewing
    project, 78–81; bookbinding project,
    81, 98; artistic and professional
    programs, 82; impact assessed, 83, 87,
99–100; opposed, 85–86; historical
    project, 88–100; layoffs required, 93,
    96, 98
World War I, food production, 21
Wright, Thomas C., businessman, 159;
    depicted, 159
Wylie, E. W., Inc., St. Paul, contractor,
    143; truck depicted, 144

Zimmerman, Searle A., cashier, 18, 150;
    reminiscences, 57, 62, 152, 168;
    depicted, 150

PICTURE CREDITS

The photographs and other images used in this book are from the collections of the Otter Tail County Historical Society and the Minnesota Historical Society and appear through the courtesy of the donors listed below.

From the Otter Tail County Historical Society collections — page 13 (courtesy of Winifred Chesborough), 15, 26 (courtesy of Conrad Toso family), 35 (both courtesy of Harvey D. Smalley, Jr.), 44 (courtesy of Conrad Toso family), 58, 60 (courtesy of Solveig Henrikson Christopherson), 65 (both), 67 (both courtesy of Harvey D. Smalley, Jr.), 77 (both courtesy of Jack Maurin), 79 (courtesy of Adeline Karst), 80 (top), 86 (courtesy of Conrad Toso family), 92, 104 (courtesy of Madeline Davis), 105 (both courtesy of Madeline Davis), 107 (courtesy of Madeline Davis), 112, 120 (both courtesy of Harry T. Burau), 126 (courtesy of Winifred Chesborough), 131 (courtesy of Jorolf Ronnevik), 139 (courtesy of Lake Region Co-op. Electrical Association), 144 (both courtesy of Mrs. Howard Carlson and E. W. Wylie, Inc.), 150 (courtesy of S. A. Zimmerman), 151 (courtesy of Fergus Falls National Bank), 155, 157 (courtesy of Roy Hintgen), 159 (courtesy of Otter Tail Power Company)

From the Minnesota Historical Society collections — page 11, 17, 18, 25 (both), 29, 39, 50, 74, 80 (bottom), 84, 85, 90, 97, 135, 149 (W. T. Oxley, photographer), 158